The Captivity of Innocence

The Captivity of Innocence

Babel and the Yahwist

André LaCocque

CASCADE *Books* · Eugene, Oregon

THE CAPTIVITY OF INNOCENCE
Babel and the Yahwist

Cascade Books
An Imprint of Wipf and Stock Publishers
199 W. 8th Ave., Suite 3
Eugene, OR 97401

www.wipfandstock.com

ISBN 13: 978-1-60899-353-6

Cataloging-in-Publication data:

LaCocque, André.

    The captivity of innocence : Babel and the Yahwist / André LaCocque, with a
Foreword by Wayne G. Rollins.

    xvi + 190 p. ; 23 cm. — Includes bibliographical references and indexes.

    ISBN 13: 978-1-60899-353-6

    1. Babel, Tower of. 2. Bible. O.T. Genesis XI—Criticism, interpretation, etc. 3.
Bible. O.T. Pentateuch—Criticism, interpretation, etc. I. Rollins, Wayne G. II. Title.

BS1238 B2 L33 2010

Manufactured in the U.S.A.

. . . the myth tries to get at the enigma of human existence, namely, the discordance between the fundamental reality—state of innocence, status of a creature, essential being—and the actual modality of the human, as defiled, sinful, guilty. The myth accounts for this transition by means of a narration.

Paul Ricoeur, *The Symbolism of Evil*, part 2, par. 3

Pyramids and skyscrapers—monuments more lasting than bronze—suggest how much of the world's 'economic' activity is really a flight from death.

Norman O. Brown, *Life against Death:*
The Psychoanalytical Meaning of History, 100

[The Tower of Babel] exhibits an incompletion, the impossibility of finishing, of totalizing.

Jacques Derrida, "Des Tours de Babel," 104

Contents

Foreword

THIS VOLUME IS THIRD in a set of magisterial portraits of the mind of J, the Yahwist narrator at work behind the scenes in Genesis 1–11. André LaCocque dubs him "the singer of tales." LaCocque's first volume focused on J's tales of Adam and Eve,[1] the second on Cain and Abel,[2] and the present volume on "Babel."

In his exploration of the works of J, LaCocque takes us to a place previous biblical scholarship has rarely visited—the conscious and unconscious depths of the human psyche and the archetypal images, symbols, myths, codes, and poetry generated in the desire to tell us how things are (ontology), how we are (anthropology), and how or what God is (theology).

LaCocque does not travel alone in this enterprise. He is accompanied by a host of phenomenologists of religion, literary critics, philosophers of language, psychologists, and psychoanalysts cited regularly in this work. The list includes, among others, Sigmund Freud and Carl Jung, post-Freudians Jacques Derrida and Norman O. Brown, Ernest Becker, Hans-Georg Gadamer, Mircea Eliade, Rollo May, and Abraham Maslow, object-relations psychologist David Winnicott, Viktor Frankl, and LaCocque's friend, colleague, and collaborator, Paul Ricoeur. Each is enlisted in the task of unconcealing the monumental strategies and themes at work in the images and tales of the biblical text.

This is not to say that LaCocque overlooks classical biblical scholarship. Far from it. In 2005, LaCocque edited a collection of essays, *Guide des nouvelles lectures de la Bible* (Paris: Bayard), covering new fields of

---

1. *The Trial of Innocence: Adam, Eve, and the Yahwist* (Eugene, OR: Cascade Books, 2006).
2. *Onslaught against Innocence: Cain, Abel, and the Yahwist* (Eugene, OR: Cascade Books, 2008).

biblical scholarship that have sprung up since the 1970s. The list is remarkable in its scope. It includes the appropriation of models from the
disciplines of literary, rhetorical, canonical, feminist, cultural, anthropological, social scientific, and psychological criticism. It features new
readings of the biblical text from liberationist, ideological, postcolonial,
imperialist, political, postmodern, and global perspectives. Adding these
synchronic readings (contextually oriented) to the earlier diachronic
(historically oriented) approaches of source, redaction, textual, historical,
and archeological criticism, LaCocque brings each to the task of describing and deconstructing the world of J.

Three topics play center stage and are at the heart of LaCocque's work
in this volume: *myth* (chapter 3), a *psychoanalytic approach* (chapter 4),
and *deconstruction* (chapter 6). A word is in order about each.

LaCocque approaches *myth* with a maxim coined by Paul Ricoeur
and borrowed from Immanuel Kant: "Le symbole donne à penser" ("The
symbol gives rise to thinking"). With this mantra LaCocque draws attention to the multiplicity of meanings and ambiguities that hover in-
corrigibly around any given image, whether a serpent in a garden, the
murder of a brother, or the construction of a tower that aims to pierce
the tissue of heaven. In LaCocque's own words: "The story of Babel is
more than an archaeological report (say, on the Babylonian ziggurat);
more than an etiological theory (on the diversity of languages and on
the name of Babel/Babylon); more than a historical reminiscence (about
the Babylonian melting-pot of the sixth century BCE); and, needless to
say, more than entertainment. Genesis 11 speaks to our *imagination*. It
belongs to *mythos*" (p. 69).

The storytelling power of *myth*, according to LaCocque, is rooted in
the perception that *mythos* unveils the "depths of the human soul" (p. 91).
To be sure, LaCocque tells us, there was a real ziggurat in Babylon and
there was a "megalomaniac ambition to subdue the whole world to its imperial dictation" (p. 159), but in the hand of the J author, "the Babel story
has become an object of art," weaving a "web of significations" (p. 140)
that give pause to the reader in the realization that more is there than first
thought or imagined.

LaCocque appreciates the irony that although the Tower of Babel
story is never revisited by later voices in the Hebrew Bible, it has enjoyed
reincarnations in literary and artistic expression over two and a half millennia by artists who found in it "a paradigm of the human condition."

LaCocque adds: "At the level of imagination, no translation is necessary. The readership of the tale is immediately universal and timeless" (p. 1).

The truth of LaCocque's observation struck me while reading a *New York Times* article of December 14, 2009, by Claudia Thomas, "Dubai Grows Up." It surveyed the immense economic difficulties and the housing bubble that had affected the utopian, multi-billion-dollar venture of the state of Dubai, with islands shaped like palm trees, and the world's richest horse track. But as I followed the litany of extravagances, through fountains visible from space, and a shopping mall that sprawled across two million square feet, I stopped reading involuntarily at the phrase, "the world's tallest tower." "No translation was necessary." LaCocque's work explains in fascinating detail why this is so.

A second reality at the heart of LaCocque's work is *psychological biblical criticism*, the discipline of reading the biblical text through psychological or psychoanalytic lens. Psychological criticism re-emerged in the early 1970s after a long exclusion from biblical studies that had stretched from Albert Schweitzer's dismissal of psychoanalytic studies of the life of Jesus in 1913,[3] to the 1970s, when biblical scholars began to recognize what the rest of the culture had come to understand: that no human artifact, including the Bible and the history of its interpretation, can be fully understood without consideration of the nature and habits of the human psyche that produced it.

The fundamental thesis of psychological biblical criticism is that although the Bible can be seen as part of an historical, social, and cultural process, it is also part of a psychological process in which unconscious as well as conscious factors are at work. These factors are alive and active in the biblical authors, in the communities they represent, in the stories and materials they preserve, in biblical copyists, translators, and publishers, in biblical interpreters and preachers, and in the long range biblical effects that the Bible works, for good and for ill, in individuals and entire cultures.

Psychological biblical criticism dares also to suggest that as palpable as the historical, social, and cultural factors are in giving birth to the Bible and its interpretations, in the end the psychic factors may turn out to be the pre-eminent determinants of *what* is recorded in the text of the Bible, *why* it was remembered, *how* it is said, *to whom* and *for what purpose* it

3. Albert Schweitzer, *The Psychiatric Study of Jesus: Exposition and Criticism*, trans. Charles R. Joy (Boston: Beacon, 1948 [1913]).

is said, *how it is read, how it is interpreted, and how that interpretation is received, shaped, and translated into the life of the community and culture.*

A third reality at the heart of LaCocque's work is *deconstruction*, the act of attempting to discern the unconscious scenarios and sub-plots at work in the story of Babel and the way it is told, with the recognition that the truth unconcealed in the story through deconstruction applies also to the storyteller's world and our own.

Since the rebirth of psychological biblical criticism, André LaCocque has been an exemplar of the application of psychological insight to texts in the Hebrew Bible, beginning with *The Jonah Complex* (1981) co-authored with his son Pierre-E. LaCocque, and amplified in his psychologically as-tute study of *Esther Regina: A Bakhtinian Reading* (2008). On the back cover of LaCocque's volume on Cain and Abel, Walter Brueggemann epitomizes LaCocque's contribution to the field as the work of a "genera-tive and restless mind that always seeks a new angle on the text" and as "an urbane intellectual who knows the world of myth and the critical claims of psychology."

LaCocque's remarkably detailed and intriguing study of the nine verses in Genesis that contain the story of "Babel" can be compared to a well-woven oriental rug that draws polychromatic skeins of thread to-gether into meaningful patterns. LaCocque presents the story of Babel, not only as constructed in the Bible and by the hand of J, but also as de-constructed under the lens of the careful reader who discerns profound, undisclosed but immediately recognizable truths about the human con-dition then and now.

—Wayne G. Rollins

Acknowledgments

I WANT TO EXPRESS my deep gratitude to my editors, K. C. Hanson and Jeremy Funk whose diligent and thorough suggestions have considerably improved the language and the general quality of my book. It has also been a pleasure to work along the years with Wipf and Stock Publishers. Their openness and congeniality are most appreciated.

Abbreviations

Ancient Sources

Alex.	Alexandrinus
Ant.	Josephus, *Antiquities of the Jews*
b.	Babylonian Talmud (*Babli*)
3 *Bar.*	3 *Baruch*
C. Cels.	*Contra Celsum* (Origen)
Deut. Rab.	*Deuteronomy Rabbah*
Gen. Rab.	*Genesis Rabbah*
j.	Jerusalem Talmud (*Yerushalmi*)
J	the Yahwist
Jub.	*Jubilees*
Met.	*Metamorphoses* (Ovid)
mss	manuscripts
Num. Rab.	*Numbers Rabbah*
P	the Priestly writers
PRE	*Pirqe Rabbi Eliezer*
QG 2	*Questions and Answers on Genesis* 2 (Philo)
R.	rabbi
Sam. Pent.	Samaritan Pentateuch
Sib. Or.	*Sibylline Oracles*
Tg. Jon.	*Targum Jonathan*
Tg. Neof.	*Targum Neofiti*
Vat.	Vaticanus

Modern Sources

AB	Anchor Bible
ABD	*Anchor Bible Dictionary*, edited by David Noel Freedman. 6 vols. New York: Doubleday, 1992

ANET	*Ancient Near Eastern Texts Relating to the Old Testament*, edited by James B. Pritchard. 3rd ed. Princeton: Princeton University Press, 1969
ATANT	Abhandlungen zur Theologie des Alten und Neuen Testaments
BKAT	Biblischer Kommentar, Altes Testament
BZAW	Beihefte zur Zeitschrift für die alttestamentliche Wissenschaft
Enc. Jud.	*Encyclopedia Judaica*, edited by Fred Skolnik and Michael Berenbaum. 2nd ed. 22 vols. Detroit: Macmillan Reference USA, 2007
ETR	*Etudes théologiques et religieuses*
GBS	Guides to Biblical Scholarship
HKAT	Handkommentar zum Alten Testament
HSM	Harvard Semitic Monographs
ICC	International Critical Commentary
ITC	International Theological Commentary
JAOS	*Journal of the American Oriental Society*
JBL	*Journal of Biblical Literature*
JNES	*Journal of Near Eastern Studies*
JPS	Tanak: Jewish Publication Society
JSOTSup	Journal for the Study of the Old Testament Supplement Series
KBL	Ludwig Köhler and Walter Baumgartner, *Lexicon in Veteris Testamenti libros*. 2nd ed. Leiden: Brill, 1958
LCBI	Literary Currents in Biblical Interpretation
NICOT	New International Commentary on the Old Testament
NPNF²	*Nicene and Post-Nicene Fathers* (Series 2)
NRSV	New Revised Standard Version of the Bible
OBO	Orbis biblicus et orientalis
OBT	Overtures to Biblical Theology
Or	*Orientalia*
OTL	Old Testament Library
PittsTMS	Pittsburgh Theological Monograph Series
SBL	Society of Biblical Literature
SBLSymS	Society of Biblical Literature Symposium Series
SBT	Studies in Biblical Theology
S.E.	*The Standard Edition of the Complete Psychological Works of Sigmund Freud*, translated from the German under the general editorship of James Strachey, in collaboration with Anna Freud, assisted by Alix Strachey and Alan Tyson. 24 vols. London: Hogarth, 1953–1974

SHR	Studies in the History of Religions
TCS	Texts from Cuneiform Sources
VAB	Vorderasiatische Bibliothek
VT	*Vetus Testamentum*
VTSup	Supplements to Vetus Testamentum
WBC	Word Biblical Commentary
WTJ	*Westminster Theological Journal*
ZAW	*Zeitschrift für die alttestestamentliche Wissenschaft*
ZTK	*Zeitschrift für Theologie und Kirche*

CHAPTER ONE

Prologue

Introductory Remarks

THIS BOOK IS THE third volume of a trilogy based on three successive Genesis myths—in the noblest sense of the word—created (or
reported in new terms) by the Yahwist and set in the primeval era. In the
first essay, I studied the myth of Adam and Eve in Genesis 2–3;[1] the second
essay engaged the story of Cain and Abel;[2] and now the present volume is
about Babel in Gen 11:1–9.

As we shall see, the author of Gen 11:1–9 is the same as in the above-
mentioned stories. Furthermore, it is a striking point that in parallel with
the latter, the tale is never again explicitly mentioned in the rest of the
Hebrew Bible. The present narrative on Babel has not stirred any echo
in the Hebrew Bible, in spite of its intrinsic power of evocation, as the
Wirkungsgeschichte (foreground) of the text attests. Nevertheless, the as-
tounding response that the myth of Babel has since received in a variety of
literary compositions and with all forms of art for over 2500 years is itself
an indication how much the "singer of tales" and his readers share a common interest in the story of Babel and see in it a paradigm of the human
condition. At the level of imagination, no translation is necessary. The
readership of the tale is immediately universal and timeless. This point is
particularly well articulated by rhetorical and reader-response criticism.
It "suggests an increased attention to myths" and "raises again acutely the
issue of the unconscious in rhetoric."[3] Such "complicity" between text and

---

1. LaCocque, *The Trial of Innocence: Adam, Eve, and the Yahwist.*
2. LaCocque, *Onslaught against Innocence: Cain, Abel, and the Yahwist.*
3. Kennedy, *New Testament Interpretation through Rhetorical Criticism,* 158.

audience renders possible the meeting of horizons—of the text and of the reader—as Hans-Georg Gadamer says; or, in the words of Paul Ricoeur, it makes possible the reader's "appropriation" of the message.

Had J composed the story of Babel in the Solomonic era (tenth century BCE), as the classic source criticism proposed more than a century ago, the absence of textual heirs in the Bible would remain extremely puzzling. This means that, once again about this myth of Babel, the complex problem arises of the nature, the time, and the integrity of J's narratives in the primeval history. It is an issue that source criticism, tradition-historical criticism, and literary criticism attempt to solve. To this we shall soon turn.

But first, let us note that within the abundant symbolism displayed by J in the first chapters of Genesis, this chapter on the tower of Babel comes as a grand finale.[4] When we were dealing in the preceding two volumes of the present trilogy with Adam and Eve, or with Cain and Abel, we saw that J's set of symbols displayed in both these narratives has for the last twenty-five centuries belonged to a collection of universal classics. Now, the symbolism enshrined in the Babel story is no less classic and universal. By this I mean that its validity and "modernity" has not diminished through the ages. At least two elements contribute to its continued relevance: the intrinsic psychological and existential power of J's images, and the thrifty way adopted by the author to "sing" his tale.[5]

About the latter point, I have addressed in the preceding volumes the deceptive simplicity of J's narratives. Their surface plainness hides an unfathomable depth. Suffice it here to recall the endless interpretations of Genesis 3. J's economy of words is striking. There is in Gen 11:1–9 no superfluous word, although so much is said by means of the extant terms. Greater amplitude given to the composition would have probably deflected the reader's attention to the story's aesthetic rather than to its dynamic message.[6]

4. Bloom calls the story "a summit of J's art." He concludes his speculative development on "Babel" with the words: "we are scattered unless, like Abraham, we hear and answer a call" (Bloom and Rosenberg, *The Book of J*, 191). Alter speaks of the "mesmerizing effect of these ancient stories" (*Genesis*, xxvi).

5. See Lord, *The Singer of Tales*. The ascetic brevity of our tale (9 verses) may be an indication that the written version of it served originally as a basis for oral performances, which would elaborate upon its elements.

6. Speaking of "the combat myth in biblical sources," Fishbane says that it is told in a "highly condensed epitome" (*Biblical Myth and Rabbinic Mythmaking*, 64). This is valid also as regards the Babel story. Fokkelman states, "[The narrator] succeeds in making his

About J (Source Criticism)

From the point of view of vocabulary and theme, it appears that the literary unit of Gen 11:1–9 was composed by J. Let us review with Theodore Hiebert some textual characteristics that definitely point to J's authorship of Gen 11:1–9: divine anthropomorphism (see vv. 5–7); the name YHWH given to the deity (see vv. 5, 6, 8, 9); "a concise, colorful style"; a typical phrase, such as "YHWH came down to see" (see v. 5; cf. Gen 18:21; Exod 3:8; 34:5); the roots *puṣ* as in Gen 9:19 ("scatter," also *naphaṣ*, vv. 4, 8, 9; cf. Gen 10:18; Exod 5:12, etc.) and *ḥalal* ("begin", v. 6; cf. Gen 4:26; 6:1; 9:20, etc.); expressions like *habah* ("come!" vv. 4, 7; cf. Gen 38:16; Exod 1:10), or *ʾiš ʾel reʿehu* ("a man to his neighbor," vv. 3, 7; cf. Gen 15:10; 31:49; 43:33), *hen* ("behold," v. 6; cf. Gen 3:22; 4:14; 15:3, etc.).[7]

John Van Seters draws the same conclusion. He tallies Gen 11:4, 8, 9 (on the "dispersion" theme) and the expression "over the whole surface of the earth" in Gen 9:19. The use of the word *ʾadam* in 11:5 is also characteristic of J. As to the Babelians' ambition to make a name for themselves (11:4), it "relates the story of Babel to Genesis 6:1–4, whereas the statement that the city and the tower are 'just the beginning of their deeds' (*haḥillam laʿaśôt*, v. 6) recalls the theme of 'beginnings' in 9:20 and 10:8."[8]

Hermann Gunkel in his commentary *Genesis* saw in the text of 11:1–9 the mixture of two separate traditions: one about the city and one about the tower. Claus Westermann rightly rejects this critical stance in his massive commentary on Genesis.[9] But Westermann considers the connection of the text with Babylon secondary, because the connection with Babylon inserts a historical place into the report on the primeval origins of things. I do not agree with him on this point (see chapter 3 below). We find there precisely the reason why the text does *not* mention Babylon by name; it substitutes for it a generic term, "Babel." (In Hebrew and Aramaic, no word other than *Babel* designates Babylon.) This substitution distances the story from history proper; the text features a term that is to be understood as a paradigm.[10] Along the same line of thought, the tower in

---

general theological vision visible in the particular and in showing the universal in the individual" ("Genesis 11.1–9, the Tower of Babel," 41).

7. Hiebert, "The Tower of Babel," 29–58.

8. Van Seters, *Prologue to History*, 180–81; Witte insists rather upon the parallel between 11:6 and 3:22 (*Die biblische Urgeschichte*, esp. 87–88).

9. See Westermann, *Genesis 1–11*.

10. So, the curse of Canaan, which in Gen 9:25–27, e.g., is given a more universal sense. In Genesis 11, we could say that there is only one Babylon, but there are many

question here, which designates, as we shall see, the *Etemenanki* ziggurat of Babylon, is called simply a "tower" for the sake of similarly fulfilling a universal symbolic purpose.

. Let us also note that, in contrast to the P genealogies that frame the Babel story, Gen 11:1–9 has little if anything to do with the origins of Israel proper. While in the persons of Adam, Eve, Cain, Abel, Seth, Noah, and his sons and daughters we are able to recognize the people's ancestors, Gen 11:1–9 is deprived of such ancient popular heroes. In fact, at face value, the tale could have originated from any people in the world.[11] When the tale of Babel is considered within the context of Israel's "antiquities,"[12] however, we realize that J is speaking of a situation dramatized by the exile in Babylon of the sixth century, and as a prologue to the election of Abraham as father of the Israelites.

In the first two volumes of this trilogy, I have addressed the problem of the personality, date, and purpose(s) of J. I refer the reader to the introductions in each of these monographs. But from the new perspective afforded by the Babel story, some aspects have come into sharper relief. One might recall that according to Hermann Gunkel, J was a compiler of old traditions, especially of *Sagen* ("legends") and folktales (particularly about a city and about a tower).[13] Made up of independent traditions initially, their *Sitz im Leben* (setting in life) is to be thought of as premonarchical tales. These eventually coalesced into a consolidated historiography with the rise of the state (tenth century). J, continues Gunkel, nevertheless had a decisive hand in such a literary conversion. In the story of Babel, J read the received tradition as an etiology of the origin of languages, a feature common to ancient Near Eastern folklore.

Martin Noth contributed to the discussion with his hypothesis of an extant literary *Grundlage* (G) to which J, on the whole, added little

---

Babels! Van Wolde, in her "The Tower of Babel," 99, notes that Babel "is a single name which expresses multiplicity and confusion." Primeval history is also primal history, says Anderson (*From Creation to New Creation*, 167). See also Seybold, "Der Turmbau zu Babel," 453–79.

11. But for the very important use of the divine name *YHWH* rather than the more general *Elohim*. Consistent with Second Isaiah's theology, J claims the universality of YHWH's lordship. On the prophetic influence [especially in their oracles of judgment] upon the Yahwist in Genesis 11, see Van Seters, *The Pentateuch*, 60: "With respect to the dating of the Yahwist, I found that the closest affinities were with Second Isaiah"; and Schmid, *Der sogenannte Jahwist*.

12. See Van Seters, *Prologue to History*.

13. Gunkel, *Genesis*.

of his own. In the primeval history, however, J was highly creative—an idea that Gerhard von Rad picked up. He saw J as a historian and theologian endowed with a creative genius. J wrote during the time of the Solomonic "enlightenment" of sorts (tenth century BCE); his aim was to theologically legitimize the reign of David's son. Such an understanding of J prevailed for a long time. But contemporary research has tackled the problem anew. John Van Seters, among others, questions the consensus initiated by Gunkel's conclusions and states that indeed there was an oral tradition in Israel, but it continued "throughout the biblical period."[14] In other words, the oral stage of a tradition does not say much about its relative age. If there was an oral story of the city and tower of Babel, it may as well have originated during the exile in Babylon or as the creation of J at that time.[15]

Dating the J source has become a burning problem today. In the first two volumes of my trilogy, I have definitely adopted the conclusions of several modern scholars and shown that J cannot have composed his primeval history before the exile in Babylon. In the light of Gen 11:1–9, things become even clearer. The text simply cannot predate the sixth-century exile, when the Judean captives were filled with awe before the city of Babylon and its ziggurat. The entire story is built on this theme. Thus J ends the narrative cycle of the primeval time as he had started it in Genesis 2–3: from the exile from Eden eastward (that is toward Mesopotamia)[16] to the exile to Babel/Babylon, that eventuates with the expressed hope that the Babelians themselves will be dispersed.[17]

It may be, however, that we have to make a distinction with Martin Noth between the J at work in the primeval tradition and the J at work elsewhere. Schmid's lapidary statement may be right: "J in Genesis and J

14. Van Seters, *The Pentateuch*, 47; he cites Niditch, *Oral World and Written Word*.

15. On the postexilic date of the narrative as an independent piece, see Oduyaye, "Balala-balala," 81. Fishbane also considers the story of Babel an independent piece (*Text and Texture*, 35).

16. See LaCocque, *The Trial of Innocence*, 258. "Eden, the first home of mankind," Fishbane says, "is the archetypal expression of the experience of sacred geography in the Bible." As to the tower of Babel, it is "the paradigmatic antitype of Eden," and Abraham is "a new Adam" (*Text and Texture*, 112).

17. More on the date of J below, under the subtitle, "Setting in Life." The idea defended by some scholars that Israel itself is implicitly included in the divine verdict of dispersion loses some of its sting as Israel is *already* dispersed and exiled (one thinks of Haman's declaration in Esth 3:8). The point is less that the Israelites will be scattered along with the Babelians than that the Babelians will be scattered like the Israelites.

in Exodus are different J's."[18] In Genesis 2–11* there is a remarkable alternation of literary units ascribed to P and others ascribed to J.[19] Van Seters sees documents supplementing documents, and I subscribe to this. For Rendtorff, P came as a later supplement, a statement that may be right or wrong, the question of the chronological sequence of P and J being today still debatable. At any rate, we seem to be on a solid ground in thinking that the final editor/redactor of the Pentateuch took the P tradition (and its genealogies) as a foundation and the J tradition of *Sagen* as a "zooming" device to bolster details of the P narrative.[20]

We must never lose sight of the double context of the story of Babel. It obviously is a piece of J's work on the primeval era. But a different context is also provided when we take into consideration the final patterning of the book of Genesis. Then Genesis 11 is sandwiched between Genesis 10, mainly from P, and Genesis 12, mainly from J. On this intertextuality, Bernhard Anderson's chapter on the Tower of Babel narrative is very helpful.[21] The Priestly editorial work in the Pentateuch is primordial. Typically its material is interrupted by J's traditions illuminating a point made earlier by P. So, Anderson says, Genesis 1—2:3, for instance, precedes the insertion of J's Gen 2:4b—4:26. Genesis 5 with P genealogies precedes a block of J's (6:1—7:8) "that, at its outset (6:1) reaches back to an earlier, indefinite point in time." After the table of nations, the tower of Babel story "resumptively reverts to an earlier time before the proliferation of Noah's sons into ethnic and linguistic groups."[22]

Thus Gen 11:1–9 comes, like earlier units in Genesis 2–3 on Adam and Eve or Genesis 4 on Cain and Abel, as an insert interrupting the genealogical note sounded in 10:32 and its continuation in 11:10. The final redactor has interspersed the P traditions with Yahwistic stories, that is, with a kind of magnifying glass on some details of P composition.

18. Schmid, "The So-Called Yahwist and the Literary Gap," 35. We may even make a distinction between the Yahwist composer of the primeval history and the one of the patriarchal traditions. Gerhard von Rad's intuition that the primeval traditions were the last to be added to Israel's epic narrative is fundamentally correct (see von Rad, *The Problem of the Hexateuch*, 63–67; see also Westermann, *Genesis 1–11*, 2).

19. When an asterisk (*) follows biblical chapter references, it indicates that within the specified chapter range, only J material is of interest.

20. *Pace* Van Seters. The pattern is particularly clear in the sequence of Genesis 1 and Genesis 2–3 . See more about this issue below.

21. Anderson, *From Creation to New Creation*, 174. See also Fokkelman, *Narrative Art*, 41 n. 53: Genesis 11 comes as an explanation of the people's scattering off after Noah.

22. Anderson, *From Creation to New Creation*, 174.

Markus Witte calls these inserts "theological excurses," or "theologization of the historical exposé."[23] In this combination of perspectives, the tale on Babel exposes a hubristic human effort to prevent humanity from being scattered—as it is effectively in Genesis 10—by building a universal metropolis (11:4).

On the Alternation of P and J (Redaction Criticism)

In spite of their divergences, modern scholars like Rolf Rendtorff, John Van Seters, Christoph Levin, and others consider the J stories as "supplements" to the P redaction of Genesis.[24] As I already said, I would not conclude from this that one of the two sources is younger or older than the other. But a redactional combination of the two is incontrovertible. So, within chapters 1–11 of Genesis, the alternation of the two sources is striking:

A/ parametrical perspective provided by P in Gen 1—2:4a
(in 2:4a the genealogy of earth and heaven)

B/ focal perspective provided by J in Gen 2:4b—3
(focus on the human)

A/ parametrical perspective provided by P in Gen 4:1–2
(the genealogy of Adam)

B/ focal perspective provided by J in Gen 4:3–16

A/ parametrical perspective provided by P in Gen 4:17–22
(the genealogy, continued)

B/ focal perspective provided by J with Gen 4:23–24

A/ parametrical perspective provided by P with Gen 4:25—5:32
(the genealogy, continued)

B/ focal perspective provided by J with Gen 6:1–8

A/ parametrical perspective provided by P with Gen 6:9–10
(the genealogy of Noah)

B/ focal perspective provided by J with Gen 6:11—9

23. Witte, *Urgeschichte*, 98.
24. See Rendtorff, *The Problem of the Process of Transmission in the Pentateuch*; Van Seters, *Prologue to History*; Levin, "Das israelitische Nationalepos: der Yahwist," 63–86. For Van Seters, to recall, the work of J is a prologue to the Deuteronomistic history.

A/ parametrical perspective provided by P with Genesis 10
    (genealogy, continued; Table of Nations)

B/ focal perspective provided by J with Gen 11:1–9
    (focus on Babel)

A/ parametrical perspective provided by P with Gen 11:10–32
    (the genealogy of Shem, followed by a focal perspective in J's
    story of Abraham in Genesis 12ff.).[25]

The oft-repeated remark that Gen 11:1–9 should have been set before
Genesis 10 (the table of nations) is ill inspired.[26] The redactional arrangement of the pericopes, as we just saw, took precedence over the inner
chronology: a P genealogical list precedes a J focal description highlighting a specific aspect of the general picture. In Gen 11:1–9, the focus falls
on Babylon and on what was experienced as its babbling language. This
in turn becomes paradigmatic of the diversity of human languages—and
thus we are sent back to the situation described in Genesis 10. The eventual arrangement of Genesis 11 following Genesis 10 is intentional and
purposeful. The final redactor of the Pentateuch clearly wanted to end the
primeval history on a negative note and introduce Abraham in Genesis 12
as the initiator of a new history, the history of promise and fulfillment.

Therefore, when Bernhard Anderson writes about the quasi-inde-
pendence of the pericope on Babel, "of its dissonance with the previous
Table of Nations (chapter 10)" and with "the ensuing Shemite genealogy
(11:10–26)," his judgment must be taken with a grain of salt.[27] It is correct at least as regards the integrity of the J insert when considered on its
own merit. This point is buttressed by the strikingly adroit structure of
the pericope (see below). And it is true that taken in isolation, the Babel
story seems to say little about a pattern of promise and fulfillment, dear
to Gerhard von Rad. Things nevertheless appear different when the perspective broadens to include Genesis 12 as fulfillment of an implied, and

25. The same alternating movement between P and J can be shown, e.g., in Genesis
25–35. In Gen 25:1–18, a P genealogy of Abraham is followed by J's focus on Jacob and
Esau in 25:19–34 and on Isaac in 25–26. Genesis 26:34–35 is P's, followed by J in 27:1–45
(focus again on Jacob and Esau). P in 27:46—28:9 precedes J in 28:10—35:8 (the story
of Jacob). P again in 35:9–15 comes before J in 35:16–21 (the death of Rachel, Reuben's
incest); as usual, the pericope ends as it started, with P (35:22–28). See also de Pury, A
Farewell to J? 57.

26. Ibn Ezra (twelfth century) already said about this issue, "Biblical chapters are not
always in chronological sequence" (Ibn Ezra, Genesis [Bereshit], xvii).

27. Anderson, From Creation to New Creation, 168.

sometimes distorted, promise in Genesis 11. The theme of name/fame comes into particular relief when Gen 12:2 is paired with Gen 11:2, for instance.[28] When eventually J turns to Israel's history with Abraham, "he does not utilize ancient Near Eastern myth but instead has recourse to Israel's old traditions."[29]

From highlighting the builders of Babel to focusing on the people's patriarchs and matriarchs, however, the contrast is stark. We shift from a plot psychology to a character psychology. The builders indeed remain carefully anonymous. The sole character in Gen 11:1–9 is God himself. But with the call of Abraham, we leave cosmology and enter history, the incipient history of a nation as projected to its ancestors, their faith, their hopes, and their actualization of a divine promise. Because of the complexity of the Yahwist's heroes, with their struggles, their failures, their victories, they are as alive as any Dostoevsky character, and their lives demand interpretation—as do the people of Babel, but collectively.

As to the ostensible temporality inherent in the story, there is actually no clue that the events took place in the primeval history other than the pointer in verse 1. But as the actual model for the city and tower of Babel is undoubtedly the Babylonian ziggurat seen by the Judean exiles in the sixth century BCE, the reader must make a distinction between the suggested chronology (in the primal time) and the actual one (during the exile). J's choice of the prehistorical setting serves the purpose of making the story semi-mythic and definitely paradigmatic.

Structure of the Story on Babel (Narrative Criticism)

Already in his 1949 commentary on Genesis Umberto Cassuto lists the impressive occurrences of stylistic tropes in Gen 11:1–9: alliterations, paronomasias, wordplays, "the recurrence of similar words in close association," etc.[30] The story is neatly divided into two movements, the second one as a sharp contrast to the first. Robert Alter calls the style of the tale "a game of mirrors."[31] He even sees the eventual multiplication of languages as already reflected in the very style here, which is "blurring . . . lexical

28. Genesis 12:1–4 has been rightly seen as the focus of J's composition. "This text is undoubtedly formulated by J and is not borrowed from older material," says Brueggemann, "Yahwist," 973b.

29. Ibid., 974b.

30. Cassuto, *A Commentary on the Book of Genesis: 2.*

31. Alter, *Genesis*, 47. In 1968 Isaac M. Kikawada aptly called the structure of Gen 11:1–9 "an hourglass-shaped story" (see "The Shape of Gen 11:1–9," 18–32).

boundaries" (between *šem* ["name"] and *šam* ["there"], between *ḥeimar* ["tar"] and *ḥomer* ["mortar"], etc.). On the model of the ziggurat, the construction of Gen 11:1–9 is in the shape of a pyramid or mountain:[32]

                              i/YHWH's deliberation
              h/YHWH comes down————————h'/let us come down
          g/the tower's top in heaven—g'/on the surface of all the earth
          f/a name for ourselves————————f'/He called its name Babel
          e/lest we be scattered————————e'/YHWH scattered them
      d/let us build a city————————————d'/they stopped building the city
      c/settlement in Shinar————————————c'/YHWH scattered them
  b/one language for all————————————b'/YHWH confounds their language
  a/all the earth————————————————a'/over the face of all the earth*

* This parabolic composition recalls the fundamental structure of the human mind, according to Lévi-Strauss. It is built in terms of binary oppositions like high/low, wasteland/building, human/divine, centripetal/centrifugal, etc. (Lévi-Strauss, *Structural Anthropology*).

kol ha'areṣ appears in vv. 1 (twice), and 9 = 3 times;

'al penei kol ha'areṣ appears in vv. 4, 8, and 9 = 3 times;

śafah appears in vv. 1, 6, 7, and 9 = 4 times;

'eḥad/ 'aḥath appears in vv. 1 and 6 (twice) = 3 times;

32. On the structure of the story, see Cassuto, *A Commentary on the Book of Genesis: 2*; Fokkelman, *Narrative Art*, 11–45; Kikawada, "The Shape of Genesis 11:1–9"; Fishbane, *Text and Texture*, 36, 38; likewise in Preminger and Greenstein, *The Hebrew Bible in Literary Criticism*, 278. Already in 1926, Johannes Pedersen had tried to refute Gunkel's attempted division of the tale into a *Stadtrezension* ("city recension"—cf. "to get a name") and a *Turmrezension* ("tower recension"—cf. "not to be scattered," the tower serving here as a lighthouse of sorts). Gunkel saw also a doublet in v. 5: YHWH descends, and in v. 7 he is about to descend (see Gunkel, *Genesis*; and Pedersen, *Israel, Its Life and Culture*, 248–49 and note). The very equilibrium in the striking structure of the text would shed a grave doubt on Gunkel's argument, but see now Baden, "The Tower of Babel," 209–24. Although himself convinced of the unity of the canonical text of Gen 11:1–9 , Baden convincingly demonstrates that the perfect balance invoked by Cassuto, Fokkelman, Kikawada, and others in favor of the redactional unity is an insufficient argument that does not by itself defeat Gunkel's double recension. Baden, however, adds, "Genesis 11:1–9 shows none of the hallmarks of a composite text" (217). He rejects the alleged doublets like *wayyehi* in verses 1 and 2 as they "represent two functions of the verb" (a verbal predicate and a temporal clause respectively), see Gen 12:10–11 (J). As to the double descent of God in verse 5, it expresses two successive movements (217 n. 28). So, Baden sees in the present version a combination of "much older independent *traditions*," and he refers to von Rad, *Genesis*, 48.

šam appears in vv. 2, 7, 8, and 9 (twice) = 5 times;

root *lbn* appears 3 times in v. 3 ;

root *bnh* appears in vv. 3, 4, 5, and 8 = 4 times;

ʾ*amar* appears in vv. 3, 4, and 6 = 3 times;

ʿ*ir* appears in vv. 4, 5, and 8 = 3 times;

root ʿ*aśah* appears in vv. 4 and 6 (twice) = 3 times;

root *puṣ* appears in vv. 4, 8, and 9 = 3 times.

Alliterations:

V. 3: *nilbenah, lebenim; hallebenim, leaben;*

niśrefah, liśerefah; ha ḥemar, la ḥomer.

V. 5: *banu, benei;*

Vv. 7 and 9: *nabelah, babel, balal.*

The punchline is *babel* in v. 9; its name is a derisive derivative of *balal*—"confusion"—(instead of "gate of the divine" in Akkadian [*bab-ili*]; cf. Gen 28:17 [Jacob's saying], Isa 13:2 [possible allusion to {one of the gates of} Babylon], Jer 51:53 ["Though Babylon should climb up to heaven"], a sarcastic response to the "name" that the people of Babel wanted to make for themselves [v. 4]). Clearly, J has pondered each word of his short story. He has come with such a balanced text that it can be called a prose poem.

Miller, for his part, elaborates upon the *middah keneged middah* (measure for measure) of sin and punishment in the story of Babel. Rather than seeing with J. P. Fokkelman the exercise of the talion (on the model, e.g., of Gen 9:6 and 1 Sam 15:33), Miller sees the sequence of sin and punishment here both in terms of the instrumentation (common language/building city and tower)—as in 2 Samuel 12; Amos 7:16–17; and Hos 10:1–2, 13–15—and also in terms of the result or intention frustrated in the judgment (see "futility curses" in Amos 5:7, 10–11; Hos 4:7–10; Mic 2:1–5).[33]

---

33. Fokkelman, *Narrative Art*, 11–45; Miller, *Genesis 1–1 1*, 35–36. But see Jer 50:15, 29; 51:6! The fact is that Babel is a coercive dictatorship that, like the scorpion, bites itself to death, see Isa 14:20: "You have destroyed your own land/ You have killed your own people."

Setting in Life (Old Literary Criticism = Historical Criticism)

For more than a century, the conclusion of Julius Wellhausen regarding a Solomonic setting in life of the source J was taken as definitively established. It is only recently that Solomon's time as an era of enlightenment and the cradle of J has been rightly questioned. [34]

In fact, all indices point to the sixth century and the Judean exile in Babylon as the time of the J composition of the primeval history. When Persia succeeded to Babylon as a universal empire, the first governor of Yehud appointed in Jerusalem was named Zerub-babel ("Born in Babylon"), an indication of the degree of assimilation of the Judean exilic elite to Babylonian society. This no doubt reflects a more general situation when exiles from a medley of nations did settle for good in "Shinar" and adopted its "one language with identical words" as if Babel was the *axis mundi*. J associates Cyrus's edict allowing the exiles to return to their respective countries and to their diverse languages with the ruin of Babylon, its city and its ziggurat.

This did not mean, however, that for J such spreading of nations and multiplicity of languages was ideal. On the contrary, the plurality of languages epitomizing the human dispersion in the world is also a loss of something that needs to be eventually retrieved with the advent of "one language with identical notions," only this time not in Babylon. What the world is in need of is the election of Abraham (a subjective and objective genitive). "Shinar" was definitely a deceiving and deleterious cul-de-sac. It led nowhere but to confusion, to ruin.

Retrospectively, we had better understand the mention in the text of "all the earth" initially finding a spot to settle in Babylon. The insistence of the tale upon topos also makes a lot of sense, for in the sixth century some may have thought that the eschatological hope, originally focusing on Jerusalem, had found its fulfillment at its antipode, in (by tradition) the wicked, blasphemous, and idolatrous Babel. The reality divulged by the exilic prophets and by J is that "the internationality of the human race" is hubristic; its common language is a parody of the true human language, it

---

34. See in particular von Rad, *The Problem of the Hexateuch*, 69. Von Rad thought that J was the creator of the Hexateuch, while nowadays de Pury and Römer think that the postexilic P is responsible for the first literary patterning of the Pentateuch (see de Pury, "Le cycle of Jacob," 78–96; and Römer, *Israels Väter*).

is babble; its unified purpose is usurpation of the divine; its achievement ends up in ruins and its phalanstery in an archipelago of human units.

The story of Babel concludes J's survey of pre-Abrahamic humanity. From the start, the humans have looked to any means to retrieve immortality. But all issues of flight from death are blocked; all escapes are circular and lead nowhere. All monuments to human prowess crumble. All social consolidations under the same flag and in the name of the same slogans drown their adherents. A common stupidity smothers them to death. J's protohistory (a universal condition that forever permeates human existence) started with a vacuum (Gen 2:5) and ends with vacuity (11:8–9). Now, as Rabelais said, "Nature abhors a vacuum." It calls for and is eventually filled by the triumphant breakthrough of Genesis 12 reporting Abraham's departure and trajectory (cf. Gen 11:1).[35]

Babel–Babylon (Archaeological Criticism)

There were some twenty-nine ziggurats erected over the country of Mesopotamia; archaeology has so far discovered nineteen of them. The word *ziggurat* is a transcription of Akkadian *ziqqurratu*, from the verb *zaqâru* = "to rise high" (!). One of the most famous of them was the tower-temple of Ur built in the second half of the third millennium. The one in the city of Babylon was imposing as well. The so-called *Etemenanki*, a ziggurat dedicated to the god Marduk, had (or was supposed to have) seven terraces built on top of each other. Its total height was 91 meters, the ground floor measuring 91 by 91 meters, according to Herodotus, who counted eight levels.[36] The building history suggests that the construction took over a century and was perhaps never completed. Started under the Sumerians, it was rebuilt by Nabopolassar (610 BCE). The text of dedication of Nabopolassar is interesting. He states that he was commissioned by Marduk to rebuild the Babylon ziggurat: "I must anchor its foundation in the lap of the underground and make its summit like heaven."[37] In Sumerian, *Etemenanki* means "Tower of the Foundation of Heaven and Earth." The destruction of the ziggurat *Etemenanki* is echoed

35. The idea of itinerary, so frequent in the patriarchal-matriarchal stories would be absent in the primeval history were it not for the mention of the migration of humanity in Gen 11:1. This movement serves as a connection as well as a foil to the ancestors' peregrinations.

36. Herodotus *The History* 1.181–82.

37. See Langdon, *Die neubabylonischen Königinschriften*, 60, lines 38–39.

in late Israelite documents: *Jub.* 10:20–21; Josephus *Ant.* 1.116; *Sib. Or.* 3:117–29; *3 Bar.* 3:5–8.

Interestingly enough, King Nebuchadnezzar (who acceded to the throne in 605) mentions in his inscriptions regarding the *Etemenanki* that he mobilized people from all corners of his empire. "Such a cosmopolitan labor force, speaking many tongues, might have encouraged the association of the tradition about the development of languages with the construction of the tower."[38] In fact, in Mesopotamia, the very building of a city was a divine enterprise. The city literally reflected its model in heaven and the king as a builder was the agent of the gods. So the attribution of a name to the town is from the outset a liturgical feature closely associated with the construction.[39]

Babel as a name solicits our attention. It raises the issue of the *axis mundi*, for it means "the gate of the divine." We shall return to the name of the city (transformed by J into a noun designating "confusion") in the section on deconstruction. Meanwhile we note that the Babelians gather in a city, which they build themselves with artificial materials (that is, Babel is no divine construction, with genuine material). Their ultimate achievement is a tower, a rigid monument erected upwards as a channel of communication with the divine, with a guaranteed stability and permanence. From an Israelite perspective, the tower is an assault on the divine, because it is linked with a religious illusion. J's God is not reached by any human construct; he comes down by choice and establishes relations by covenanting with persons. He is not the God of the *Etemenanki* but of Abraham, Isaac, and Jacob.[40]

The god of the *Etemenanki* (a heavenly god) is present in ancient Near Eastern myths considered by several scholars to be close parallels with J's story. Samuel Noah Kramer, in particular, has published an English translation of "Enmerkar and the Lord of Aratta," in which he sees (in lines 136–56) the description of an original harmony, with no threat from any corner: "Man had no rival" (line 140), and he spoke "to Enlil in one tongue [the Sumerian language]" (line 146). But Enki in his wisdom "changed the speech in their mouths, [brought?] contention into it, into the speech of man that (until then) had been one" (lines

---

38. Van Seters, *Prologue to History*, 183. In Ezek 43:13–17, the prophet envisions a ziggurat of sorts for the altar on which sacrifices are made, with each of its levels being around one meter high and some 50 centimeters narrower than the inferior level.

39. See Jacobsen, "The Eridu Genesis," 518.

40. See in particular Alt's "The God of the Fathers."

154–55).[41] Unfortunately, this alleged Sumerian parallel is probably to be discarded. Kramer's translation of this text (made in 1968), especially of lines 136–55, was biased. Bendt Alster interprets the oneness of language in the Sumerian document as a prophecy about the coming submission of all lands to the Sumerian god Enlil. So "Enmerkar" may not be a bona fide ancestor of Gen 11:1–9 after all.[42] However, the strong influence of the Babylonian versions of the flood on Genesis 6–8 leads Van Seters to state that J was responsible for the integration of the Babylonian traditions into his work.[43]

I remain personally skeptical as to the authenticity of any "reconstruction" of the earliest Babel story. True, J could have known the Sumerian epic, for example; but the work of any writer naturally echoes themes found elsewhere without this being a sign of dependence in the first place. J, like all other authors, does not work in a "splendid isolation." Literary themes are floating around, ready to be used by anyone. J, for all we know, may well have created his narrative on Babel out of nothing (relatively speaking). The veritable source of J's inspiration was what he saw with his own eyes in Babylon, the land of his exile.

J's Polemic against Babylon (Ideological Criticism)

The tale is to be read as a moral didactic parable or, as I said earlier, as a prose poem.[44] Its use of divine anthropomorphisms and of hyperboles about the size of the tower, for instance, adds tension and repulsion for the arrogant purpose of the builders.

One important feature is that the story takes place outside Israel. As in the preceding J stories, YHWH is presented as the ruler of the whole cosmos and most particularly of the historic enemy of Israel (temporarily) triumphant. This universalism of J in the primeval history[45] does not detract from the fact that from an ideological critical point of view, J wrote for Israel—to show, among other things, that the election of Abraham

41. Kramer, "The 'Babel of Tongues,'" 108–11.

42. Alster, *Wisdom of Ancient Sumer.* See Bost, *Babel*, 105–14. Seybold, all the same, sees in "Enmerkar" an ancient redactional basis of Genesis 11; see "Der Turmbau zu Babel."

43. Van Seters, *The Pentateuch*, 122. See also Uehlinger, *Weltreich und "eine Rede."*

44. Other examples include the Cain and Abel story and the book of Jonah.

45. See especially Rose, *Deuteronomist und Jahwist.* In 1928 Kurt Galling had already interpreted J's patriarchal narratives as a universalistic prologue to Moses's story (Galling, *Die Eräzhlungstraditionen Israels*).

(and through him, of the people of Israel) is the saving divine intervention in a world in process of reverting to chaos.[46] "The last enemy to be
destroyed" is, contrasting with the anonymous people in the time of the
flood, a specifically historical one: Babylon, that is, the most powerful
entity in the ancient world, which claimed to be the sole legitimate and
efficient agent of law and order.

In a polemical vein, J named the Babylonian claim an instance of
hubris and filed it in the incrementally growing catalog kept since the
beginning of history. Babel is the apex of arrogance. It involves the har-
nessing of all humanity for a single purpose devised by a totalitarian regime, with all the means it can muster. The opposite course is the oneness
of the world under the universal lordship of YHWH: in Genesis 10, all
humanity has common ancestors. Thus Genesis 11 appears as a flash-
back, about which Hamilton coins the word "dischronologization."[47] But
this sequence of chapters is the effect of the literary sources distribution
between J and P (see the above section on the alternation of P and J).

Speaking of chapter sequence, the relationship of Genesis 11 and 12
is decisive. The divine chastisement, it will be shown, is commensurate
with the crime, but it does not remain without repair. There is a shift from
the punishment of humanity in Gen 11:8–9 to the blessing of a people
(*goy*), epitome of all nations, in Gen 12:3 (whose textual background is
found in Gen 9:19; 10:5, 20, 31–32). The divine guidance of Abraham
in 12:1 contrasts with the massive migration mentioned in 11:2. In this
verse, the Babelians were looking for a land to settle; in Genesis 12, God
himself bestows a land on Abraham. Whereas Gen 11:9 brings the confusion of all tongues, the human retrieves the language of communication
in Gen 12:8 (Abraham "invokes the name of YHWH"). The ambitious
name making of the Babelians is reversed in God's making great the name
of Abraham (12:2).

Theodore Hiebert's protest that the primeval Babel story does not
address all humanity is shortsighted.[48] True, J writes for the Israelites,

46. "This is the first instance of obedience to God in the J history," Conrad L'Heureux
writes (*In and Out of Paradise*, 56). He adds that in contrast with J's primeval history,
where *God* is the one to be blessed (Gen 9:26), in the case of Abraham there are no less
than five mentions of God's blessing him (57).

47. Hamilton, *The Book of Genesis: Chapters 1–17*, 349–59.

48. Hiebert, *The Yahwist's Landscape*, 77–78 (contra a consensus of scholarship).
Hiebert is still dependent upon the "Pan-Babylonianism" of Gunkel, leaving aside,
however, its basic "myth and ritual" ingredient (see Gunkel, *Creation and Chaos in the*

not for the Babylonians, and his tale of Babel must be read within the
perspective of its sequel in Genesis 12.[49] The vocation of Abraham in response to the megalomania of Babylon looks ludicrously inadequate, it
is also true. One individual, coming from the same general area as the
Babelians, seems an impossible foil to Babel's mobilization. He is "centrifugal" and will find a land that God, not he, has selected for himself and
his descendants. His peregrination takes him in the contrary direction
from those who went "eastward" in Gen 11:2 (*miqqedem*). Later on, his
kinsman Lot also chooses to "journey eastward" (*miqqedem*); see Gen
13:8–13.[50] But all this does not detract from the universalism displayed by
J in these chapters. I refer the reader to chapter 4 below and to the section
"A Deconstructive Approach."

Inaugurating the history of salvation after the primeval "prologue,"
Abraham is to leave Chaldea and go to the Promised Land. Within this
context, Genesis 12 celebrates liberation by means of a first exodus and
a first wandering in the desert toward a redeemed identity. Leaving Ur,
Abraham is leaving "the land of Shinar," the locale of confusion and
arrogance,[51] and initiates the ruin of the "tower," the deconstruction of
the empire. "All these themes seem to point very clearly to the concerns

---

Primeval Era; and now, Gunkel, *Israel and Babylon: The Babylonian Influence on Israelite
Religion.* The polemics against Babylon in our text are emphasized by Benno Jacob,
Umberto Cassuto, Gerhard von Rad, and others. It stands to reason that in his description of a landscape, J would have used elements well known by his audience: the hilly dry
land of Judah, for instance. This does not in the least affect the universal scope of J. Van
Seters states that by applying to humanity in general principles familiar to the prophets,
their "natural religion . . . is given universal scope" (*Prologue to History*, 191).

49. Suffice it here to refer to Gerhard von Rad, Claus Westermann, Robert Alter, and
many other scholars proposing the same idea. (Alter calls attention to the radical change
of orientation from the primeval stories to the patriarchal sagas. While the former look
toward the past, the latter's direction is toward the future [see especially Gen 49:1], Alter,
Genesis, xliv.)

50. That Lot made the wrong choice is confirmed by the fact that he falls captive to
four kings, including "Amraphel of Shinar." Two of the other kings, of Sodom and of
Gomorrah, fall into "bitumen pits" (Gen 14:1, 9–10)!

51. See Isaiah 47 ("You [Babylon] shall no more be called tender and delicate . . .
your shame will be seen . . . [you] who sit securely, who say in your heart, 'I am, and
there is no one besides me.' But evil shall come upon you . . . and ruin shall come on you
suddenly. . . those with whom you have labored . . . they all wander about in their own
paths; there is no one to save you" [NRSV].) Revelation 17:5 reads, "Babylon the great,
mother of prostitutes and of the abominations of the earth." Contra Crüsemann, "Die
Eigenständigkeit der Urgeschichte," 11–29.

of the exilic community."[52] Hiebert does not take sufficiently into account the dramatic caesura that inaugurates the history of *Israel*. Abraham is more than another link in the chain of human generations. He is not independent of humanity's origins, but he is the Particular that transforms and reorients the Universal.

And not only Abraham, but also Jacob. In a judicious comparison of our text with Gen 28:10–32 (the story of Jacob's ladder), Michael Fishbane states that Jacob's vision is a "counterpoint to the hubris of the tower building on the plain of Shinar." Jacob's staircase spells "promise and hope—not doom and dispersal . . . For indeed this place was for him a sacred center, a 'cosmic mountain' linking heaven and earth (v.18). It was, as he says, a Beth-el, a 'house of God' and a 'gateway to heaven' (v.17) . . . a 'House of Elohim' (vv. 20–22)."[53]

Another parallel needs to be drawn: this time with the previous stories by J in Genesis 2–9*. I am alluding to the guilty party's nonrecognition of sin.[54] The textual silence on this point is indeed comparable with the lack of repentance from Adam and Eve, from Cain, from the "sons of God," and from humans at the time of the flood. True, there appear at times redeeming characters like Abel, Seth, and Noah; but J reports no dramatic event that would divert the catastrophic course of history. Even Noah does not intercede for his fellow human beings. The contrast of these unrepentant characters with Abraham in Genesis 18 is stark and deliberate.

Critique of the Empire (Sociopolitical Criticism)

Here, I intend to focus on a couple points that emphasize J's revulsion toward the empire.

I will insist all along on the intrinsic textual scorn vis-à-vis the robotization of the Babelians. They share not only one language but also

---

52. Van Seters, *Prologue to History*, 190. On the basis of the interruption in the constructions of Babel (Gen 11:8–9), Markus Witte goes so far as to evoke the failed attempt of Alexander the Great to rebuild the Esagila in Babylon. Then the common language and the common project of the builders in Babel reflect "die Praxis Alexanders" to found cities and to call them by his own name, as well as the Hellenistic "uniformization" of culture (in contrast to the Persian plurality of languages; see the book of Esther). See Witte, *Die biblische Urgeschichte*, 321.

53. Fishbane, *Text and Texture*, 113.

54. Contrast this with stories in the books of Daniel, Jonah, Judith, and others.

uniform concepts. All their energies are mobilized for the construction of monuments to their own glory. The traditional linking of the Lamech-like Nimrod the Kushite with the construction of Babel (see Gen 10:8–12) goes in the same direction.[55] This and the likeness of the material used in Babel and by the pharaohs for the erection of their pyramids and other mausoleums bring the Bible to condemn equally Babylonian and Egyptian megalomania. As a symbol of this, in the tale of Babel, the tower evidently plays a major role. The prophets concur in their condemnation of human lust for power and glory; see Isa 2:12ff.; 30:25; cf. Ezek 26:2ff. (against Tyre).

The very anonymity of the throng of builders, whose uniform thoughts show their function in the story as a collective mass, runs against the ideal process of individuation, of which Carl Jung speaks: that is, growing to a full psychic wholeness. Jung writes, "A sane and normal society is one in which people habitually disagree, because general agreement is relatively rare outside the sphere of instinctive human qualities."[56] But what we have here is all but a parody of a "sane society." The Babelians do not aim for self-individuation but self-deification. For J, this amounts to self-alienation and self-dissolution. The whole scene of Gen 11:1–9 is a scene of confusion, starting with a confusion of the mind or psyche. "Babel-Confusion" (11:9) is the ultimate unveiling of what had been going on since the beginning in the valley of Shinar; it is not just an "arresting development."

For, since the beginning, the Babelians wanted much more than just a "there" to settle in. They wanted to build an empire.[57] The expressed mention of a tower at the center of their city says it all. As we saw earlier, the tower of Babel is a ziggurat, a temple dedicated to Marduk, but it is also a stronghold, the redoubt of a fortified city, and we understand Walter Brueggemann when he speaks of a "fortress mentality."[58] Such

55. Besides Jewish tradition as a whole, see also Milton, *Paradise Lost* [1667], book xii, lines 38–39: for Milton the tar used for building Babel is "a black bitumous gurge" that "boils out from underground, the mouth of hell."

56. Jung, "Approaching the Unconscious," 59.

57. Derrida ("Des Tours de Babel") says that Babel "was establishing its empire, which it wanted universal, and its tongue, which it also attempts to impose on the universe. The moment of this project immediately precedes the deconstruction of the tower" (105–6). Derrida calls the Babel endeavor "a colonial violence" that God interrupts as well as "the linguistic imperialism . . . [as God] subjects them [the Babelians] to the law of a translation both necessary and impossible" (111); see chap. 6 below.

58. In Dan 11:31, the sanctuary is a mountain fortress. See the close reading we offer of v. 5 below; see also Brueggemann, *Genesis*, 100.

an introverted withdrawal implies one people, one metropolis, and one state religion. For Klaus Seybold, we have here an implicit critique of the David-Solomon empire.[59] Seybold cites Judges 9; 2 Samuel 7; and Psalm 2; but these texts are all late. So if we maintain these parallels, they pull Gen 11:1–9 to a late date as well.

The scattering of "the same language"—no doubt the one of the ruling party—implies the shattering of the empire and its monoglossic culture. Genesis 11 is a satire of the imperial cultures that Abraham and Sarah are commanded to leave behind. Oduyoye contrasts Genesis 3 and Genesis 11. While Genesis 3 illustrates intellectual hubris, Genesis 11 is a comment on political hubris.[60] So if we prolong this line of thought, we might retrace the Yahwist's narratival development in Genesis 2–11* by focusing on human hubris throughout his composition: Genesis 3 illustrates ethical hubris (a matter of good and evil); Genesis 4, psychological hubris (the other is hell on earth); Genesis 6, religious hubris (playing the angel); Genesis 6–9, the will-to-power hubris (a culture of violence); Genesis 11, political hubris (playing God).

On the Matter of Relevance

Why tell the story of the Tower of Babel at all in the twenty-first century? A narrative of the quality of the Tower of Babel story makes its message immediately universal, because it is presented as a human experience mirroring innumerable similar experiences. The story makes paradigmatic a situation or an event that otherwise could have appeared as an isolated incident in time and limited in scope.

The aesthetic response of Alberto Manguel is valid, according to which, "They [the readers] want words to name the comforts of peace but also the confusion, destruction and desperation brought on by our ambitions."[61] This statement parallels what Bronislaw Malinowski earlier had said of myth: "Belief . . . whether in magic or in religion, is closely associated with the deepest desires of man, with his fears and hopes, with his passions and sentiments."[62] J's motivation, however, goes further than this;

---

59. Seybold, "Der Turmbau." Vogels speaks of "un pouvoir centralisateur qui supprime tout pluralisme," et d' "impérialisme" (*Nos origines*, 185).
60. Oduyoye, "Balala-balala."
61. Manguel, *The City of Words*, 84.
62. Malinowski, *Magic*, 144.

he wants his readers to realize that, among other things, they participate in Babel's building. "Babel" then becomes the symbol of all of our constructions and fabrications, with their inexorable outcome: confusion (of our life messages) and scattering (of all the pieces of our projects).

PART ONE

CHAPTER TWO

Construction

Working Translation

IN WHAT FOLLOWS, I provide a working rendition of the Hebrew text on Babel, as it is needed at this point, before proceeding later with a translation dictated by the exegesis of the text:[1]

1. *It so happened that all the earth had one language with the same utterances.*

2. *And on their journey from [to] the east, they found a depression in the land of Shinar. There they settled.*

3. *They said one to the other, "Come! Let us brick bricks that we'll flame in the flame." Brick was to them like stone, and bitumen was to them like mortar.*

4. *They said, "Come! Let's build us a city with a tower whose top (is) in heaven. Let's make us a name, lest we be scattered over the face of all the earth."*

5. *YHWH descended to see the city and the tower that the humans were building.*

6. *YHWH said, "Behold, (they are) one nation and (there is) one language for all. This is what they have started to make, so that henceforth no(thing) will be inaccessible to them (in) all that they will plot to make.*

7. *Come! Let us descend and confound there their language, so that they will not hear [understand] the language of one another."*

1. See chapter 5, below, "Translation."

8. *YHWH scattered them from there over the face of all the earth, and they ceased building the city.*

9. *This is why He called its name Babel ["babble"], because there YHWH confounded the language of all the earth, and from there He scattered them over the face of all the earth.*

Linguistic Notes (Philological Criticism)

Verse 1

Literally, the Hebrew text says, *all the earth was [has is expected] one lip [speech]*. Umberto Cassuto refers to the same construction in Pss 109:4; 120:7; and elsewhere. So, what characterized humanity was their one speech. Most translations into English understand the following expression, *debarim 'ahadim* as pleonastically repeating "one language/speech."[2] But the economy of words in Gen 11:1–9 is so tight as to exclude all "trimmings." The unexpected use of the word *debarim* here should put the reader on alert. I translate, "with a few subjects/utterances," as an indication of the severe limitation of interests on the part of the crowd. The subject of their discourse was narrow; they all were talking of identical things.[3] Rashi (after *Tg. Jon.*) understands, "one plan, a common counsel," and A. B. Ehrlich, "a limited vocabulary."[4] Ibn Ezra states, "The learned and the ignorant in those days spoke alike."[5] André Wénin goes in the

2. It can be said about this expression's usual translation what Jacques Derrida observed about the translation of *pharmakon* in Plato's *Phaedrus*, namely, that translators "have turned *pharmakon* [alternatively, *debarim 'ahadim* Genesis 11] on its strange and invisible pivot, presenting it from a single one, the most reassuring of its poles" (Derrida, *Dissemination*, 97; quoted in Sherwood, *The Prostitute and the Prophet*, 180). See also Collins's critique of Sherwood's work in *The Bible after Babel*. A summary of Collins's favorable assessment is on p. 22: "Sometimes, she strains in this effort, but on the whole it is enlightening.")

3. *'Ahadim* in the sense of "a few" appears five times: here plus in Gen 27:44; 29:20; Ezek 37:17; and Dan 11:20. In the *Iliad*, Nestor and Odysseus "speak the same," i.e., show the same purpose (3.127ff. See Snell, *Poetry and Society*, 19). Strikingly, at the level of Homer's works, the unanimity is always for the accomplishment of an action. Now, the mentality reflected in Genesis 11 is arguably closer to Homer's than to modern times'. In Genesis also, the unity of language is both conditioned by and conditioning the unity of action, namely, the building of Babel. That is why, when the common language is broken up into languages, the common action is also discontinued.

4. See Ehrlich, *Genesis und Exodus*. Cassuto thinks that these renderings are forced, and he refers to Ezek 3:6; but there the term is *lašôn*, not *debarim*.

5. Ibn Ezra, *Genesis [Bereshit]*, 137–38.

same direction. He writes that humanity uttered "le même discours . . . des paroles identiques . . . une pensée unique." He stresses the repetitiveness of their sayings, "to brick bricks, to flame in the flame . . ." They speak to no one else but themselves. Their "we" is autistic.[6] (When God duplicates the human "we" in v. 7, whatever is conveyed here by the plural form indicates a *communication* with someone else, whether human or angel.)

As to the "one language" that they spoke, it is not said which one it was. Rashi thought of the Hebrew, which he identified also with God's word in creating the world. Most interesting is j. *Megillah* 1.9 for which they spoke all kinds of languages with each one understanding them all.[7]

'Aḥath/'eḥad: four times in the text, v. 1 (twice) and v. 6 (twice). Thus, J. P. Fokkelman says, "The primary importance of the unity of language has been made manifest stylistically and structurally."[8]

Verse 2

The people in the story are migrating *miqqedem* (basically, "from the front"; cf. Isa 9:11; Job 23:8). Are they coming "from the east" or going "eastward" (see KBL, 823; cf. Judg 6:3, 33)? Redaq (Rabbi David Qimchi, twelfth and thirteenth centuries) saw here an allusion to the use of the term in the story of Adam and Eve ("east of Eden" in Gen 3:24). He says that these people came from the place where Adam was created. He therefore understands the phrase as "eastward," that is toward Mesopotamia coming from Palestine (where Eden lies according to Genesis 2–3).[9] Umberto Cassuto also understands the term as an orientation point from Israel's perspective.[10] In contrast, Abraham of Ur will migrate westward (12:4).

Ironically, the action occurs in a valley. (Settling in a valley contrasts with erecting a huge tower that will compensate for the absence of mountains in Mesopotamia.)[11] The valley is called *Shinar*, a name found again in Gen 10:10 (in association with the sinister Nimrod), in Gen 14:1, 9 (where the "king of Shinar" is one of Abraham's foes), Josh 7:21 (where a coat from Shinar is an item in Achan's booty), Isa 11:11 (in which place a remnant of Israel is scattered). "The land of Shinar" in Zech 5:11 is the place where

---

6. A. Wénin, *D'Adam à Abraham*, 219, 223.
7. See Acts 2:6.
8. Fokkelman, *Narrative Art*, 27.
9. See LaCocque, *The Trial of Innocence*, 64–66.
10. Cassuto, *Genesis*, 240; cf. Gen 13:11.
11. Herodotus describes Babylon as a "great plain" (*The History* 1.178, 193).

"the woman in the basket of Wickedness" is set to dwell. Significant is the text of Dan 1:2, where "Shinar" is used in a clearly disparaging way; the context comments about "the treasury house of his [Nebuchadnezzar's] gods" and again associates Babylon with an idolatrous shrine. "Shinar" is here set in apposition to "home of his gods," that is, a pagan temple.

In ancient Israel, valleys are seen with a certain suspicion (see, for example, the plains of Moab in Numbers 22; Sheol evidently is underground and is foreshadowed by the Hinnom valley in Jerusalem). God's locales of predilection for his epiphanies are mountains: Sinai, Horeb, Nebo (set in opposition to the plains of Moab, says Deut 34:1), and Zion. Nothing good is expected to happen in a valley (cf. the valley of death [Ps 23:4]). The Israelite aversion to valleys explains the Aramaeans' taunt that YHWH is a God of mountains, not a God of the valleys (1 Kgs 20:28, the word here is ʿamaqim).

Benoseʿam ("on their journey"). Let us note with J. P. Fokkelman that the people arrive "there," "more or less accidentally" as indicated by the verb *nasaʿ* ("to journey") "typical of nomadic mobility."[12] Unsatisfied with the horizontal plane, they open up a vertical one (v. 4). Fokkelman continues with the remark that the divine response to the vertical axis "has immense consequences for the horizontal plane . . . After the maximum concentration maximum 'decentration' sets in."

Šam ("there"). The insistence of the text on the spatial dimension of the story is striking (see chapter 3, below).

Verse 3

ʾIš ʾel reʿehu ("a man to his companion") appears also in v. 7 (*ʾiš šephath reʿehu* ["each the language of his companion"]). From the J source, see also Gen 15:10; 31:49; 43:33.

Habah ("Come!") appears also in vv. 4 and 7 (see also, from J, Gen 38:16; Exod 1:10). The people use the exhortative to gather all their energies for a common purpose; God repeats it in v. 7 in a parodic way. From this locution, Bernhard Anderson concludes, however, that the Babelians are "acting in democratic concert."[13] But the point is elsewhere—in the unanimity of their project, consistent with the uniqueness of language and purpose. There is here no praise for their creativity. Bruno Snell

12. Fokkelman, *Narrative Art*, 44.
13. Anderson, *From Creation to New Creation*, 172.

reminds us that "nothing can be brought into being that has not previously been thought out—and that means formulated in speech."[14]

Parallel to the cohortative *habah*, which is also put in the mouth of God in Gen 11:7, the verse is morphologically in the plural: "let us descend and let us confound." The plurality of the culprits affects the divine party's discourse.

On the paronomasias of *nilbenah lebenim* and *niśrephah liśrephah*, followed by *hallebenah le'aben* and *haḥémar . . . laḥomer* (four pairs of words), see above under "Verse 1."

Niśrephah liśrephah (We'll flame in the flame): the redundant form stresses the high quality of the bricks (not sun-dried) as they plan to build an enduring city and an enormous high-rise tower, necessitating sturdy material. On *ḥemar* and *ḥomer*, see respectively Gen 14:10 and Exod 2:3; Nah 3:14 and Exod 1:14. What J finds noteworthy is the substitution of construction materials in Babylon: instead of stones, bricks; instead of (hardened) clay, bitumen.[15] The accent is on the artificiality of the enterprise: counterfeited materials to build the sham mountain that the ziggurat imitated. This purely *human* production parallels the Hebrew slavery in Egypt, according to Exod 1:14 (where incidentally the words "bricks" and "mortar" are found).[16] So even the term "brick" in Genesis 11 is loaded with bad memories in Israel. After all, the Babylonian king was molding the first brick, called the "cornerstone," of the upcoming temple; the king's name was branded on the brick, and v. 4 here ("let us make a name for ourselves") may allude to that practice.

Requirements for altar building in ancient Israel show that the purpose for a constructed object determined the type of materials employed (both for building and for tooling; see Exod 20:22–26; 27:1 = 38:1; 2 Chr 4:1). Note from these passages the naturalness of the materials. Using iron tools would "pollute" the altar, according to Exod 20:22; cf. Josh 8:31.[17]

---

14. Snell, *Poetry and Society,* 10.

15. Ironically, a modern Iranian missile's name *Sajjil* means "baked clay"!

16. See *3 Bar.* 3:5: a group among the builders forces others to build the tower after "they plotted"—says the text—its construction. The parallel with the Egyptian slavery is evident. "The store cities ("fortified cities" in LXX) of Exod 1:11 may have been interpreted as a tower," says H. E. Gaylord Jr., translator of *3 Baruch,* 659.

17. According to Dante (*De Vulgari Eloquentia* 1.7.4–5), "Nimrod" attempted to overcome nature and its divine author.

Verse 4

'*Ir umigdal* (a city and a tower): Although the tower is absent in v. 8 (but present in v. 5), there is no reason for belittling the importance of the tower in Genesis 11. The people want to build a city with a tower "whose top is in heaven." To be stressed is the ludicrous paradox of building such a column in a valley or a depression. About its height let us note that the existence of a Near Eastern cliché (i.e., "its top in the sky") does not justify taking this expression at face value.[18] For the Babylonians, reaching up to the divine was always the rationale for constructing a ziggurat. From Israel's viewpoint, however, the same words become offensive and blasphemous; they reveal "an arrogant revolt against divine authority."[19] Israel stresses God's descent from his abode to meet humans where they are (in Genesis 11, see vv. 5 and 7; and also Exod 19:11, 18, 20; 33:9; 34:5; cf. Mark 1:10).

Pierre Auffret calls attention to the construction of the units '*ir umigdal* (in which the *waw/u* is clearly cementing the two words), and *wero'šo baššamayim* ("and its head in heaven," where the *waw* marks a caesura, in contrast with a continuum that the expected '*ašer* would indicate). So *wero'šo* refers to the city, whose summit, thanks to a tower, will reach heaven.[20]

Wero'šo baššamayim ("and its head in heaven") is set in contrast to the mention in the second part of the story of "on the surface of all the earth" (11:8, 9). In Deut 1:28, we find again the expression "up to heaven" (said about fortified cities of the Canaanites), and it could therefore be understood as simply pleonastic. But the description belongs to the panicky report of the spies after their foray into Canaan. The spies' panic in Deut 1:28 contrasts with Caleb's mien (cf. Num 14:24) and does stir up God's wrath (Deut 1:34–40). Deuteronomy 9:1 (*ubeṣuroth baššamayim*: "and its fortifications [as high as] heaven") is a quotation from the spies'

18. About the height of the tower let us note that the existence of a Near Eastern cliché ("its top in the sky") does not prove that the expression in the Bible is merely metaphorical. A shift in semantic fields in most cases entails a shift of meaning. There is a world of difference between the English word *skyscraper* and the Soviet conclusion that Sputnik did not find any god up in the sky. Besides, it may well be no cliché at all. The phrase, says Theodor Gaster, was common among many ancient cultures to describe human hubris. The fitting punishment was the confusion of languages (*Myth, Legend, and Custom in the Old Testament*, 135).

19. To quote Hiebert, "The Tower of Babel," 37, who rejects this possibility.

20. Auffret, *La Sagesse a bâti sa maison*, 81.

report in 1:28. Moses says it ironically, and the connection might become more transparent if this part of Moses's speech were put between quotation marks. Furthermore, if any doubt remained as to the negativity of the image, it is brushed aside by texts like Dan 4:17, 19 (said ironically of the sham greatness of Nebuchadnezzar): the "tree" will be felled! Along the same line of thought, Dan 8:10–12 says that the goat's horn (that is, Antiochus Epiphanes) grew as high as the host of heaven—but the horn will be broken (vv. 22, 25). Therefore it may well be that J's expression here in Gen 11:4 is also ironical. In Jer 51:53, J's metaphor is replaced by a military scene wherein Babylon, which "should mount up to heaven," falls prey to destroyers sent by YHWH.

Wene'eseh lanu šem ("And let's make a name for ourselves"): noteworthy is the paronomasia of *šem* (name) and *šam* (there) in the story. The same combination is found again in other texts speaking of the Name of God dwelling "there" (that is, in the Jerusalem temple), especially in the Deuteronomistic tradition. In this tradition, the expression *šemô šam* becomes a leitmotif (see Deut 12:11; 14:23; 16:2, 6, 11; 26:2; see also *šemi šam* in Jer 7:12 and Neh 1:9). Within this intertextual configuration, the Babelians' purpose sounds blasphemously arrogant (on *šem*, see Gen 6:1–4; Prov 22:1).

Genesis 11:4, according to Hiebert, does not address "pride or imperial pretensions" but "cultural uniformity."[21] But "cultural uniformity" itself may be a manifestation of pride and imperial pretensions! The fact that here God "does not speak about the tower" responds to the dictates of the story structure, as v. 6 "mirrors the opening sentence of part 1" and thus addresses the very circumstantial condition for the building of the city and the tower.[22] Any argument from silence is unwarranted. At any rate, God declares that the situation created by the Shinar throng cannot be permitted to develop further.

True, there are texts where making a (good) name is positively stated. But Abraham does *not* make a name for himself in Gen 12:2. Neither does Abishai in 2 Sam 23:18 or Benaiah in 2 Sam 23:22 or again Uzziah in 2 Chr 26:8, 15. God can of course make a name for himself (Josh 7:9; 2 Sam 7:23 = 1 Chr 17:21; Neh 9:10), but we are then in a totally different domain. In Zeph 3:19–20, *God* is the agent and Israel is the beneficiary.[23]

---

21. Hiebert, "The Tower of Babel," 43
22. Ibid.
23. Note with Cassuto, *A Commentary on the Book of Genesis: 2*, 231 (mentioning

The same is true in Isa 63:12; Jer 32:20; Ezek 16:14; 34:29; 39:13. Second Samuel 18:18 and Isa 48:19 clearly belong to another idiom. In Gen 11:4, the very anomalous and disturbing reflexive form "let us make . . . for ourselves" arguably is indicative of a misplaced pride on the part of the builders. They want to be the agents of their own eminence.

One text, however, deserves notice as possibly paralleling Gen 11:4 with a positive assessment. See 2 Sam 8:13: *Weyaʿas David šem* ("David made a name"). But the parallel with Genesis 11 is stronger in the English translation ("David made a name [for himself]") than in the Hebrew text. The latter does not say that David wanted to make a name for himself (intention), but that his fame spread (result). The difference is substantive.

Pen naphuṣ ("lest we be scattered"): "In the Bible, the root *puṣ*," says J. Severino Croatto, "always conveys a negative sense . . . [T]his is the same verb widely employed by the Prophets, especially Ezekiel, in oracles of punishment or promise within the context of the exile . . . . [I]t denotes the loss of identity . . . [I]t has to do with the dissolution of Babylon itself by means of the same weapon (the scattering over the whole earth) used by Babylon at the time of the destruction of Judah and especially of Jerusalem."[24]

On the negative sense of the locution, see Ezek 11:16–21; 12:15; 20:33–38; in the primeval tradition, see Gen 9:19 and 10:18.[25] In fact, the verb *puṣ* is a *terminus technicus* describing the 587 exile (see Deut 4:27; 28:64; 30:3; Jer 9:15; 13:24; 18:17; 30:11; Ezek 11:17; 20:34, 41; 28:25; 34:6, 12). As to the use of the verb in the hifil (factitive) mode with YHWH as its subject, it again occurs only in late Deuteronomistic texts like those in Deuteronomy already cited.

The people are conniving for fear of being scattered, but that is exactly what will happen in the future, so that their state of fear appears

Zeph 3:9), that the reestablishment of the one language (*śaphah berurah*, pure language) of humanity at large is concurrent with bringing the proud low (v. 11). In this prophetic text also, the one speech serves to communicate ideas that Zephaniah ingeniously summarizes as "calling on the Name of YHWH."

24. Croatto, "A Reading of the Story of the Tower of Babel," 220–21. Croatto cites Isaiah 47 as a parallel text. Croatto, incidentally, sees also in the unity of the Babelian language "the essential instrument for domination wielded by any imperial project" (204).

25. Anderson sees in Genesis 9 and 10 "no suggestion of scattering being an act of divine judgment, as in the Babel story (see also Isa 33:3)" (*Creation to New Creation*, 176). But, in the Genesis texts invoked, the scattering is set in a specific context regarding Canaan. And Isa 33:3 is certainly negative enough! Genesis 10:32, which is also cited as affording a general and neutral meaning, uses precisely another verb (*parad*).

prophetic. Hence, Rav Shimon ben Chalafta (ca. 210 CE) invoked Prov 18:7 "a fool's mouth is his ruin!"[26] Of this Gen 11:8 will provide an illustration. The verb *puṣ* is present in both places, as well as the phrase *ʿal penei kol haʾareṣ* (over the face of all the earth; already found in Gen 1:29 [creation], and 7:3 [the flood]; see also 8:9), to be once more repeated at the end of the story (v. 9). Let us note that the KBL gives as the basic meaning of *puṣ* "*zerbrechen*, break asunder."[27] It can be used in military parlance for the sorry fate of the enemy (Num 10:35; 1 Sam 11:11; Ps 68:2). The derivative noun *thephuṣah* has a negative meaning (see Jer 25:34 and Zeph 3:10). Further on, the verb *naphaṣ* in Gen 9:19 (a cognate of *puṣ*), already mentioned, is at least as much negative. Its basic meaning is "shatter" and may describe an action of dashing to pieces (KBL refers to Jer 13:14; 48:12; Ps 2:9; 137:9). For the sense of "pulverize," see Isa 27:9 and Jer 51:20–23.

Verse 5

Wayered YHWH ("and YHWH came down"). The irony is striking. In spite of the dimensions of the tower, whose top is in heaven, YHWH has to descend to see it. God's descent from heaven is not punitive per se (see Exod 19:11, for example), but, in Genesis 11, the divine descending movement evidently reverses the human ascending one in part 1 (vv. 4–5).[28] So here once again the sense of the expression depends on the context.[29]

Lireʾoth ("to see"): J's use of this verb in his narratives is important, and often in connection with the theophany (then in the passive form in the sense of "to appear" [to someone] as in Gen 12:6–7; 18:1; 26:2, 24). In the transitive form, we are syntactically on a different ground; but not from a semantic point of view. God sees and God is seen refer both to a divine way of communication. God reveals himself, and the truth of human ambition is revealed to him. J's use of the lexeme conveys a deeper sense than just a simple anthropomorphism. With God's vision of things, we expect the unveiling of the veritable Babelian purpose in building city

26. See Zlotowitz and Scherman, *Bereishis* = *Genesis*, 337.

27. KBL, 755.

28. See von Rad, *Genesis*, 149; see also Sarna, *Understanding Genesis*, 250; Hamilton, *Genesis 1–17*, 354; Gowan, *When Man Becomes God*, 27. Rollins states, "The holy can be imagined as a transcendent being with personal attributes . . . (e.g., 'an eye to observe our ways')" (Rollins and Kille, *Psychological Insight into the Bible*, 109).

29. On the divine descent in J texts, see also Gen 18:21; Exod 3:8; 19:11; 34:5; and note the dramatic setting of each occurrence of the expression.

and tower. Here God's vision is of the same quality as in 7:1 where it is
said that God "saw" that Noah was a just, or in Exod 2:25, where God is
said to have seen the people's misery.

> *'Et-ha'ir we'et-hammigdal* ("the city and the tower"): Two edifices
are identified. Building a city would not by itself stir God's concern (see
Gen 4:17), but the additional immense tower divulges the true purpose
and identity of the city, and it gives away the motive of the builders. Verse
6 will spell out God's reaction; the standpoint is definitely ethical (*yazmu*
[v. 6]: "they connive, they plot").

> *Banu benei* ("the sons of [x] . . . were building"): the paronomasia
adds itself to other similar samples in the story. In v. 4, e.g., *šamayim*
("heaven") was in assonance with *šam* ("there"), itself in assonance with
šem ("name"), etc. Strictly speaking, the verb's form in the past tense
would indicate that the construction was completed. Verse 8 below indicates that such is not the case; I therefore translate it with "were building."
The perfect tense is justified as God's action succeeds the human one. It
must not be translated by "had built."[30] The same grammatical use of the
past tense followed by the future is present in vv. 5 and 7 for the descent
of God.

> *Adam.* The use of this word to designate humanity in general is char-
acteristic of J.

Verse 6

Hen ("Behold"). This is also a characteristic term in the work of J: see Gen
3:22; 4:14; 15:3; Exod 4:1; 5:5; 8:22, etc. In all these cases, *hen* introduces
a rhetorical reflection occasioned by regret or sorrow.

> *'Am 'eḥad* ("one nation"): This is the first use of the lexeme *nation* in
the Bible. First of all, it stresses the kinship that binds the builders like in
a single clan. Second, the word emphasizes J's shift in perspective from individuals like Adam, Eve, Cain, Abel, Seth, Noah to human collectivities
or to an undifferentiated "people." The human actors in this myth remain
carefully anonymous. They act and they are addressed as a throng, whose
dispersion will be collectively experienced as a fatal blow.

> *Weśaphah 'aḥath* (and one language). See v. 1 above.

> *Wezeh haḥillam la'asoth* ("this is what they have started [they have
profaned] to make"): They started or they profaned; there is indeed

---

30. *Pace* Croatto, "A Reading of the Story of the Tower of Babel," 211.

ambivalence in the root *ḥll*. In the context of terms entirely negative, the allusion to blasphemy is not to be overlooked.[31] The thematic parallel with Gen 3:22 is evident. In both cases, the Yahwist's God opines that humans have only *started* with a behavior that needs to be nipped in the bud. The verb *ḥalal* in 10:8 has become decidedly negative (in connection with Nimrod), as it is here in 11:6.

We ʿattah ("and now"): Regarding the interjection *we ʿattah* (generally translated into English by "then" or "now"), the best study has been written by H. A. Brongers.[32] The following developments I credit to him. The time adverb appears 275 times in the Bible (in Genesis alone, twenty-seven times). It comes always in direct discourse, generally introducing a first or second person in a cohortative form. With the prefix *we-*, it solicits attention to a present situation as an outcome of the past or as prefiguring the future. It should not necessarily be translated "and now." It indicates a turning point: "and now/but now/from now on/*henceforth*." It does so in Gen 11:6; see 2 Sam 2:6; 2 Kgs 12:7. It can mean "therefore" as in Gen 21:23. The adverbial use of *we ʿattah* is a caesura in text and in time. That is why I see v. 6 as the pivot between the two parts of the story, rather than v. 5, as several critics prefer.[33] For in Gen 11:6, the interjection announces the drawing of a line between the human endeavor and the divine decision to keep human history in check. True, the Babelians do not repent, but the U-turn implied in the Hebrew word for "repentance" (*thešubah*) is implicitly present, albeit as God's initiative.

As to the combination of *hen* and *we ʿattah* that so closely recalls Gen 3:22, it would already by itself demonstrate that, for J, the Babel builders' hubris falls in line with the primeval couple's desire to be like God. Their dispersion at the end is the collective pendant of Adam and Eve's expulsion from paradise.[34]

Lo᾽ yibbaṣer mehem ("it is not inaccessible to them"): the expression is found again only in Job 42:2 (*welo᾽ yibbaṣer mimkha mezimmah*

31. In the general sense of "beginning," the root was already present in four other texts: Gen 4:26 (the time of Seth and Enoch); 6:1 (time of the impure mix with angels); 9:20 (the drunk and naked Noah); 10:8 (Nimrod). Only in Gen 4:26 is it not an aborted beginning, but the midrash reads this text negatively: they started to call *men and things* by the name of YHWH! (See Neher, *L'Exil de la parole*, 117).

32. Brongers, "Bemerkungen zum Gebrauch des Adverbialen *weʿattah* im Alten Testament."

33. So, e.g., Fokkelman, "Genesis 11:1–9," 22–23.

34. On the fall of the arrogant city, see Jer 50:31; cf. Isa 13:9. On the impending dispersion, see Isa 47:15; cf. Jer 51:2, 6, 9, 45.

["no purpose of yours {God's} can be thwarted"], NRSV). Once more, what is appropriate only to the divinity is applied by and to humans (see above on the "name," v. 4). Humans try to be "like God," a confirmation of our reading their project as self-deification. Note in both Genesis 3 and Genesis 11 the presence of the root *zmm* ("to purpose to do"). In Job, the design is God's; in Genesis 11, the design is of those who want to play God (cf. Gen 6:5–6; Hab 1:11, 16).

Kol ʾašer yazmu laʿasoth ("all that they will purpose to make") corresponds to the *debarim ʾaḥadim* of v. 1; they were driven by a unique purpose. While the root *zmm* appears to be present in both positive and negative contexts, it remains in Pss 37:12; 140:9; and Prov 30:32, as well as in Deut 19:19 and Ps 31:14, that the agent of the action is the wicked. Psalm 17:3 is more difficult. It should be rendered, "I plan/ concoct [things], but my mouth does not go beyond [that]." In Jer 4:28 and 51:12, in Lam 2:17 and Zech 1:6, God is the agent of a negative action. In Zech 8:14–15, God again is the agent, and his plans are alternatively for weal and woe, but there is clearly a play on words, making *zmm* an ambivalent concept. See the important text of Jer 51:11–12, on the divine intention to destroy Babel; compare for the idea, Jer 50:45–46.

In summary, *zmm* is uniformly used negatively (with the possible exception of Zech 8:15 where *God* is the agent). Finally, only one other text might be considered an exception: Prov 31:16 speaks of "the virtuous woman" considering buying a field. Here the agent is "virtuous," and her aim is laudable. But the use of the term under consideration is a poetic license, as the verse belongs to an alphabetically set pericope (31:10–31) under the letter *zayin*. I therefore maintain that in Gen 11:6 the verb is to be read with the sense of plotting or scheming.

Verse 7

Nerdah ("Let us go down"). See above, v. 5.

Wenabelah šam sephatham ("and let us there mix up their language") says God. *Nabelah* is in paronomasia with *nilbenah lebenim* ("Let us make bricks") in v. 3 and *nibneh* ("Let us build") in v. 4. The alliteration with *babel* is crucial. (Similarly, *ʾiš . . . reʿehu* ["one another"] reverses the use of the same terms in v. 3.) The root *bll* ("to mix"), as a matter of fact, builds a pun with "Babel" of which it provides here a forced etymology. The message is clear: the truth is that the great Babylon, the "gate of the divine," is the epicenter of universal confusion, a gate to human breakup. True, consistent with the previously explored vocabulary of the Yahwist, the use of the verb *balal* is not always negative. The context may at times point to the mixing of ingredients for the daily sacrifice in the shrine as in Exod 29:40; Lev 14:10; Num 6:14; and others.[35] It means also "to moisten," even "to anoint" someone with oil (see Ps 92:11). But in texts that can really be tallied with Gen 11:7, the sense is definitely negative: Hos 7:8 says Ephraim is confusedly mixed with nations (cf. Hos 9:1). Isaiah 64:5 presents a confession in the first-person plural in which the term means "to be rotten" or, at least, "to be withered." There is no surprise, therefore, in finding the LXX translation of the verb in Gen 11:7 as *syncheō* ("to confuse"). After the "mixing up," people will not be able to understand one another.

Let us note about the verb *wenabelah* its surprising vocalization. Rabbi Yoseph ben Isaac (twelfth century) in *Bechor Shor*, reads here a feminine niphal (passive) form: "their language will become withered."[36] In Wisdom literature, the same verb is rendered by "to become senseless, foolish" (see Job 30:8; Prov 30:22, 32). J's choice of this term is deliberate. In Gen 10:5 and 32 P uses another verb *parad* ("to divide, to separate [from each other]"), as in Prov 18:18 or Ruth 1:17, with a somewhat more mitigated effect. The Yahwist's aim is to both deride the pretensions of Babylon and insist on the serendipitous advent of Abraham that will be a blessing for all (scattered and disoriented) nations (Gen 12:2). Read in succession, all the J stories in the primeval era display a sliding scale of human sinfulness.[37] Far from being an exception, Genesis 11 comes as the apex of human depravity, if only because now J points to an actual and demonic chronotope: Babylon of the sixth century. Such a precision comes in contrast with the preceding J situations (the "fall," a paradigmatic fratricide, the mixing of species—of heavenly beings and earthly beings, and the flood) that are all imaginary and ahistorical (that is, not experienced by the audience/readership in the exact terms of the myths).

---

35. See KBL 130

36. See Isa 24:4; (19:3); cf. *3 Bar.* 3:8; and the *Zohar ad* Gen 11:7.

37. *Gen. Rab.* 38.6 judges "the generation of the dispersion" as more wicked than the generation of the flood. See Sasson, "The 'Tower of Babel,'" 214–19. Sasson also states emphatically that Genesis 1–11 is preparing the way for the advent of Abraham in Genesis 12. Note that, contrary to what happens in the preceding J's stories, there is here no divine mitigating of the punishment.

So, Abraham's response to his call does occur in a world in disarray. According to J, the great divide between the primal age and the *Heilsgeschichte* is not Babel but Abraham.[38]

On *šam* ("there"), see "Verse 2," above, and especially from chapter 3, below, "The Story of Babel as Myth."

Lo' yišme'u: We translate this, with Water Brueggemann, as "they will not listen." God will make them break all relationships.[39] On this very basis, the rabbis of old elaborated on an ensuing chaos with an accompanying disregard for human life.

Verse 8

Wayyaphes ("and he dispersed"): Again here the root *pus*, see v. 4 above. And again the locatives *šam* ("there") and *'al penei kol ha'ares* (over the face of all the earth). The dispersion precedes the confusion of languages because, structurally, the matter of location was the most relevant detail in the settlement of the people at Shinar (v. 2). Although mentioned first, the unicity of their language (v. 1) has been used as an instrument for thwarting their impending dispersion, thus giving priority to the latter (v. 4). Isaac Kikawada refers to Sumerian parallels.[40] But, as Kikawada says, the point to be stressed is that the dispersion is caused by YHWH, the God of J's Israelite audience.

Miššam ("from there"): it is the third time that we encounter the word *šam*. It appears again two more times in v. 9, an amazing total of five occurrences within nine verses. The boomerang-like movement in the tale goes from *šam* to *miššam*, and, as we shall see in v. 9, from "name" to shame; from topographical concentration to dispersion; from one single language to the multiplication of languages.

J's stress on the spatial dimension of the myths started already in Genesis 2–3 with the Garden of Eden (see 2:8, 10, 11, 12; 3:23).[41]

38. For J, humanity in the primal era was monotheistic, even Yhwhistic. The scattering of the builders in Genesis 11 is thus not just geographical and linguistic, but also religious. Its redemption starts with Abraham in the next chapter; the story of Babel is a set-up for Abraham's story. Isaac Kikawada says about Gen 11:1–9 that "thematically, it might be a conclusion, but rhetorically it was a transition to the main subject of his [J's] work" (Kikawada and Quinn, *Before Abraham Was*, 70).

39. Brueggemann, *Genesis*, 103. Again in Acts 2 the accent is on *hearing*, as Brueggemann astutely says (see Acts 2:6, 8, 11, 14, 37).

40. See Kramer, "The 'Babel of Tongues'"; and van Dijk, "'La confusion des langues.'"

41. I shall focus below on spatiality in Genesis 11. The similarity of vocabulary with Genesis 2–4 calls for notice: the word "earth," for instance is present in 2:4, 5a, 5b, 6,

Wayaḥdelu ("and they stopped/ceased"): The verbal root *ḥdl* means "to lag behind," hence "to cease doing something," especially, as in our text, with the preposition *le-*. An interesting shade of the word conveys the idea of "to give up, to drop," as in Judg 9:9, 11, and 13, or "to stop attending to something," as in 1 Sam 9:5.

Libnoth haʿir ("to build the city"): The absence of the tower here, which some critics exaggeratedly stress,[42] is simply due to a hendiadys with the city.[43] It is evident that the interruption of the construction of one is also the interruption of the other.[44] The end of the narrative comes with a play on words with *Babel/Babylon* (not on the tower), because only the city receives a name here, in contrast with the tower, which remains unnamed. But what could J have called it? We know today that its Akkadian name was *Etemenanki*, which means "foundation of heaven and earth." Such scientific precision has no place in fiction.

Verse 9

ʿ*Al-ken* ("therefore"/"that is why"). Croatto states, "the formula 'therefore' is typical of the etiological conclusions of myths."[45] See also above "Verse 7." More needs to be said about etiologies; see the section on "A Close Reading of Verses 8–9" below.

Qaraʾ ("He called"): God is the subject of the verb. It is followed by an editorial explanation of the name *Babel*.

Šemah Babel ("its name Babel"): There is, therefore, the Babylonian name for the city ("Gate of the Divine"[46]), and there is YHWH's name for it ("Confusion"). The former appellation corresponds to the human project in part 1 of the tale; the latter to the divine scrambling action in part 2. As the tale focuses on the theme of language, the emphasis is on *interpretation*. Babylon can be seen these two different ways, but one understanding is right and the other is wrong. That is, the narrated, sequential

---

11, and 13. See also: "one/unique," "build," "and now, lest"; "from [to] the east," "make," "called," "saw," "head/top," "name," "there," heaven," and "heard."

42. Above I mentioned Gunkel, Skinner, van Wolde, and Anderson. See also Hiebert, "The Tower of Babel."

43. So also Witte, *Die biblische Urgeschichte*, 91 n. 56), who indicates his agreement with Budde, *Die biblische Urgeschichte (Genesis 1—12,5)*. See also Uehlinger, *Weltreich*, 314, 377; Seebass, *Urgeschichte (1,1—11,26)*, 272.

44. See LXX, Sam. Pent., and *Jubilees* ad loc.

45. Croatto, "A Reading of the Story of the Tower of Babel," 216–17.

46. Perhaps itself a popular etymology.

arrangement of events (first the Babelian angle, then YHWH's) can also be interpreted as a vision of simultaneous events.[47] From the Babylonian, shortsighted perspective, "all the earth"—meaning all of Babylon—speaks one language and shares the same concepts (v. 1). In other words, what could possibly be intelligibly spoken beside the Babylonian language? And what projects are there that be more worthy than the construction of the city and tower of Babylon?"[48] In contrast, the Israelites see Babylon as nothing but a "Babel," a babble of language put at the service of a vast cock-and-bull construction soon to be devastated (see again Jeremiah 51). Eventually, the tower will only reach a ridiculously low height when compared with the initial purpose of the builders. From its pretension to verticality (the very sense of the word *religion*) as *axis mundi*, J brings it down to a flat horizontality, a *stagnum mundi*; and from a city-magnet for "all the earth" (vv. 4, 8, 9a, 9b = four times, the cipher of the universe), to the epicenter of an explosive dispersion of the nations. Such a concentration of power will eventually break apart and be diffused across the whole earth.

A Close Reading of Genesis 11:1–3

Verse 1

"*It so happened that the whole earth was [of] one language.*"[49] That is, the unity of language was the central characteristic as well as the cement of the whole earth in those primeval times. The single human language is a remnant of the harmony that prevailed in Eden. As a divine instrument put at the disposal of Adamic humanity, it had the marvelous property of making everyone and everything understandable.[50] Adam communicates

47. This can also be applied to the "sequence" of Genesis 10 and Genesis 11. As a myth, the Babel story may be read somewhat independently from the Genesis 10 context, alongside of which the myth comes cumulatively.

48. In Isa 47:8, 10, as we saw above, Babylon says, "I am, and there is no one beside me." See also Jer 51:44.

49. See Isa 19:18; in an eschatological context, see also Isa 19:22 and Ezek 3:5–6.

50. Aristotle's *On Interpretation* comes to mind, according to which human communication is possible only when words have one single sense (see *Metaphysics* G1006 b 7, cited in Ricoeur, *Freud and Philosophy*, 32. Manguel states, "Language is our common denominator" (*The City of Words*, 5). He adds perceptively that language is "a shared instrument based on common and conventional representation of the world [among people convinced that] their points of reference . . . [are] the same and that their utterings [translate] . . . a similar perceived reality" (8).

also with animals and nature in general. So, at least the speaking of one language went through the original trial of innocence and remained intact. This is the highly positive background against which the myth will unfold. The higher one is, the farther one falls . . .

Later in the tale, as a matter of fact, this kind of consolidating mortar will crack, and the one language will become a mosaic of languages. This happening will ruin the universal construction and make obsolete the earlier unique monolingualism of "the whole earth," a phrase that will be then in need of a new definition.

Now, in the ancient cosmogonies there is ominously one other unity, the unity of chaos (while creation produces diversity). Within this perspective, the Babel construction might be considered a return to chaos, and, at the chaos level, it is not unexpected that the protagonists of any action would be undifferentiated. We note with Ellen van Wolde that those who are speaking the one language are "neither introduced nor described in more detail than 'they.'"[51] They are only once identified by a generic name *benei ʾadam* (v. 5), which allows J to make an alliteration with *banu* ("they built").

As a sequel to the present verse focusing so strongly on discourse, the tale will soon feature a contrasting and heavy silence from the Babelians. Indeed, the very insistence of v. 1 upon language makes us all the more sensitive to the absence of human discourse once the builders have started building. Construction has become a substitute for speech. A shameful enterprise to be hushed up? Or a kind of ritual with a muted message? Even when the work (*opificio*) is interrupted and the workers dispersed, not one word is uttered—not in surprise, protest, anger, or sorrow.[52] It is a silence that speaks volumes: after the sacred silence of the ritual comes the sullen silence of emptiness. The Babelians are dumbstruck. The speakers would not understand each other anyway. If they do speak at all, it is with a plea not to be killed, a plea that remains "a voice crying in the wilderness." Murder is not far off.[53]

---

51. Van Wolde, "The Tower of Babel" 96.
52. "Newly born monster or full-fledged monster, Nero in the past or in the future is always Nero" (Poulet, *Etudes sur le temps humain*, 111 [my translation]).
53. See Neher, *L'Exil de la parole*, "Tout se passe [in Gen 4:8] comme si l'oblitération du dialogue était source de meurtre" (103). Recall that Freud stressed the muteness of the death instinct (see *Beyond the Pleasure Principle*, 7–64).

J has a keen sense of the nature of silence. Right after the serpent's discourse, Eve remains speechless while facing the tempting tree in Gen 3:6, "a wonderful picture," in Gerhard von Rad's words.[54] And so, we return to the story of Cain and Abel; here as well is a striking absence of discourse when frustration takes Cain to fratricide (4:8). In the field Cain is about to express in words his grievances to his brother, but then decides on their uselessness; and he kills Abel without a word, thus intensifying the horror of the crime.[55] But while in the story of Cain and Abel there was a conflict between the two brothers about the sacrificial ritual, in the Babel tale there is strikingly no human conflict: doesn't the crowd have one language, and is it not moved by one intention? As to the ritual, in Genesis 11 it amounts to a liturgical parody, for all the people are as obstinate as oxen working away at the same task—a task that is the opposite of sacrifice.

The mention of one language for the whole earth is strongly emphasized by an additional statement regarding humanity's *debarim ʾaḥadim*. As indicated above,[56] this expression does not just mean "the same words." It rather characterizes a discourse that Mikhail Bakhtin called "monoglossia" (as opposed to the polyglossia of healthy communication and dialogue), or again "single-voicedness."[57] *ʾAḥadim* in the lexeme under consideration sets a restrictive limit to the generally multidimensional quality of the discourse. Babelian humanity spoke one language with a monoglossic, that is, monologic meaning. As André Neher notes, "Toute la terre était d'un seul bord et vivait les mêmes histoires! Le monolithisme totalitaire de la civilisation de Babel."[58] Here the norm is sameness, pre-

54. Von Rad, *Genesis*, 72.

55. See also Gen 4:16 about Cain's silence following God's sentence. In *Onslaught against Innocence*, I have drawn parallels with Greek texts like *The Illiad* and *The Odyssey*.

56. See "Linguistic Notes," above.

57. Carol Newsom characterizes the monologic in this way, after Bakhtin: "Even if such propositions or systems of thought are actually the product of many minds, they can be represented as capable of being spoken by a single voice or comprehended by a single consciousness. Not so dialogic truth" ("Bakhtin," 24).

58. Neher, *De l'hébreu au français*, 43 ("The whole earth was of the same brand and lived through the same histories! The totalitarian monolith of Babel's civilization"). David Banon paraphrases: "Hélas, toute la terre parlait un même langage et avait une même idéologie" ("Babel ou l'idolâtrie embusquée," 6). Reference can be made to the monoglossic Persian absolutism described in the book of Esther. Dante understood that *debarim* was not simply "words." For him, the languages resulting from the eventual splitting are the guild idioms (so, the architects had their language, the stonecarvers theirs, etc.). To

vention of diversity (v. 4), a uniformity that fits the "finalized" product of Babel's construction. The ensuing deconstruction amounts to a renewed prodding toward "unfinalizing" the move by shifting from a tower (a substitute) to the constitution of the self.

This is also how Dostoevsky used the Babel metaphor in the famous chapter of *The Brothers Karamazov* on the Grand Inquisitor; and Franz Kafka in his story called "The Wall of China" (ca. 1918). "The few topics" of the Babelians' prattle refer to a mobilization of all resources (see *3 Bar.* 3:1–8) for the realization of a unique project, that is, a unitary empire ("all the earth") with a unitary purpose. In the words of George Orwell's "Principles of Newspeak," "So did the fact of having very few words to choose from . . . [T]he Newspeak vocabulary was tiny . . . Each reduction was a gain, since the smaller the area of choice, the smaller the temptation to take thought."[59]

Verse 2

"And on their journey from [to] the east . . ." The text remains rather vague, as we said earlier. "From [to] the east" says little geographically. J wants to keep his story within the frame of a mythic space. Eventually, Babel is Babylon, but the chronotope is set here with an aura of mystery so as to readily include all the "Babels" of human history. As the east is the sunrise spot, it is indicative of a beginning, as in Gen 2:4; 4:1; 6:1; 9:1. All these beginnings, however, end in failure, and Gen 11:1–9 will be no exception. Only Gen 12:1 is the authentic starting point of history with the promise of a glorious *Endzeit*.

A review of the use of *qedem* in Genesis primeval stories will allow us to be more specific about a move that can be described as a centripetal spiraling movement since Genesis 2–3. Eden is "in the east" and is, of course, a mythic place. The same may be said of the city of Henoch, which is *qidmath ʿeden* (4:16). Space is again mythically between heaven and earth in Genesis 6, where the circle narrows somewhat with the repeated

---

each field belonged its idiom. Initially there was no problem with mutual understanding (*De Vulgari Eloquentia* 1.7.6–7).

59. Orwell, *Nineteen Eighty-Four*, 308. An "Occitan" poet, P. Grosclaude (*Un cóp sera*, quoted in Bost, *Babel*, 195–96), evokes with horror a coming time when people will be "all identical, with the same words to express the same things, with only one history, only one point of view, with one face. We'll be all alike like bricks, and with all those bricks we'll build a tower that we'll call Babel."

mention of *ba'areṣ* ("on the earth": 6:4, 5, 6). Where did Noah live? "On the earth" (6:11 [twice], 12 [twice], 13 [twice], 17 [twice]; 7:4, 6, 10, 12, 14, 17, 18, 19, 21 [twice], 23, 24). Then the texts harp on the theme "on the face of all the earth" (*'al penei kol ha'areṣ*) in 7:3; 8:9; or "from/on the face of the ground" ([*me*]*'al penei ha'adamah*) in 6:7; 7:4, 23; 8:1, 3, 7, 11, 13, 14, 17 [three times], 19; 8:8. The *'adamah* is again present in 8:13, 21, 22; 9:1, 2, 7, 10 [twice], 11, 13, 14, 16, 17, 19, 20. All this shows the immense importance of space, and particularly of "the earth," in the early J chapters of Genesis. Nevertheless, the geographical terms remain on the whole too general. Only Mount Ararat in Gen 8:4 is more precise, but this place is out of Israel's purview; this place is exotic and more or less legendary. Again, in Gen 11:1–9 see vv. 1 and 9 for "all the earth," and vv. 4, 8, and 9 for "on the face of all the earth." With *Babel* J takes his readers to a veritable chronotope; the spiraling move has landed at a single locus. The contrast with the earlier context is striking.

In summary, irrespective of the division between literary sources in the primeval stories, Genesis 6–11 uses the word *'ereṣ* a staggering sixty-four times, *'adamah* eight times, and the term *qedem* eight times. *Babel* is unique (with the exception of in Gen 10:10) to Gen 11:1–9.

In Gen 11:2 humanity is going eastward, prolonging the initial migration since the exit from Eden. To them, Shinar and hence Babylon is in the east, that is, farther removed from the original Garden. Their settlement in the east is already in and of itself a token of their rebellion against God. The text says *wayeševu šam* ("and there they installed themselves").[60] They do so in a mood of defiance. Something like, "If we are not welcome any longer in Eden, we'll build a place of our own in Shinar. And if God shuts the gate of the Garden with Seraphim, we'll bypass this hurdle and construct for ourselves a vertical channel of communication with the divine, a *Bab-ilum*, of which we'll have control and disposition." As was seen earlier, the lexeme *there* appears five times in Gen 11:1–9.

They found a depression in the land of Shinar. The choice of a topographical depression as a place to build a tower to heaven is paradoxical. But "as there is no new life without death," so Karen Armstrong says, "[t]here can be no ascent to the highest heaven without a prior descent into the depths of the earth."[61] An *axis mundi* requires the bridging of the

60. In *Gen. Rab.* 38, 2. Rabbi Yitzhaq goes so far as to say about 11:1, "wherever you find the word *yašab* [to settle], there Satan plays the game."

61. Armstrong, *A Short History of Myth*, 26; see also 37. In Mesopotamia, the sanc-

inferna and the *caelum*—which recalls Gen 6:1 on the impure commerce of the "sons of God" with "the daughters of men."[62]

Shinar (*Šingi-Uri* in Sumerian) designates Sumer and Akkad, that is, the expanse of the Babylonian empire's hub. In the Bible, it includes the whole of Mesopotamia (Gen 10:10; 11:2; 14:1, 9; Josh 7:21; Isa 11:11; Zech 5:11; and Dan 1:2).[63] J's choice of this term rather than just *Babylon* marks again a certain distance of the tale from too precise chronotopes (although the verse here is crammed with spatial designations: seven words out of nine in Hebrew).

There they settled. The bitter irony of their settlement followed by their dreaded dispersion will soon become clear. The contrast is not only set with their eventual fate "all over the earth," but with Abraham's migration in Genesis 12.

Verse 3

Come! Let us . . . John T. Strong, in his article in response to Theodore Hiebert,[64] rightly stresses the parallel between Gen 11:3 and Gen 1:26, where the cohortative form is also present. He concludes, "The humans' use of the cohortative, in effect, characterizes them as intruding into God's role as one who can create by fiat." Strong then argues that the declaration in Gen 11:4 to the effect that the construction of Babel is intended "to make a name for ourselves" amounts to "defacing the image of God . . . scratching off the name of God and replacing it with their own name." The final scattering of the Babelians is the "equivalent of shattering the image of God."[65]

Now, within the context of J's primeval history, remarkable is the shift from the divine/human dialogue in the preceding stories to a "dialogue

---

tuaries of Nippur, Larsa, and Sippara were called *Duranki* ("link between heaven and earth"). The city of Babylon was allegedly built as *bab-apsu* (the Gate of Apsu = the freshwater sea flowing under the earth = the netherworld). We thus better understand why J set the building of the tower in a depression.

62. See Origen *Contra Celsum* v, 30; Augustine *Civitas Dei* xvi, spoke of Nebroth (= Nimrod) *the giant*. The same idea is found in John Calvin's *Le livre de Genèse* 240; see also Dante *De Vulgari Eloquentia* 1.7.4–5, cited in Bost, *Babel*, 146–47.

63. Daniel 1:1–2 specifically links the land of Shinar with Nebuchadnezzar of Babylon, the destroyer of Jerusalem.

64. Strong, "Shattering the Image of God."

65. Ibid., 632–33. Strong's comparison of a J text in Gen 11:3 and a P text in Gen 1:26 is not without its problems, especially since Strong maintains the classic Documentary Hypothesis chronology.

with alternate voices" (Martin Buber) in vv. 3–4. This deterioration of the relationship between God and humans is to be emphasized.[66] Given the absence in Gen 11:1–9 of any individual with whom God can converse, God has no other.choice than to speak to himself (vv. 6–7). The Babelians have chosen to lose themselves in a collectivity in order to protect their anonymity.

Let us brick bricks. Stones were not unknown in Mesopotamia. In his description of Babylon, Jean C. Margueron states, "[There was] a bridge spanning the Euphrates upon seven piers of bricks joined by bitumen and caped with paving stones."[67] The extensive use of bricks is, however, confirmed by Herodotus (*The History* 1.179): "They [the Babylonians] made bricks of the mud . . . [which] they baked in ovens. Then, using hot asphalt for cement . . ."

Bricks that we'll flame in the flame, the biblical text says, thus echoing Herodotus's report.[68] Thus, these people from the east initiate a human activity that is fated to be imitated throughout history. As in ancient societies the hunters, for instance, model their behavior on that of the primeval hunter, now the brick makers, the builders, the creators of civilization, will duplicate the archetype set by the crowd of Genesis 11. Indeed, the invention of the brick-and-tar combination is creation that associates the humans with the gods.[69]

So even before the biblical text mentions a city with its tower, the reader already knows that the story will be about a human attempt at imitating the gods. Nothing here will be innocent. Innocence is not only on trial or under attack; it is now scorned, dragged in the mud—as it will be again later in Egypt by the pharaohs, who are also builders.

Of interest is Herodotus's description of Babylon's ziggurat:

> In the midst of the temple square there was built a solid tower,
> in length and breadth one stade, and on this tower was mounted
> another, and another still on the top of that—eight of them in all.
> The ascent to these has been constructed circularly, on the outside,

66. See de Pury, "La tour de Babel et la vocation d'Abraham," 87.

67. Margueron, "Babylon," 564b.

68. The mention of bricks substituting for stones is imbued with certain sarcasm when we remember that in the ancient world "[a] stone was a common hierophany," as Armstrong (*A Short History of Myth,* 17) reminds us.

69. In numerous myths the world over, gods are the initiators of human activity, whether by making the first gesture or by inventing the original tools—the pickaxe for instance.

around all the towers. Halfway up the ascent there is a halting place and seats to rest on, where the climbers sit and rest. In the last tower, there is a great temple, and in the temple there stands a great bed, well covered, and by it is set a golden table.[70]

In addition to appearing here, *bitumen* is found again in Gen 14:10 and in Exod 2:3 with various connotations. *Clay* appears more often. Exodus 1:14 draws an ominous parallel: the Egyptians "make bitter" the life of the Hebrews "by forced labor with mortar [*ḥomer*] and bricks [*leb-enim*]" of clay.[71]The natural symbol of the mountain is here perverted by the artificiality of the material. This denaturalization is also "denatured-ness." The symbol is distorted in the sense that it keeps a trace of its arche-typal straightforwardness but acquires a supplementary and unnatural dimension. The ziggurat is a mountain without being a mountain. Hence the term used by J to designate it: a "tower," that is, a construction (with bricks and tar). While the mountains are God's creation, the ziggurat is a human fabrication. As such, it exacerbates, so to speak, the symbolism of *axis mundi* and of the phallic. The sham mountain is bald and naked, with a symbolism brutal and inexorable.[72]

In conclusion, there is something of an underpinning violence in the materials of construction invented by the Babelian technology. Are we thus to infer that the central element of space in the narrative will be forced, even raped, by the builders? Space from the onset reacts negatively to the Babelian project: it has no stones and no mortar to offer! But the Babelians will circumvent this absence with an artificial presence: bricks will serve as stones and bitumen as mortar. The coercive enterprise has become unethical and unecological. It is what Babylon must sacrifice on the altar of its obsession with space (note the recurring lexeme "there"). One cannot swallow swaths of territory and concurrently fulfill ethical demands. As soon as the human desire is oriented toward ever more power, the desire is perverted and perverting. The Hebrew prophets do not give their audiences the benefit of the doubt about this. As for J, he follows the same vein and puts into God's mouth the statement, "If this is how they have begun . . ." (v. 6).

70. Herodotus, *The History* 115.

71. In the book of Job, the phrase "houses of clay" is a metaphor for human bodies (4:19; 10:9, e.g.).

72. On the bald mountain, see Isa 13:2; cf. Jer 51:25 ("burned-out mountain"). Becker wrote, "Culture is in its most intimate intent a heroic denial of creatureliness" (*The Denial of Death*, 159).

A Close Reading of Genesis 11:4

Come! Let's build us a city with a tower. This is what they had in mind. They exhort each other using the cohortative plus a verb in the first-person plural. This formation appears once more in Exod 1:10, where we find again an evil discourse followed by a motivation introduced by *pen* ("for fear that") and the mention of "the earth." The irony of God's repeating the same discourse pattern here in 11:4 and in 11:7 is unmistakable. In both verses, we come across a performative speech act, whose effect is to engage speaker and hearer alike. "Let us" even in the mouth of God has the expected effect of inviting the reader to participate in the planned action. The Babelians sent their invitation; God sends his counterinvitation.

Again about the plural form of the Babelian exhortation we note the redundant "let *us* build *to us*." The stress is clearly on "us," us alone. Now, in the Babylonian myth *Enuma Elish* (tablet vi), the Anunnaki (lesser gods) are those who say to Marduk, "Let us build a shrine whose name shall be called . . . ," to which Marduk responds, "Like that of lofty Babylon, whose building you have requested / Let its brickwork be fashioned / You shall name it the Sanctuary." So, the Anunnaki "raised high the head of the Esagila equaling Apsu / Having built a stage-tower as high as Apsu . . ."[73] J uses irony in having common people build the "Esagila," and sarcasm in giving to "lofty Babylon" the name *Babel,* with the meaning "Confusion."

Esagila in Sumerian means "the structure with upraised head," Ephraim Skinner notes.[74] He adds, "The Akkadian for 'they raised its (Esagila's) head' (*ullu resisu*) is merely a play on Esagila."[75] In the so-called Weidmer Chronicle, the god Marduk wishes, "May Esagila, the majestic shrine, be [. . .] to the limits of hearth and earth! . . . May the city be famous!" Further on (19) we read, "Raise up to the sky the top of Esagila, the palace of heaven and earth [. . .] (20). May its foundation be fixed like sky and earth for ever!"[76]

City and tower form a hendiadys.[77] Archaeology has shown that city building started in Mesopotamia around 4,000 BCE. The relative fragil-

---

73. See *ANET,* 68–69.

74. Skinner, *Genesis,* 75–76.

75. Ibid., 76.

76. See Grayson, *Assyrian and Babylonian Chronicles,* V, no. 19; Hallo and Younger, *Canonical Compositions from the Biblical World* (note Alan Millard's contributions to this volume, listed in the bibliography); Glassner, *Mesopotamian Chronicles,* 263ff.

77. In 1949 Cassuto too stressed the inseparability of city and tower (see Cassuto,

ity of the building material required periodic rebuilding.[78] The ziggurat in question in Genesis 11 is in Babel/Babylon, which was rebuilt in the seventh and sixth centuries BCE by Nebuchadnezzar (at the time of the Judean exile). The "tower" (*Etemenanki*) necessarily remains unnamed in the Hebrew text. The first literary references to the *Etemenanki* are from the seventh century, according to Speiser.[79] In Genesis 11, its top is supposed to reach up to God's abode, and as to the means summoned to build it, first the crowd of people looks like the depersonalized, ant-like army of a dictatorship;[80] and second, the mob is armed with what amounts in an Israelite's conception to an ersatz of material. The rabbis of old derided that crowd, saying that no one among them deplored the accidental death of a worker at the tower, but all would grieve for the loss of a brick.[81]

A tower whose head (is) in heaven. There is a wordplay with *šam* and *šem* and *šamayim* ("there"/"name"/"heaven").[82] There is no reason, as we saw earlier, for trivializing this Babelian motivation to reach heaven. The rest of the story contrasts this haughtiness with the horizontality of the final dispersion ʿal penei kol haʾareṣ ("on the surface of all the earth"). The mythical motif of a column reaching heaven is not unique. Recall that the Greek mythological Titans did pile Mounts Pelion and Ossa on top of Mount Olympus in a futile attempt to reach and attack the gods in heaven.[83] So in spite of a particular Jewish tradition's preference to understand

A *Commentary on the Book of Genesis* 2, 237, 248). See Speiser, *Genesis*, who insists on the *literary* Mesopotamian sources of J here, rather than the architectural. He refers to *Enuma Elish* 6.62. But the one does not exclude the other. Besides, Speiser wrongly places J in the eleventh and tenth centuries BCE, and such a date for J would make the Israelites' seeing the ziggurat in Babylon improbable.

78. See Leick, *Mesopotamia*, 268.

79. Speiser, "Word Plays on the Creation Epic's Version," 54. Gunkel, we recall, claimed a dual origin for the J tale—one source for the story about the city and another for the story about the tower; he thought that the tower was originally scornfully named *pits* or *puts* after the human dispersion. See Gunkel, *Genesis*, 92–96, and a critique in Westermann, *Genesis*, 1:174 . In *Jub.* 10:26, the tower is called *catastrophê!*

80. The expressed purpose of erecting the tower shows that we are in the realm of propaganda, where the goal of action is "not symbolic of a belief but the demonstration of the belief itself" (Manguel, *The City of Words*, 139).

81. See *PRE* 24 (Rabbi Pinhas [fourth century CE]). Recall that Karl Marx spoke of a *Verwertung* (valuation) of things at the expense of the *Entwertung* (devaluation) of human nature (see Marx and Engels, *Kleine ökonomische Schriften*, 97–99, cited in Brown, *Life against Death*, 238).

82. Remarkably, as the story concludes in 11:9, the text continues with the mention of Shem: "These are the generations of Shem . . ."

83. See Homer *Odyssey* 11.315–16; a motif picked up by Virgil in *Georgics* 1.281.

the expression "in heaven" as pointing to an impressive structure (as in
Deut 1:28 and 9:1, as we saw above),[84] the reading of J. P. Fokkelman,
among others, is to be adopted.[85] We must remember that for the above-
mentioned tradition, the whole Pentateuch dates from the Mosaic time,
long before Israel in exile witnessed the Mesopotamian ziggurats.[86]

Genesis 11:4 reflects the antiquarian conception of a three-level
cosmology. Heaven or the divine abode is way above the (flat) surface of
the earth.[87] The point here is not only cosmological but metaphoric. The
tower is supposed to reach in height the divine abode, wherever it may
actually be. The perfect balance of the two parts of our story demands that
God come down from (metaphoric) heaven (rather than from the sky!).

Furthermore, as far as the people of Babel are concerned, their
encounter with the sacred is symbolized by the climbing up to heaven.
From a phenomenological point of view, heaven is an interesting choice
of a spatial object (although unreachable). It certainly speaks volumes
about a religious mentality looking, by means of cosmic symbolism, toward a nonproblematic, fathomable, indubitable, and interpretation-free,
certainty—an idol.[88] This is a religious system that fits a dictatorial political regime as a hand fits a glove. By contrast, J's encounter with the sacred
is mediated by story and history—by the story of the tower of Babel and
the history of Abraham in the next chapter (Genesis 12), for instance.
With this approach, of course, everything becomes problematic and un-

---

The Targum to Gen 11:4 paraphrases it as "an armed idol at the top to fight God." For
David Oradia Sphorno (fifteenth and sixteenth centuries), "to make a name" is "to make
a god."

84. See, e.g., Sarna, *Understanding Genesis*, 72–73; Jacob, *Das erste Buch Moses*;
Cassuto, *Genesis*, 242.

85. Fokkelman, *Narrative Art*, 19–20.

86. With Gowan, *From Eden to Babel*, 29, the appropriate parallels are found in Isa
14:1–21 and Ezek 28:1–19 (both texts use mythic language). In Deut 26:15, God is asked
to look down from heaven (cf. 1 Kgs 8:27; Ps 113:5–6). Besides, *šamayim* even understood as pointing to the *sky*, this (the sky) is God's abode: see Lam 3:44; Job 22:13 [14];
Luke 11:13 [mss Alex., Vat. etc.]; Matt 5:34. *Šamayim* is never just topographic in the
Bible. In Matt 11:23, it denotes the height of human arrogance.

87. As Jeffrey Stout states, "people who lived thousands of years ago don't deserve
epistemic blame for believing that the world was flat . . . Given the reason and evidence
available to them, it was rational to believe that the world was flat . . . But it wasn't true
millennia ago that the earth was flat" (Stout, *Ethics after Babel*, 29–30). In other words,
we must distinguish between the *justification* of a proposition and the *truth* of it. The
distinction is fundamental. It flies in the face of literalism.

88. "The Tower of Babel stood (while it stood) as a proof of our belief in the unity of
the universe" (Manguel, *The Library at Night*. 23).

fathomable, and the God worshipped is invisible although reaching out to humans "down there." An iconoclastic revolution.

Let's make us a name. It would be hard not to discern here a narcissistic desire of autonomination at the expense of God's Name (see Gen 4:26). In the *Epic of Gilgamesh* the hero is frustrated in his hope for self-deification. So, on his return to Uruk, he builds monuments, a substitute for immortality. Albert de Pury says that the expression in Gen 11:4 corresponds to the Pauline use of the Greek verb *kauchasthai* ("to boast"), indicating a self-glorification reminiscent of that from the fools in Pss 52:1 and 74:4; see Rom 3:27; Phil 3:7ff. Indeed, the crowd attempts to initiate a *Heldensage* (a "hero legend") through a daring exploit, a far cry from Hebrew ideal. Vladimir Propp says that in a tale, performance of a difficult task (M) leads to a performers' "transfiguration" (T), even to apotheosis.[89] About *whose head (is) in heaven* Propp notes that this clause denotes a "transgression" (δ) of a tacit "prohibition" (γ). Furthermore, both psychoanalysts and Marxists tie up language and work. Language, they say, makes work possible: a central concept in the Babel story.

Once more, the self-glorification of the Babelians recalls Genesis 6. Genesis 6:4 mentions the *ʾanšei hašem* ("people of name/of renown"), who are also the gigantic offspring of the impure mix of male angels and human females. Then those hybrid creatures are called "heroes" (*gibborim*). Now, remarkably, the only other pentateuchal instance of the term "hero" (*gibbor*) occurs in Genesis 10 about Nimrod (10:8–9), where again the central motif is human hubris. In his turn, Nimrod makes one think of the anti-hero Lamech in Gen 4:23–24, whose fame is built on violence. All of these "heroes" of J are striving for autonomy, narcissistically considering the world "a theater for heroism," said William James.[90] The obedient Noah serves as a foil to such heroes (see Gen 6:22 and 7:5, 9, 16).

Of course, a more potent foil is Abraham. To him, as we recalled above, God declares that he will make his name great (Gen 12:2)—a blessing repeated in behalf of David (2 Sam 7:9)—and that his descendants will fill the earth. Significantly, Shem is an ancestor of Abraham (see Gen 11:10–26).

Lest we be scattered over the face of all the earth. Now they express their angst about being separated from their own constructions, that is, from their sham paradise and, in fact, their motherly projection. From

89. Propp, *Morphology of the Folktale*, 68 (in French, *Morphologie du conte*, 83).
90. James, *The Varieties of Religious Experience*.

this perspective, their eventual dispersion is the equivalent of the father's prohibition of incest.[91]

This revealing motivation is to be read against the background of Gen 11:2. There the crowd is changing its collective identity from nomadism to sedentary life. "Lest we be dispersed" implies that it was their situation *ante* (in v. 2, they are still on the move): lest we be dispersed *again*. They were dispersed before the move described in 11:2 (a situation portrayed in Genesis 10), but it is not what they want; they look for settlement in one place. There is thus no opposition here to Genesis 10. The Babel story starts with dispersion and ends with dispersion. In both cases the scattering is unwanted, but the similitude ends here, for while the first diffusion was a fact of nature (or of the divine fiat), the second dissemination is imposed as a punishment and a way of control. The new identity that the Babelians constructed for themselves is rejected and destroyed.

Squeezed between two comparable decentralizations, the building of Babel and its tower appears as a parenthetical and failed attempt to contravene the divine law. The autonomous Babylonian state had recourse to exiling entire communities into its power base in Mesopotamia. Now J, paralleling the prophetic movement of his time, foresees the dismantling of Babylon and the disbanding of the exiles: a curse for the Babelians and a blessing for the Judeans.

But at first the people of the east come with a common desire for homogeneity and a fear of being scattered. Clearly, their consolidated social body has forebodings and realizes the fragility of its organization.[92] But "speaking one language" (*śaphah 'aḥath*), the group is able to concoct a double feature: a city where "all the earth" (v. 1) will dwell, and a tower reaching to heaven (v. 4). On both the horizontal and the vertical axes, Babel claims to omnipotent absolutism. The "concentrationary" Babel presents what Charles Foucault calls "force relations." Babylonian power is not innate but the outcome of a plot: "Let us . . . , and let us . . . , lest . . . ." *Babel* is the name of a conspiracy. At its basis are a certain philoso-

91. After all, Otto Rank in his magnum opus, *The Incest Theme in Literature and Legend*, 12, said the incest fantasy is "of surpassing importance in the psychic life of the creative writer" (quoted in Rudnytsky, *Reading Psycho-Analysis*, 59). Parenthetically, Rank has demonstrated the legitimate application of psychoanalysis to literature. On this, he was preceded by Freud's inroads, such as in "Delusions and Dreams in Jensen's *Gradiva* (1907) or "Creative Writers and Day-Dreaming" (1908) and, of course, in his analysis of the Oedipus myth (see *The Interpretation of Dreams* [1900]).

92. In reality, the fear of dispersion is fear of death, a central theme in Genesis 2–11.

phy or ideology (11:4)[93] and a certain technology (11:3). In this scheme, the city corresponds to the bricks used in v. 3, and the tower corresponds to the bitumen that holds the whole project together. For the city will not be enough to consolidate the society; it must share a common feeling of *power*, which the temple-tower is meant to provide. If building a city with its tower may be in itself deemed innocuous, the builders' discourse sheds light on their conniving.

Both city and tower will be instrumental in keeping the people in a compact block like a beehive. They all will live in a city, Babel, and the tower will serve as an umbilicus, pumping life from heaven. Corresponding to this architectural duality of city and ziggurat, the Babelians' expressed motivation is also double-sided. Babel is antidispersion (hence the city), and it is the concentration point of fame (hence the tower). The two faces are consolidated into a centripetal uniformity. The ultimate goal is clearly oneness, sameness. The people all speak one language; they share the same words/concepts; they live in one place; and their ambition congeals in scaling the magic mountain.[94] In the background is the "Myth of the Center" as exposed below (in chapter 3).

Sameness, however, in all of its aspects highlighted in the tale, is fated to become utterly confused. The unique city of the Babelians' dwelling is to be replaced by a scattered humanity across the whole world. The fame-making project is made impossible. The one language (*śaphah*) explodes into a multiplicity of languages and, hence, a multiplicity of concepts (*debarim*).[95] Centripetal uniformity is transformed into a centrifugal diversity. Sameness is no more. J rejects as blasphemous both the ideology and its accompanying technology (hence the rejection is attributed to YHWH in 11:6). Jacques Derrida would say, Babel is the sign of contriving, which is the sign of an ideology, which itself refers to a will to power, which signifies a rebellion against God . . .

93. In his *Structural Anthropology*, Lévi-Strauss has shown that all human systems of communication are the fruit of the human mind. Language and society are mutually creative. Language is a social fact, and society is a speaking community. (On this score, the parallel is striking between language as a social fact and society as a speaking community, on the one hand, and the mutuality of Israel's people and their traditions, on the other hand.)

94. Raimundo Panikkar sees in the tower of Babel story a mirror of the universal desire for having one God, one church, one empire, one civilization, one party, and one technology ("The Myth of Pluralism").

95. "Jede Sprache ist ein Versuch" (Wilhelm von Humboldt, quoted in Steiner, *After Babel*, 83).

A Close Reading of Genesis 11:5–7

Verse 5

YHWH came down to see the city and the tower. In this verse the divine initiative corresponds to the enterprise of the people of the east. Here lies the crucial difference between Israel and the nations. Israel sets religion (*re-ligere*, "binding up [heaven and earth]") on its head—symbolized here by the divine climbing down, countering the human climbing up. No narrative makes it more evident than Gen 11:1–9. True, the motif of the divine descent looks embarrassingly anthropomorphic, but it certainly makes its point crystal clear. The comparison often made between the tower of Babel and Jacob's ladder in Gen 28:10–17 should not belittle the differences between the two texts. The dreaming Jacob does not climb up the ladder "reaching to heaven." Angels are climbing down and going up, and YHWH definitely takes the initiative (see v. 13).[96]

God descends to *see* what is happening down in Babel.[97] Such a divine move might have initiated a theophany, as in Exod 19:11 for instance, where YHWH descends in the sight of all the people, who, for their part, may not ascend the mountain (Exod 19:12, 23).[98] Again in Exod 19:18 and 20, YHWH is said to descend the mountain, and he invites Moses to ascend.[99] In Genesis 11, however, YHWH's descent is purposely no theophany (but only secretly for J). The crowd tries to force the theophany (11:4), but the attempt backfires, and the people are sent

---

96. See the remarkable distinction between religion and faith in Karl Barth's *Church Dogmatics,* especially "The Revelation of God as the Abolition of Religion," in *The Doctrine of the Word of God* I/2:284–361. Barth writes, "the revelation . . . contradicts every religion of works and therefore all religions as such" (ibid., 311).

97. God's leaving heaven to see what the humans are doing evokes the midrashic tradition, according to which the divine Shekhinah exiled itself to heaven because of the successive sins of humanity; but seven righteous men brought her back from heaven, the last one being Moses (see *Num. Rab.*, Naso, 13,2; cf. *Deut. Rab.*, Ki Testse, 6,14).

98. *Targum Onkelos* changes the anthropomorphism of God's descending to see, into an act of revelation; active verbs of seeing and hearing are put in the passive forms. We are, of course, at the opposite of an inactivity (*otiositas*) of the creator-god of sundry religious cosmogonies. There, as Gerardus van der Leeuw states, "[Der Urheber] lebt nur in Vergangenheit: er *hat* immer getan, er *wird* nie tun" ("[The ancestor] lives only in the past: he has always *already* done, he *will* never do again"), cited in Pettazzoni, "Myths of Beginnings and Creation Myths," 32 n. 18.

99. There is thus a striking movement of ascending and descending by both God and Moses (as well as Aaron), that in part recalls Jacob's ladder in Genesis 28, which we mentioned earlier.

back to themselves—and to their mutual *incommunicado,* that is, to their mutual lack of *"phany."* They do see one another, but what they see and hear alienates them from one another. Truly, Babylon's sightliness has become unsightly.[100] Now, as in a nightmare, people happen to talk in foreign languages that exclude rather than include their neighbors from human life-saving conglomeration and centralization. They are left without a center of being.

The divine move of descending is also ominously present in Gen 18:21 (to Sodom and Gomorrah). In that case also God expresses his intention before the act, and there again God goes down to check a city and its sinfulness. In both these Genesis texts, there is no theophany in the sense of revelation. In prophetic texts, like Isa 63:19—64:1, the theme of God's descent is tied to the divine Name and also to a purpose similar to the one in Genesis 11: to counter human hubris (see 1 Sam 5:11; 14:20).

How does God come down? On a cloud, as in Ps 104:3? J does not give us any clue. But the symbol of the tower is close to the one of the chimney, which like the tower is a conduit for the communication between heaven, earth, and hell. Perhaps it is not unwarranted to imagine God using the stair-shaped tower of Babel—meant for the human ascent to heaven—for his descent to thwart the human project.

Before leaving this theme of divine *kenosis* (self-emptying) of sorts, let us note the biblical selection of the senses of vision and audition above those of touch, taste, and smell—although none of these is excluded. God is said to enjoy smelling the smoke of sacrifices, for instance, in Gen 8:21. Similarly using the divine senses he touches the mountains in Ps 144:5, or the mouth of Jeremiah in Jer 1:9. Speaking of God's tasting anything, however, would be too trite, for God's senses keep a definite distance from an object. He hears and sees, he understands and pities. As far as Israelite worshippers are concerned, the sense of hearing is prominent. They are under the imperative to hear the Word of God.[101] Conversely, God hears the groaning of his people (see Exod 2:24); and more important, he *sees* their affliction or their general human turpitude. Here in Genesis 11 the sense of divine seeing takes prominence (see Gen 1:4, 10, 12, 18, 21, 25, 31; 6:5; Exod 3:4; 2 Kgs 14:26; Isa 59:15–16). Although we should not

---

100. Phillips, paraphrasing Levinas, writes, "Totality is interrupted in the moment when transcendence, infinity, God, ethics, speaks" ("Levinas," 155).

101. Remarkably, psychoanalysis is the most oral/aural of all modern disciplines; see Mahony, *Freud and the Rat Man,* 135.

overemphasize a statistical difference between Israel and its surroundings, with Israel's neighbors' stress on other senses such as touching and
being bothered by human noise, nevertheless the privileged role given in
Israel to both divine and human hearing and being seen is highly remarkable. The active seeing is not exclusively God's but tends to be among his
attributes.

And the tower. It is possible to discern with J. Gerald Janzen still
another shade of meaning in the word *migdol*; that is, a "temple-tower"
whose significance is in part defensive—the redoubt of a fortified city, to
which the inhabitants retreat when the city walls have been breached.[102]
(As the proverb has it, "The name of YHWH is a *migdol ʿoz* [a tower of
might]; / The righteous runs into it and is safe.")[103] On this score, it is interesting to connect the verb *puṣ* ("disperse") with the widespread motif,
in the Bible and in texts celebrating Hammurapi's kingship for example,
of the scattering of a people or its army by enemy forces. The niphal verb
yibbaṣer ("to be inaccessible") in v. 6 is then taken in the sense that this
root frequently has, alluding to defensive fortifications: "Now nothing
that they propose to do can be defended against." That is, with such a
fortified city as a base for empire, no other power will be able to withstand
their imperial aggression. As for the word *mezimmah* ("purpose"), it may
indicate "indistinct speech," as when a group of plotters "put their heads
together" and speak in tones that "outsiders" are not able to make out.

Which the Adamites [the humans] were building. The builders here
are designated with a general term of "sons of man [Adam]" or "humans."
As this text and other texts show, the expression is used to sharply contrast
humanity (earthlings) with the divine realm (see 1 Sam 26:1; 1 Kgs 8:39; Ps
33:13). In Gen 6:2, 4, the phrase has been changed into "daughters of man"
in opposition to the "sons of God." The same background of the incompa-
rability of the divine and the human is decisive here as in Genesis 6.

As I mentioned earlier, there is alliteration of *benei* ("sons of") and
banu ("built").

---

102. I borrow most of the present paragraph from a personal email communication
with Professor J. Gerald Janzen from April 20, 2009.

103. See Prov 18:10; cf. Judg 9:45, 51; 2 Kgs 9:17; 17:9; Isa 5:2; Jer 51:53. I refer to
Wallis, "Die Stadt in den Überlieferungen der Genesis," 33: the city entails "die Festung,
Zitadelle, den Tempel, den Markt."

Verse 6

In this verse starts a divine soliloquy, which is an infrequent occurrence in the Bible. It is found again in Gen 2:18; 3:22; and 6:7. Remarkably, in three out of these four cases, the soliloquy is an introduction to punishment. The problem, of course, is how J knows about this intimate reflection of God. For, while the reason behind God's descent ("to see") seems at least to contradict the idea of a divine omniscience, the "singer of tales" who reports the divine inner thinking appears endowed with what God is lacking! Only a myth can come with such a paradox.

"*Behold, (they are) one nation and (there is) one language for all.*" With this, we return to one of the main themes in J's narrative: namely, the theme of hubris, or the will to power ("*sicut Deus*"), as in Genesis 3 and 4 and again in Genesis 6. Isaiah 14:14 is especially relevant here: Babylon boasts, "I will ascend to the top of the clouds, / I will make myself like the Most High."

"*This is what they have started to make [they have profaned doing], so that henceforth no(thing) will be inaccessible to them (in) all that they purpose to make.*" Strikingly, in each case presented by J of a human enterprise to usurp the divine status, God takes the threat very seriously. True, in Pss 2:4; 37:13; and 59:9, God is described as laughing at such human attempts at self-deification, but not so in the Yahwist's work. God does not laugh when Adam and Eve follow the advice of the serpent to enthrone themselves (see Gen 3:5; cf. 6:13), and now again when Mesopotamian humanity reaches out toward his abode. In both cases, we should be sensitive to the implicit acknowledgment of the human *techne* as capable of (almost?) promoting humans to the rank of divinity.[104] The chasm between the divine and the human does not appear that unsurpassable after all. What the Priestly source (P) calls the *imago Dei* seems to entail the tremendous human capacity to challenge the Creator. It is only at the divine threat that the sea waters flee before him (Ps 104:9; Job 38:8–11), and it is only because God sets limits for them and for human megalomania that the horrible does not (should not) occur.[105]

104. We remember Friedrich Nietzsche's *The Gay Science* evoking "the madman." He asks, "Must we ourselves not become gods simply to appear worthy of it [our killing of God]" (181)?

105. In a letter to Eva Cassirer, Rainer Maria Rilke wrote, "What horror to think that the world has fallen into the hands of men!"

The verb translated by "started" can also mean "to profane." As Gen
11:1–9 is replete with plays on words and with irony, it is not unwarranted to discern behind God's declaration the profanation that the Babel
enterprise implies.[106]

The city of Babylon with its tower is seen as only a beginning point
that bespeaks the unbridled ambition/hubris of the builders. In other
words, the erection of Babel is only a token of human evildoing that needs
to be blocked before it goes out of control. Once more we realize how ill
advised it would be to have a minimalist reading of the tale. True, as we
said, it may be that the construction of a city, even with a "tower," is in
principle more or less innocent, but this is certainly not the case in J's
understanding of Babel. Building Babylon is evil, and it augurs a very bad
future with more and worse evils. It must be nipped in the bud.

The striking stylistic parallelism of Gen 11:6 with Gen 3:22 definitely
points to the intention of the Babel builders to construct an antiparadise.
But from this one also they will collectively be excluded just as the primal
couple was *in illo tempore.* Here as there, God thwarts the human quest
for immortality, and the scattering of peoples and languages that follows
prevents humanity from perpetrating the sin of sins: that is, deicide. It
is thus without surprise that we find in the Talmudic tractate *Sanhedrin*
71b that the "good" thing in the dispersion was that they could not plot
evil together. According to Ibn Ezra on Gen 11:8, it was for human good
and blessing that God dispersed them, for so they "filled the earth" (Gen
1:28).

J makes clear that what motivates God's protection of his divinity
is not jealousy; it is care and compassion. Psalm 33 comes to mind; in v.
10 YHWH ruins the plans of the nations but, significantly, the rest of the
psalm stresses God's care (*hesed*; vv. 18, 22).[107]

Verse 7

Come! Let us descend and confound there their language. The plural form,
in the imitation of the Babelian discourse in the first part of the tale, could
involve the angelic court in heaven; indeed, J has deployed some kind of
angelology in Gen 3:24 and 6:1–4 (cf. also 2 Sam 24:14; 1 Kgs 22:19ff.;

106. See Neher, *De l'hébreu au français,* 117. This is probably also valid as regards the
other texts with the same root in the primeval history: Gen 4:26; 6:1; 9:20; 10:8.

107. We can also think of the ambivalence in Jonah's being swallowed by the sea
monster but spewed out on land to fulfill his mission.

Isa 6:8; Ps 82:6; Job 1:6ff). Furthermore, to the unique location of human settlement in Shinar, God now responds with a unique divine "landing" in Babel. The supererogatory presence of the locative "there" sends us back to v. 1, when the people had decided to settle "there," that is, in Shinar.

Incidentally, let us state here that there is no dogmatic lesson to be drawn from the use in this text of the plural form or from the divine descent over Babel or over Sodom in Genesis 18. In Gen 11:7, J is displaying irony.

Let us confound. Jerome T. Walsh calls attention to the wordplay implied in the root *nbl*, which also means "fool." Here it is as if God fooled them in their language (as they had fooled themselves in thinking that their construction would prevent their dispersion).[108] Interestingly, the same root (*nbl*) is also used with sexual connotations (see Gen 34:7; Judg 19:23; 20:6; 2 Sam 13:12; Hos 2:12); in other words, the confusion of languages is also an act that is susceptible to be interpreted as a rape.

So that they will not hear [listen to, understand] the language of one another, YHWH scattered them. Indeed, the two phenomena are tied together. Language is more often than not a geographical datum. J did not need be a linguist to conclude his story the way he did. He merely reported a fact of experience. For that matter, even within the same language family, words progressively adopt different meanings, so that, for instance, there is a world of difference between "to engross" in English and *engrosser* in French! The builders of Babel, we may imagine, continued to use the "same words" (11:1) but with different meanings—until they could "not understand one another's speech" (11:7).

On Language and Langue

Gerhard von Rad argues that the intervention of God is "prophylactic." I would not overstress this somewhat minimalist view. But it remains clear that to the arrogant Babelian scheming, God set a limit according to the model of the limits that we see in Psalms and Job regarding the sea and other potential threats to the goodness of creation. Here the erected fence is human language(s). In place of the unity of language, there will be a multiplicity of languages—and, we should say—a splitting up of language itself as conveyor of rationality. For the myth invites us to an epistemological reflection on human reason as it manifests itself through instrumentation

108. Walsh, "Genesis 11:1–9," 94 nn. 12–13.

imbued with logic. As Jean-Pierre Vernant says, "Modern epistemology has convincingly demonstrated that, in any scientific field there is, it is impossible to part the different forms of thinking, its tools and its language, in short the very objects of thinking."[109] Thus, the splitting of language is also a split in rationality. There are, so to speak, as many logics as there are languages. Bruno Snell refers to Wilhelm von Humboldt, according to whom, "language is not only an implement which represents given objects, but . . . each language has a special intellectual system in which each peculiarity is determined by the whole."[110]

Originally, thinks J, there was a unique *śaphah*. Therefore—but by now in a hidden way—all human logics have a common denominator. We might say that a proof that J is right is that any idea expressed in any language (the so-called donor) is translatable into any other language (the so-called recipient). Ultimately, the failure of the Babel's construction is due to an accidental disregard for or obliviousness to the original root.[111] It is "accidental" by opposition to an absolute loss. On the model of innocence in Genesis 2–3 and Genesis 4, which must be constantly retrieved and lived through, the "unity" of the *debarim 'aḥadim* (a sort of oxymoron insisting simultaneously on the plurality of expressions and the singularity of meaning) must be reinvented. To achieve this, two contradictory propositions must be brought together. On the one hand, the very *multiplicity* of words and discourses clearly indicates that Truth is vanishing and beyond reach. The stream of words never compensates for the Logos that is still to be revealed. On the other hand, the Logos itself is *unique* and unlimited, but its essence must be said in multiple ways—in narratives, hymns, laws, oracles, proverbs, and chronicles. When the two terms are joined, the Logos permeates the discourse and the *debarim*, indeed, are *'aḥadim*. George Steiner beautifully writes, "The translator also is an *antitheos* who does violence to the natural, divinely sanctioned

109. Vernant, *Religions, histoires, raisons*, 79 (my translation).

110. Bruno Snell, *Poetry and Society*, 11.

111. According to Walter Benjamin, translation brings all human languages together for there is at the basis of all languages a common "pure language." Anything told in one language is also translatable in all languages. So that "a specific significance inherent in the original manifests itself in its translatability" (Benjamin, *Illuminations*, 71). The plurality of tongues goes back to a unique "archetypal language" (Franz Rosenzweig). It entails "the variety of 'histories' [as] closely related if not identical with the variety of languages" (Benjamin, "On the Concept of History," quoted in Britt, *Walter Benjamin and the Bible*, 128).

division between languages (what right have we to translate?) but who affirms, through this rebellious negation, the final, no less divine, unity of the *logos*."[112]

Babel fails because the builders miss the Logos. They aim for a status quo, with a massive tower, representation par excellence of immutability and monovalence, like an Egyptian pyramid. Their *śaphah ʾaḥath* is the outcome of an imposed unique interpretation of the real, without toleration for variance.

The multiplication of languages compels humans to discover the infinite variety of the real and of its interpretations. The construction of the tower of Babel is locally interrupted, in fact cancelled out, but the effect is universal: as after the flood, a new world is born. The unity of location is a fact of the past, and the unity of history has given birth to histories. Ever since the events of Genesis 11, the world has been in crisis. Nothing will be dearer to humans than retrieving the eclipsed unity. On all plans— familial, social, national, international—there will be unceasing attempts at rebuilding the original cohesion lost in the valley of Shinar. Vernant again writes, "The law of progress in rational thinking is through development by crises and even by great crises."[113]

Thus, the parallel between the story of Babel and the story of the flood is arresting. This time around, collective death is replaced or prefaced by an uprooting of the Babelians from monoglossia and unidimensionality. The loser in the process is the tower! And with it Babylon; and beyond it, polytheism.

At this point, an inquiry into the biblical view of the diversity of human languages does demonstrate that there is no such thing as "a simple description of a multilingual world."[114] Deuteronomy 28:49, for example, introduces a foreign nation whose threatening stance toward Israel is compounded by the fact that it speaks an incomprehensible language. Isaiah 33:19 mentions the arrogant nation (of Assyria) as speaking an "impenetrable language: they have a stammering tongue that you cannot understand" (literally, are "a people deep in lip"; cf. Gen 11:1: "all the earth

---

112. Steiner, *After Babel*, 331–32. Robert Scharlemann states, "Language is the reality to which the meaning of the word *God* refers and the word *God* is the reality to which the meaning of language points; God *is* what language *means*, and language is what God means" ("The Being of God When God Is Not Being God," 102).

113. Vernant, *Religions, histoires, raisons*, 100.

114. So Hiebert, "The Tower of Babel," 49.

was one lip"). Isaiah uses here the verb *la ʿag*, "stammering, stuttering" (cf. 37:22) in mockery. Other texts stress the same point: see especially Isa 28:9–13 and Ezek 3:5–6. Daniel and his companions are required to learn the Chaldean language (Dan 1:4). If we turn to the New Testament, we find a comparable concern with language. Acts 2:6, for example, hails the return to mutual understanding that had been destroyed in Genesis 11. First Corinthians 14 is entirely about language(s); see vv. 4, 5, 14, 19, 22, 23, 26, 27, 39, and so forth.

It is thus an anachronistic interpretation that sees in the language breakdown a felicitous occurrence. We never find any biblical text sharing such an optimistic comprehension of the phenomenon—and Pentecost becomes incomprehensible within the framework advocated by Hiebert and others.

The result of the divine intervention is paradoxical. The unity of language was clearly not bringing good results, but now that human communication has become plural, there is a dispersion of humanity all over the world—and the new result is called into question. In fact, the remarkable point in v. 6 is the following: strikingly, disintegration ferments *from within* the discontents in Babelian civilization. Almost reaching heaven eventually leaves the builders unsatisfied, and the means to become like God, namely, the single language, festers and finally explodes like the belly of a carcass. The discontentedness of civilization, said Freud, is "the sense of guilt produced by civilization."[115] On this score, once more, the parallel with Genesis 3 is evident.

A Close Reading of Genesis 11:8–9

Verse 8

YHWH scattered them from there over the face of all the earth. Danna Nolan Fewell also draws a parallel between the scattering of the Babelians/Babylonians here and the earlier one of the Judeans by the Babylonians. She adds, the "destruction of Babylon takes on eschatological proportions (see Isa 13)."[116] She goes on to evoke the city of Zion that the returnees build—with a city wall and a temple, so as not to be scattered from their center. They too gather "as one man" (Ezra 3:1)—and, according to her, part of the outcome is as deplorable as was Babel, the antitype.

115. Freud, *Civilization and Its Discontents*, 135.
116. Fewell, "Building Babel," 12.

The unity of language depends essentially on the imagined unity of the external world. As Freud said, "the conscious idea comprises both the concrete idea plus the verbal idea corresponding to it."[117] Once the Babelians' verbal idea explodes, it is a sign that the concrete idea does not coincide anymore with reality. The multiplication of languages (the verbal idea) is the outcome of a deep crisis in the Babelian worldview. The artificiality of a unified external world on the plain of Shinar is debunked. The world is revealed for what it actually is, that is, a collection of scattered pieces, each claiming autonomy buttressed by a particular tongue.

This was from the beginning the great fear of the Babelians. A fear that we start to understand when we realize that dispersion is *separation*: separation from the mother, of course, as we shall further see in a special section in chapter 4 below. Ultimately the greatest fear is of the separation par excellence, namely, death. The separation from the environment—here the constructed world of Babel—is the sure precursor of the separation from life. The initial angst of being dispersed is the deep-rooted refusal of death, its denial. More powerful than city walls, technique is the shield against death.

As long as the builders were a compact body, the demise of sundry members did not affect the integrity of the populace. The death of a wolf leaves intact the pack.[118] However, once the scattering of the Babelians occurs, the demise of an individual unveils all the horror of death—the ultimate enemy, as St. Paul said (1 Cor 15:26). Victory over death is not in a return to a newly consolidated pack. Paradoxically, the "history of salvation" starts with one individual, Abraham, who is the antitype, says the New Testament, of the central Jew (he is also the central human being, the so-called son of man).

From this perspective, the Babelians' endeavor in the first part of the tale appears to short-circuit the *Heilsgeschichte*. Had it been approvable by God, the Bible could have concluded with Genesis 11! And Genesis 11 indeed brings about some kind of conclusion or closure. It fittingly brings to the end humanity's prehistory—in a resounding failure. Hope does not settle in the greatest city of the ancient world; it rests between the shoulders of a man, unattached to that place and its local deities. The *El* element in *Bab-El* was a false divinity. The living God is Abraham's

117. Freud, *The Ego and the Id*, 36; Freud, *An Outline of Psychoanalysis*, 79–80.
118. The midrash intuited that much when imagining that the loss of a mason went unnoticed, but not the loss of a brick (see n. 81 above).

God.[119] Although I cannot concur with Ellen van Wolde about her interpretation of Genesis 11, her conclusion that "God is executing something
[here] that belongs to creation and in that sense the story of the tower of
Babel concludes the history of creation," is absolutely correct.[120] But then,
this parabolic and intertextual patterning with Genesis 2–3 confirms that
Gen 11:1–9 belongs to the progressive expansion of evil before the new
beginning with Abraham.

On that subject, let us note that until Genesis 11, the different episodes of rebellion against God, starting with the uprising in the Garden
of Eden and the provisionary ending with the flood, have displayed a
dialogical exchange between the divine and the human. The Babelians
have a language and several words and concepts, but God does not speak
to any one of them, only to himself. In fact, God's monologue breaks an
uncanny silence during the time that the Babelians were building their
arrogant city and their crazy tower. Jacques Derrida, invoking the Zoharic
"breaking of the vessels," says, "God separated himself from himself in
order to let us speak, in order to astonish and interrogate us. He did so
not by speaking but by keeping still, by letting silence interrupt his voice
and his signs, by letting the Tablets be broken."[121]

Max A. Myers writes that "in alienated religion humans worship
projections of their own instrumental activity, making the earth and their
partners over into an instrumental ensemble."[122]

They ceased building the city. Historically, it is of interest to note
that the Babylonian ziggurat went through episodes of construction and
destruction. So, it had been destroyed already in 689 by the Assyrian
Sennacherib. Then Nebuchadnezzar restored the city and the ziggurat,
which was again devastated in 460 during the war against Xerxes the
Persian.[123] On the cessation of building, see the parallel texts of 1 Kgs
15:21 and 2 Chr 16:5.

---

119. The opposite of the Babelian dispersion is found in Deut 32:8 as regards Israel.
We can also think of Num 10:35, where Moses pleads with God to scatter the enemy and
to gather his people (cf. Ps 68:2–3).

120. Van Wolde, "The Tower of Babel," 103.

121. Derrida, *Writing and Difference*, 67, quoted in Altizer, "History as Apocalypse,"
149.

122. Myers, "Toward What Is Religious Thinking Underway?" 120.

123. See Jer 50:2. The Babylonian ziggurat was first built between 3500 and 2400
BCE; see Seely, "The Date of the Tower of Babel."

We find the verb *ḥadal* ("to cease") with a sexual connotation only in one text, Gen 18:11 (regarding Sarah's menses). But in a highly symbolic piece as is Gen 11:1–9, where the tower is phallic and the city is feminine, there is at least an allusion to a cessation of insemination (see, e.g., Judg 9:9, 11, 13; 1 Sam 2:5) or to *coitus interruptus*.

In the readings of Genesis 11 by Ellen van Wolde and Theodore Hiebert, among others, the element of the tower becomes superfluous. Given that in v. 8 the tower is not mentioned, the critics in question generalize and interpret the text as if the absence of the tower would make no narrative difference. Van Wolde typically "flattens" the tower to horizontality![124] In fact, as we saw above, the striking structural balance of the story forbids such ungrounded theories. Of the two terms "city" and "tower" only one is inclusive: "city." As city construction stopped, so did tower construction. If the text of v. 8 here had something like, "they ceased to build the tower," the ambiguity would perhaps imply that the city continued to be built.

The strikingly balanced pattern, building a perfect structure in Gen 11:1–9, not only sheds light on the composition of the tale, but lays a powerful emphasis on the mythic combination of its constitutive elements. Taken individually, these elements may at times appear as commonplace or unsophisticated. As Lévi-Strauss has insisted, it is their combination that gives sense to the myth.[125]

But we may proceed one step further. The text tells us that the work was stopped, but it does not say that the city fell to ruin. In the sixth century BCE, the time of the Judean exile, Babylon was still definitely standing. The "in-situation" of the myth demanded at most the *interruption* of the construction. Applied to the city at large, it conveyed the expectation that the city would at some time be destroyed. Scores of prophetic oracles

---

124. Van Wolde, "The Tower of Babel," 100. Furthermore, there is a surprising unwillingness on the part of van Wolde to see the obvious synecdoche in the expression "all the earth" (five times in the text). If "all the earth" is speaking one language, it cannot mean anything but the whole humanity. Her effort to interpret it to the contrary is highly unconvincing (102). Van Wolde and Hiebert succumb to the tendency of reading the story as a "fiction, such as we read in a novel," instead of a myth, that is, "a living reality believed to have once happened in primeval times, and continuing ever since to influence the world and human destinies" (Malinowski, *Magic*, 100). The anthropologist insists, "The myth is believed to be the real cause which has brought about the moral rule, the social grouping, the rite, or the custom" (ibid., 108).

125. Lévi-Strauss, *Structural Anthropology*, esp. chap. 11.

speak of Babylon's annihilation. Suffice it to refer, once more, to Jeremiah 51. Verse 37 reads, "Babylon shall become a heap of ruins, a den of jackals, an object of horror and of hissing, without inhabitant." And v. 53, "Though Babylon should mount up to heaven, and though she should fortify her strong height, from me destroyers would come upon her, says the LORD" (NRSV).

Verse 9

This is why He called its name Babel ["babble"]. "[A] sneering pun, not without pleasure nor without relief," says J. P. Fokkelman, who uses also the term "sarcasm."[126] The Babelians stressed the action conveyed by the root *lbn* (*nilbenah lebenim*, v. 3), and YHWH reverses the root consonants so that it becomes *nbl* (*nabelah*, which, we remember, alludes also to folly). "Babel" becomes, under the pen of J, a metonymy, whereby one thing is associated with something else with which it shares a certain "kinship," thus a "chronotope," like "Pyongyang" for the North Korean regime.

There YHWH confounded the language of all the earth. While the tale about Babel is the expression of Israel's judgment on the temple-towers of Mesopotamia, J's etiology of the diversification of human languages in general was provoked by the strangeness and opacity of the Babylonian/Babelian language in Judean ears in the sixth century BCE.[127]

Some modern scholars see in this verse a mere etiology of the multiplicity of human languages and, more broadly, read Gen 11:1–9 as originally celebrating the Babylonian cradle of civilization. But, strictly speaking, the biblical text does not refer to a plurality of languages but to the "destruction du langage comme instrument de communication," as Paul Ricoeur rightly says;[128] see Isa 5:20. As a consequence of missing this point, all the utopists since Thomas More have attempted to retrieve a pre-Babelian unity of idiom.

Linguists retrace the blossoming of languages, along with a human dispersion over the whole earth, in a different way than Genesis. But their archaeology of languages and dialects, while a great deal more objective

126. Fokkelman, "Genesis 11:1–9," 12. Cassuto, *A Commentary on the Book of Genesis* 2, 249, speaks of "biting mockery" (in the use of the phrase "the whole earth") to describe the dispersion—a contrasting echo of "the whole earth" in Gen 11:1.

127. We already mentioned above Deut 28:49; Isa 33:19; 28:9–13; Ezek 3:5–6.

128. Ricoeur, *Histoire et vérité*, 117. Jean-Jacques Rousseau stated that Genesis 11 is an *exposition*, not an *explanation* of the plurality of languages (in *Essai sur l'origine des langues* [1755], 126).

and dispassionate than the biblical, is deprived of symbolic profundity. J is no archaeologist. The myth of Babel he narrates is a purely inductive and imaginative reconstruction without scientific claim. The ideological background of the Jewish traditions about languages is that their multiplicity means alienation from *the* language with which the universe was created and that remains "the language of the Sanctuary." The splitting of the sacred tongue amounts to a linguistic catastrophe.

The multiplication of languages (six thousand of them according to modern linguists) as a negative result of the Babelian hubris, leads George Steiner to state, "Far from being economic and demonstrably advantageous, the immense number and variety of human idioms, together with the fact of mutual incomprehensibility, is a powerful obstacle to the material and social progress of the species."[129]

Third Baruch 3:7–8 adds "blindness" to the confusion of speech—on the probable model of Gen 19:11 [J] where evil intents are also thwarted. For 3 *Bar.* 2:7 in Greek, the tower of Babel was a "war against God" (cf. *Tg. Neof.* Gen 11:4; Josephus *Ant.*1.117 calls it a "tumult"). So, the explosion of languages is not a punishment only for the Babelians, but for the "whole earth," as Adam and Eve's expulsion from Eden had been. In both cases, however, there is a silver lining to the divine intervention. The situation can be redeemed and language reunified in the eschaton (see Isaiah 13; Acts 2). In time, the dispersion will eventually give birth to different civilizations and cultures, for the benefit of all. This will blunt the cutting edge of the curse. But there is still no clue about these benefits in Genesis 11, which is steadily negative,[130] but nevertheless stands in expectation of the advent of historical newness in the person of Abraham.

And from there He scattered them over the face of all the earth. According to the P source of the primeval history, the human dispersion is a matter of divine purpose. This is again strongly stressed in chapter 10, which precedes the Babel story. But what looked natural and rather simple in P becomes highly dramatic in Genesis 11. In J, the very rebellion of humans paradoxically serves the divine purpose. If there is here also a *felix culpa*, it is merely from God's point of view. From the start, J's theology has been dialectical: the will of God is accomplished through human obedience, or through human disobedience.[131] Therefore, we already

129. Steiner, *After Babel*, 56.
130. *Pace* Hiebert and his students in *Toppling the Tower*.
131. Manguel says that beyond the penalty implied in Gen 11:9, the tale stresses "the

find here something similar to the J's pronouncement in Gen 50:20, when Joseph tells his brothers, "The evil *you* intended to me, *God* intended it for good." See also Exod 1:10–12. Evil is thus neutralized *in ovo*. It is far from being negated (as illusionary, for instance), but it is rendered incapable. In other words, with J things are never as simple as they look. J's genius is especially apparent in his multidimensional treatment of the relation between God and humanity.

Before a silver lining appears in humanity's dispersion, therefore, there is undoubtedly the occurrence of fragmentation after the wholeness celebrated in Gen 11:1–2. We should not downplay this motif, which begs to be transcended eschatologically.[132] Fragmentation characterizes the Babelian world, while wholeness is the beginning and the end of the Edenic world. This duality should not be understood merely as sequentially ordered, but as having an existential concomitance, like "life and death, blessings and curses" in Deut 30:19.

Actually we experience fragmentation only against the background of an intuited wholeness, finitude against the backdrop of the infinite, and mortality against the backdrop of immortality. We experience the scandalous confusion of the whole world's speech (Gen 11:9) because we intuit and strive after unimpeded communication with others and with the Other.

---

importance of finding a common means of communication, of understanding what the other says and of making ourselves understood . . . a function that requires both self-consciousness and consciousness of someone else" (*The City of Words*, 58).

132. "The severity of the punishment is evident in the permanence of the judgment," writes McKeown in *Genesis*, 72.

CHAPTER THREE

The Story of Babel as Myth

Tradition History

A LL THIS LEADS TO the crucial conclusion that J has promoted the
Babel/Babylon event to the level of *myth*, as we shall now further
elaborate.

Tradition history deals with what kind of message J transmits to the
following generations, and what kind of interpretation. Earlier we saw that
according to Gerhard von Rad and John Van Seters, who followed him,
J was a historian. The point has a lot of merit, but with the proviso that
ancient historians, like Herodotus, for example, had a conception of history different from ours today. They did not hesitate to mix legends with
facts. J is no exception. From this perspective, we might say that J's work
on the primeval era is less of a historian than of a "mythologist." True,
Genesis 11 is no pure myth, but sufficiently mythic to be treated as such,
though with prudence. The story of Babel is more than an archaeological
report (say, on the Babylonian ziggurat); more than an etiological theory
(on the diversity of languages and on the name Babel/Babylon); more than
a historical reminiscence (about the Babylonian melting pot of the sixth
century BCE); and, needless to say, more than entertainment. Genesis 11
speaks to our *imagination*. It belongs to *mythos*.

In order for a narrative to be mythic, at least four conditions need
be fulfilled. First, it has to send us back to a primeval time. Second, myth
shows a divine intervention in human affairs. Third and most important,
the narrative must be highly symbolic; in fact it must serve as paradigm in
the history of humankind. Fourth, myth is etiological.[1]

1. For Oden, three criteria need to be fulfilled: it must be in "story form; show . . . the

In this respect, the etiological dimension of Gen 11:9 is an important warrant for placing the Babel story in the category of myth. In some
anthropological schools, "mythical" just means "explanatory."[2] Another
warrant is provided by the restricted and "fogged" spatial area the story
is dealing with. The focus is unapologetically exclusive (see Gen 11:2). It
makes of *shineʿar* a somewhat mysterious place, not entirely to be identified with the southern half of Mesopotamia (Sumer and Akkad). The
unity of space is thus made easy, and so also is the unity of time as the
grandiose construction of Babel and its tower is literally condensed into
half of one single verse (v. 4a)! On both these scores, we face a minimizing
process of geography and history that fits the mythic. It also goes along
with J's disguised sarcasm toward Babylon.

Thus the tale does fit the mythic inasmuch as space is "used to make
the world intelligible by the translation of felt qualities into spatial images," as Rogerson says.[3] The same author refers to Friedrich Max Müller's
view of myth as "a psychological and linguistic theory which seeks to
describe how the human understanding, together with human language,
developed at the dawn of man's history."[4] As is well known, Israel used
ancient Near Eastern mythical categories to state its theology, convinced
as she was that the only appropriate language for theology is analogical.
Hence Israel's attraction to *mythos* over *logos*.[5] Eliade writes, "Images by
their very structure are *multivalent*. If the mind makes use of images to

---

signs of traditional transmission in a communal setting; and . . . refer . . . to a deity and/
or supernatural beings" ("Myth and Mythology," 949b). In *La Symbolique du mal* (*The
Symbolism of Evil*) Ricoeur enumerates the functions of myth: first, it embraces the whole
of humanity in an exemplary history; second, it indicates an orientation to the human
experience by telling its beginning and its end; third, we find in it expressed the enigma
of human existence as it stresses the discordance between the human state of fundamental innocence and the historical modality of guilt (162–63 [in French, 154–55]).

2. See Rogerson, "Anthropological Mythology," 54, 175. Such a reductionist definition of myth was already rejected out of hand by the anthropologist Malinowski in 1926
(*Magic*, 110). Malinowski, rather than using the term *etiology*, chose "justification by
precedent" of moral values, sociological order, and magical belief (see esp. 146).

3. Rogerson, *Myth*, 88 (paraphrasing Cassirer, *The Philosophy of Symbolic Forms*
2:86ff.).

4. Rogerson, *Myth*, 176.

5. Although, as Paul Ricoeur says, "Tout mythos comporte un logos latent qui de-
mande à être exhibé" (*De l'interprétation*, 27). Later on, in chap. 6, on deconstruction,
we'll see the *logos* transformed into *rhema* ("flow").

grasp the ultimate reality of things, it is just because reality manifests itself in contradictory ways and therefore cannot be expressed in concepts."[6]

In this, Eliade was echoing Carl Jung, who wrote, "Because there are innumerable things beyond the range of human understanding, we constantly use symbolic terms to represent concepts that we cannot define or fully comprehend. This is one reason that all religions employ symbolic language or images."[7]

But there was an important obstacle on J's path, namely, the mythical intrinsic tenet that primeval events *determine* all subsequent reality. Israel could not condone such a conception that blocks all divine historical initiative. That is why Israel proceeded to use a mythic material while "demythologizing" it, to use a Bultmannian term.[8] Paradoxically, we witness a historicization of myth, and a "mythicization" of history; such a process attributes to historical events (like the exodus, for instance) a paradigmatic quality.[9]

So, myth is a discourse that transcends its utterance about events that occurred "once upon a time." Its structure is permanent, embracing past, present, and future, says Lévi-Strauss.[10] He adds that it is because of this fundamental structure that myth is perfectly "translatable" into any other human culture, while languages are much more resistant to translation. Paradoxically and arrestingly, the time-transcending and translatable myth of Babel deals with the time-bound and "untranslatability" of the human languages!

Lévi-Strauss also says that myths are without a singular author, a statement that we must take with some reservation. In the tale on Babel, whatever may have been the "original" materials with which J worked, J is its creator. We may compare him with a music composer like Brahms or Schubert, for instance, who found inspiration in existing *Volkslieder*—

6. Eliade, *Images and Symbols*, 15 (italics original). Freud said that the mythological conception of the world is psychology projected onto the external world (*The Psychopathology of Everyday Life*, 164). This is echoed by Armstrong, *A Short History of Myth*, 11: "It was an early form of psychology."

7. Jung, *Man and His Symbols*, 21.

8. Brevard Childs states, "the Old Testament attempted to alter the form of myth so as to be able to use it for its own purpose" (*Myth and Reality in the Old Testament*, 7).

9. See Childs, *Myth and Reality*, 77; Hempel, "Glaube, Mythos und Geschichte im Alten Testament." See also Johnstone, "The Mythologising of History in the Old Testament"; Fishbane, *Text and Texture*, 136 ("a profound inner-biblical dialectic between the mythicization of history and the historicization of myth").

10. So Lévi-Strauss, *Anthropologie Structurale Deux*, 231.

Lévi-Strauss, we recall, is fond of such comparison between myth and music.

The tale of Babel cannot be called simply legend, because of its paradigmatic character, precisely what makes it a myth.[11] The issue of the relation of nature and culture provides a distinguishing touchstone. In the myth of Gilgamesh, for instance, the theme of the shift from nature to culture is prominent. In the myth of Babel, humanity is nomadic and ahistorical at the natural level (cf. Gen 11:2), and their quest for organization leads to the construction of a city with its tower, thanks to their capacity for invention, that is, culture. When, later on, the builders stop building, nature does not take revenge against culture. Rather, God (that is, the supernatural) intervenes. God does not take sides with nature, but with a culture of a different kind, as Genesis 12 will subsequently show. We return to the Mesopotamian myth of *Gilgamesh*, where nature is represented by the untamed Enkidu, and culture by both a whore and by King Gilgamesh. But Gilgamesh deals with his subjects in the city of Uruk "like a wild ox,"[12] that is, not much better than as under the jungle law. In short, wildness is the common denominator of nature and culture. As far as the Babelians are concerned, they also, like Enkidu, opt for culture, but remain uncouth. They are self-centered and aggressively autonomous. The society they conceive for themselves is closed and marked by uniformity. YHWH has nothing to do with such "culture," whose sole dream is to smother other cultures and to destroy Jerusalem. The conflict initiated by God's descent to the level of human affairs is a clash between one way of life and another. This cannot be conveyed by a "legend" filled with fantasy. "Fantasy," Geoffrey S. Kirk writes, "deals in events that are impossible by real-life standards; but in myths it tends to exceed the mere manipulation of the supernatural and express itself in a strange dislocation of familiar and naturalistic connexions and associations."[13] Kirk also notes, "In myths the supernatural component often produces drastic and unexpected changes in the forward movement of the action."[14]

The word *myth*, of course, may convey a negative connotation, as it does in some New Testament texts, such as 2 Pet 1:16 ("cleverly devised myths") or 1 Tim 1:4 and 4:7 ("profane myths") or 2 Tim 4:4 (in opposi-

---

11. On this, see Kirk, *Myth*, 31ff.
12. *Epic of Gilgamesh* 1.28.
13. Kirk, *Myth*, 268.
14. Ibid., 40.

tion to "truth"). This shadow face of myth reflects its ahistorical nature. In this sense, it is akin to parable, legend, fable, *Märchen*; these also belong to *mythos* in contrast with *logos*. Understandably, Aristotle treated myth with skepticism. So did Plato, who emphasized its symbolism but was openly critical. Incidentally, poetry and drama did not fare better among those philosophers. But we must be very cautious about this equation of myth with untruth, for it may divulge a psychological bias. Alberto Manguel states, "For fear of disruption and uncertainty, we attempt to relegate the maker's [the poet's] role to that of the fabulist, equating fiction with lies and opposing art to political reality."[15]

What hybridizes genre of the Babel tale is the mixture of the mythic and the historical. This is not the sole example in the Hebrew Bible. Psalm 77:17–21 and Isa 51:9–11 provide other samples. In fact, Gen 11:1–9 inserts itself into the progressive evolution from myth to history.[16] Such progression involves a series of alienations: of man and woman in Genesis 3, brother and brother in Genesis 4, angels and humans in Genesis 6, parents and offspring in Genesis 9, and now among people in Genesis 11. These oppositions recall Edmund Leach's pointing to the binary dimension of myth (following Lévi-Strauss), as it is "constantly setting opposing categories." He gives as examples "God against the world" or "good and evil."[17] Relevant to the Babel myth is the opposition between, on one hand, the earthly materials used for building the city and, on the other hand, the tower, the aim of reaching up to heaven. From this perspective as well it is clear that we should not minimize the importance of the expression "with its top in the heavens" (v. 4).

Not a pure myth, Gen 11:1–9 is a mixture of fantasy and chronicle. As fantasy, it comments about a human wave to the east (or, from the east), and about a gigantic endeavor consisting of building Babel. It comes also with a legendary etiology about the city's name and the tremendous diversity of languages in the world, corresponding to the builders' geographical dispersion. As a chronicle, it retraces, however imprecisely, the origins of the Mesopotamian city of Babylon, and it alludes to the historic ingathering—by coercion—of diverse nations into exile there.

15. Manguel, *The City of Words*, 22–23.
16. So Vogels, *Nos origines*, 183.
17. Leach, *Genesis as Myth and Other Essays*, 8. As we shall see in chap. 6, on deconstruction, it is precisely this pattern of binary oppositions that deconstruction dismantles.

With the help of these elements, J has created a story that transcends space and time. The myth sends us back to *in principio* ("in the beginning"), that is to a unique and primordial moment that reactualizes itself in ever new constructions of cities and arrogant towers, whether on the collective or the individual plane.[18] Babel is as much a symbol as were the stories on Adam and Eve, Cain and Abel, and the flood and Noah.[19] On the model of most myths of the beginning, this one speaks of the construction of a certain world, of its disintegration, and of its (potential) rebirth into a different form, while the initial form does not completely perish because of the new. Eliade's writings insist on a time-free eternal reenactment of the myth, corresponding to a conception of time that is cyclical: creation, destruction, re-creation of the same.[20]

The previous sentence signals that we should now turn to the issue of time in the biblical myth. First and emphatically it must be said that this myth comes in a context of broken circularity. After destruction, disintegration, confusion, and scattering, there is no repeat of what has been ruined; such re-creation will happen only at the end of time, yielding a form transcending anything we know—though now our hope for this re-creation guides our daily navigation like the North Star.[21] Meantime, the city and the tower remain pitifully incomplete and doomed; humanity is an archipelago; and the initial monolanguage is at best the remote ancestor of innumerable languages and dialects.

The nonrepeatability term for term of the Hebrew myth makes it unique and fundamentally demythologized, a strong determination of its compositeness.[22] Similarly, the myth of the "fall" is not deterministically repeated in never-ending cycles, but is the archetype of our discrete stumblings. The punishment by universal flooding will never be repeated (Gen 9:15), but its cause, the explosion of human violence, is not confined to a remote past: it continues to deserve the same chastisement as in the time

18. Already at the level of Kindergarten, children of both sexes build a tower with construction blocks as high as it goes until it crumbles! See my elaboration on the myth of Icarus in the section on "A Psychoanalytical Approach," below in chap. 4.

19. Eliade says that "the symbol arises, from the beginning, as a creation of the psyche" (*Images and Symbols*, 177).

20. See in particular *The Myth of the Eternal Return*.

21. Church fathers compared the cross, e.g., to a column standing at the center of the world and opening communication with heaven (see, e.g., Ephrem, "Nineteen Hymns," 224, 228). Clearly a tower of Babel redeemed and transfigured.

22. The myth of Babel, like a pearl in the oyster shell, includes its own principle of demythologization.

of Noah; Babel is in full decay, but it finds its duplication in innumerable collective and individual narcissistic "towers."

Earlier in this study, I have stressed the stasis of the tower—like that of a pyramid or an obelisk in Egypt or the Eiffel Tower in modern times. This immobility says much about the attempted escape from time. Literarily, it finds expression in Indian or Greek myths with their negation of history. J's tale of the tower of Babel stands in stark opposition to these, and it corresponds to the absence of monuments in historical Israel. While the Jews, as it has been said, carry their land on the soles of their shoes, the Babelians consolidate all their energies to wage war against the transitoriness of time and space.

Time

Following scholars like Henry Wheeler Robinson, Paul Minear, John Marsh, Thorleif Boman, and Carl Heinz Ratschow,[23] among others, Brevard Childs, in *Myth and Reality*, reminds us that "the Hebrew concept of time was primarily interested in the quality of time rather than its temporal succession . . . (cf. Hag 1:2; Esth 1:13)."

The Hebrew Bible's conception of time must be considered against the backdrop of the factor of sin; that is, of the perversion of historical reality. In Genesis 11 this human condition is metaphorically pictured as the Babelian attempt at playing God. Hence, the quality of time becomes gravely jeopardized and shows its essential need to be redeemed. Time is never neutral and never a mere succession of events. At every point of the succession, there is the need to assess its higher or lower quality, that is, either its progression (toward the eschaton)[24] or its regression (back to the forever-threatening chaos).

Now, the builders of Babel, like their counterpart constructors of the pyramids in Egypt, endeavor to freeze time. In Manguel's terms, we are set "in a non-progressive time and a non-mapable space."[25] The building is atemporal; even the process of its erection is bypassed by the text. The

---

23. See Robinson, *Inspiration and Revelation in the Old Testament,* 106ff.; Minear, *Eyes of Faith,* 97ff.; Marsh, *The Fullness of Time,*19ff.; Boman, *Das hebräische Denken im Vergleich mit dem Griechischen,* 104ff.; Ratschow, "Anmerkungen zur theologischen Auffassung des Zeitproblems," all referred to in Childs, *Myth and Reality,* 75 nn. 3–7.

24. On eschatology, see Isa 11:6ff.; 65:17; Amos 9:11ff.; Jer 4:23; 30:20; 33:7; Mal 3:4.

25. Manguel, *The City of Words,* 81.

throngs announce their intention in Gen 11:2 and the tale jumps to the near-achievement of the city in 11:5.

The next scene shows God figuratively "descending to see" (Gen 11:5), that is, to evaluate the quality of the Babelian project. His conclusion is clear. The Babelian endeavor must be stopped. But with this stalling, it is the whole of human history ("all the earth") that is diverted, and the eschaton is delayed until a new start puts history on its tracks again. True, after the flood, the human settlement in Shinar was already by itself a new start, but it backfired because of the insatiable human desire to again put God between parentheses. If God is high, they'll go higher; if he sits in heaven, they'll go up to heaven; if he has a name of glory, they'll make a name for themselves; if he rules a kingdom, they'll establish an empire by substituting their own "there" for the divine dwelling;[26] if God is one, they'll congregate in one place and speak one language with a narrow focus to their monoglossic and one-dimensional discourse. Where the means are missing, they'll invent artificial replacements.

These culturally conditioned items short-circuit time. In J's other primeval myths, we find a similar denunciation. Already in Genesis 3 the natural (leafy) loincloths of Adam and Eve are replaced by an animal skin—given by God but fitting the new human condition. In Genesis 4, it is Cain and his immediate descendants who build cities and invent tools and musical instruments. Noah builds an ("exclusivist") ark. Now, as much as J represents the unconscious by that which is not conditioned by culture, J also shows suspicion about the instinctual. There is, as a matter of fact, a deeply ingrained anxiety in the Yahwist to show the profound difference between humanity and animality. (Adam finds no animal fit to become his alter ego.)

Time and history have thus become the enemy of Babel. Time, especially qua succession of unique events, constitutes a major obstacle to mythic narrative, for the main purpose of myth is to report original cosmic events that are timeless and impervious to the vagaries of historical occurrences.[27] Consistent with this conception of unchangeability, the mythic god is eternal, static, and changeless. The Babelian ideal, symbolized by an obelisk, a pyramid, or a tower, is meant to neutralize all

26. Cf. the rabbinic *Maqom* ("place") or *Shekhinah* ("indwelling") to designate God.
27. All myth, Lévi-Strauss says, is a quest for time lost. Myth always concerns events in a remote past; although occurring long ago myths form a permanent structure (*Structural Anthropology*, chap. 11).

becoming. The eventual dispersion of humanity and the multiplication of languages is the revenge of time as it stresses human limitation, finitude, or (to use a Bakhtinian term) "unfinalizability." The Babelian hubris—a characteristic filling time and space—is humiliated (for better or for worse, as history will show).

Space

In spite of the tight stylistic pattern of Gen 11:1–9, with its purported repetitions and oppositions, and its perfect balance, there would be no major obstacle to attributing the Babel story to oral tradition. But the prominent role played by space tips the balance the other way. "Orality" is by nature conditioned by time, both in terms of the inner temporality of the narrative, and by the time-bound delivery of the tale. However, Gen 11:1–9 strongly insists on the notion of space, and its narrative distribution is itself harmonious and strikingly visual. It is likely, therefore, that we are dealing with a written composition from the outset. As I said earlier, J may well have been influenced by extant traditions, oral and written, but his authorship of the Babel piece seems beyond doubt.

Such a conclusion warrants making several assertions about J. First, J was an ingenious composer, not merely a redactor or a traditionist. Second, J's status as an independent thinker/poet presupposes a sophisticated setting. Wellhausen thought of the Solomonic era, but the (post) exilic period saw prolific literary production, and it comes with at least comparable credentials to our consideration. Third, both personal creation and the "setting-in-life" of the Babel tale make possible an explanation for the relative lack of any echo of the Babel myth in the rest of the Hebrew Bible. On this score, J is an "isolated" giant, as were many a prophet in Israel's history.[28]

Now, charismatic J's reporting of Babel's construction in the form of a myth perfectly fits the mythic mentality of the Babylonian builders. They want to assimilate and celebrate the alleged fundamental harmony of the cosmic order. They speak one language; they think the same thoughts; they concentrate people, energies, and desires around one building project; and, more decisively yet, they endeavor to bring together the present world and the world beyond. In a way, the central notion of space here

---

28. The kinship of J with Isaiah is to be underscored. See below the section "Prophetic Parallels."

aims at an absence of distance between heaven and earth, divine and human, sacred and profane, same and different—thanks to a mediatory *hieros gamos* ("sacred marriage") between the human king and the divine, like the one in the myth reported in Genesis 6.

The issue of space raises the problem of the relationship of the human to the cosmos or to *nature*. The absence of distance between heaven and earth also affects the contiguity of religion and nature. The Babelians build a mountain that is supposed to bind together the divine and the cosmic. Nature is "moralized" and imbued with virtues that reflect the divine. The gods have created the pickaxe, and their gift of it to humanity is conferring to the object a sacred dimension besides a useful one.[29] The cosmos is in fact harmonious as it obeys the laws inscribed in the stars. Everyone in Mesopotamia is born with a divinely attributed destiny; determinism rules the day.

Let us say, incidentally, it is not so in Israel. In Israel there is no complacency towards nature. Like human flesh, nature per se is neither good nor bad. It needs to be guided, humanized, and historicized, lest it become a snare, an agent for servitude, a demonic power. Genesis 1 commands, and Genesis 2 and 3 illustrate, human domination over nature or animality. When nature is not held in check, it soon dominates and enslaves. The Babelians eventually learn this lesson when it is too late.

The notion of space in Genesis 11 goes beyond its vocabulary; the story presents a typical version of the "myth of the center." From the outset, the tale illustrates a human centripetal wave. "All the earth" is rushing "from the east" (and from their initial dispersion [Genesis 10]) (?) to one place in the "Valley of Shinar," in Mesopotamia.[30] The word *šam* ("there"), we recall, appears five times in the nine verses of the tale. Nomadic humanity is described as looking, since time immemorial, for a suitable spot to settle and to put down roots of culture and religion. The whole tale is about their construction of a city and of a tower; they are looking to establish a state. It is thus not surprising that the matter of space becomes

29. See the Sumerian text *Praise of the Pickaxe* (esp. lines 9–10), in Castellino, "Les textes bibliques et les textes cunéiformes," 134. See also Kramer, *Sumerian Mythology*, 51ff.; Jacobsen, "Sumerian Mythology," 136. Instruments and tools are human inventions, according to Israel.

30. On the basis of Gen 1:28 and 10:32 (both from P), Walter Brueggemann thinks of a regathering of people in Shinar and of a rescattering as an act of judgment (see *Genesis*, 97–104). See also what I say here from an intratextual point of view about the fear of the people to be *again* nomadic and dispersed in Gen 11:4.

so important. It is all the more so because the quest for settlement is not without philosophical and psychological consequences. The selection of a center is religious, for it breaks the homogeneity of space for the sake of discovering a central and sacred axis.[31] Therefore, when eventually the dismantling occurs, it amounts to an antireligious move that is not unwelcome in Judean eyes. As we saw above, there is in a certain way an oxymoron in speaking of "Israel's religion." Prophetic Israel polemicizes against idolatry, polytheism, magic, dualism, determinism, disincarnate spiritualism, ancestor worship, escape from history—all things dear to religion. There was, after all, something right in the Roman accusation of Jewish "atheism." Everything affirmed by religions is indeed put upside down by historic Israel—like Babel's fate.[32] We find an echo of this in a declaration by Jacques Derrida: "For me, there is no such thing as 'religion.' Within what one calls religions . . . there are . . . sometimes texts, especially those of the prophets, which cannot be reduced to an institution, to a corpus, to a system."[33]

From this point of view, there is for the Israelite mentality an internal conflict among the Babelians between the ends they intended and the means they used. There is no compatibility of a temple reaching up to heaven on one hand and its construction with crass earthy means: clay (instead of the available stones) and bitumen (spurting from the ground; see Gen 14:10). Besides, the ziggurat, says G. Rachel Levy, "is coextensive with the earth, erected 'in the place of fertility' over a vast hollow, the primeval cave where the dead dwell . . . the 'Bond of heaven and earth' (Dur-an-ki) . . . thus conceived as a kind of Jacob's ladder."[34]

Of particular importance for our study is the following statement by Mircea Eliade: "The erection of an altar . . . is nothing but the reproduction—on the microcosmic scale—of the Creation. The water in which the clay is mixed is assimilated to the primordial water; the clay that forms

---

31. See Eliade, *The Sacred and the Profane*, chap. 1.

32. See my remarks on "religion" with reference to Karl Barth's *Church Dogmatics* (see chap. 2 n. 96 above).

33. Derrida, *Deconstruction in a Nutshell*, 21, quoted in Sherwood, "Derrida," 73.

34. Levy, *Religious Conceptions of the Stone Age* (see part 3, "Ziggurat and Pyramid" sec. 1: "Culmination [Egypt and Sumer])." On the point of the *axis mundi* bridging hell, earth, and heaven, see *Enuma Elish*, vi, 57–63; cf. Parrot, *Ziggurats et tour de Babel = The Tower of Babel*. The *Chaldean Cosmology* I, 10–16 reads as follows: "The Esagila that Luguldukuga [= Marduk] founded in the midst of the Apsu"; cf. Labat et al., *Les Religions du Proche-Orient asiatique*, 75.

the base of the altar symbolizes the earth; the lateral walls represent the atmosphere, and so on. . . . [All this] is equivalent to a cosmogony."[35]

Before leaving the *axis mundi* subject, I refer to other biblical texts like Daniel 4, on the great tree whose top reaches to heaven (v. 8). Nebuchadnezzar goes atop his palace and boasts about "great Babylon" (vv. 25–26); but shortly after, he becomes confused in his mind and is banned by his people to the confines of the earth, as it were. See the parallel text of Isa 14:13–14 (Babylon is speaking): "I will ascend to heaven; I will raise my throne above the stars of God . . . I will make myself like the Most High" (NRSV]).

Space, therefore, is ambiguous in (nonbiblical) myth, as it does not establish a gap between objects, but the absence of an interval between them! Space here has no surface extension. It is purely vertical, a beam inside which there is no distinction of the finite and the infinite. Indeed, mythical space is determined by "a particular content to each position,"[36] which the human experience does define. Human experience, however, is only the rediscovery of an essential quality afforded to space from the "time" of the primordial world structure, so that mythical space no less than mythical time is fundamentally *ne varietur* (fixed). When it happens that the Babelian space is utterly disrupted at the end of the J story, the disruption is experienced by the mythic mentality as cosmic, and as questioning the world structure. As in the case of the flood in Genesis 6–9, Gen 11:1–9 spells out a catastrophe on a universal scale.

The severity of the chastisement calls for further reflection. No author in the Hebrew Bible, whether ostensibly before or after David's bringing the ark of the covenant into Jerusalem (David's anointment of Zion) would mention a foreign city except against the backdrop of Jerusalem's election and holiness. Especially in the case of the arrogant and blasphemous city of Babylon, its boasting is an affront to Zion.[37] Israel's mythicizing of Jerusalem entails the demythologization and the demystification of all other spaces. No other place but Zion can claim centrality and sacrality without such claim amounting to a challenge to God's choice of Jerusalem as his "resting place" (Ps 132:13–14). Zion is *the* mountain that no ziggurat can rival; although as in all cases of a religious mountain, it is cosmic and reaches mythically to heaven while embracing the whole of

---

35. Eliade, *The Sacred and the Profane*, 30–31.
36. Childs, *Myth and Reality*, 83.
37. See, for instance, Dan 4:30–31.

humanity (see, e.g., Isa 2:2). Zion is "perfect in beauty" (Ps 50:2), a claim that Babylon usurps (cf. Isa 13:19; 14:9; Jer 51:33). Most interesting is the declaration in Ps 78:69 that *God* "built his sanctuary *like* the heights [of heaven], like the earth that he established for ever." Babel cannot compete (cf. Gen 11:4). Zion, not Babylon, is the *axis mundi* (Ps 48:1; Ezek 38:12; cf. 40:1–4), a *historically* grounded reality.[38] Decisive is the realization that "a place is never holy apart from its relation to YHWH,"[39] something utterly lacking to Babylon. Eric Burrows writes, "We find in Jerusalem itself an extraordinarily complete *counterpart* to the Babylonian pattern. The significance of this parallelism would be missed if it were seen merely as an instance of Babylonian influence on Israel: logically it implies a polemic *against* Babylonian pretensions, a counter-claim in favour of the theocratic centre of Israel."[40]

True, at times Jerusalem's relation to God is not any better than Babel's. Then the divine judgment on Zion is equitable: Mic 3:9–12 announces, "Jerusalem shall become a heap of ruins, and the mountain of the house a wooded height" (NRSV; see Jeremiah 7).

In summary, space in Gen 11:1–9 is central, because this notion fits the Babylonian empire's ambition. Great powers have no problem with duration. They assume that they will eternally endure.[41] Their problem is swallowing and absorbing space. They aim to be universal and to impose their *pax* on "all the earth."[42] J understood this well and astutely emphasized the topological dimension of Babel.

We may go one step further and characterize the Babelian space as ultimately vertical, as I said above. Both in the Yahwist story and in the exilic prophetic corpus, Babylon has an imposing height. Heaven is the limit—that is, there is no limit. The great prophets denounce the Babylonian hubris that its architecture translates (see Isa 13:13–14; Jer 51:9, 53; in Jer 51:25, Babylon is ostensibly a mountain!). The Babelian/

---

38. Childs, *Myth and Reality*, 89.

39. Ibid., 91.

40. Burrows, "Some Cosmological Patterns in Babylonian Religion," 54. Within the circumstances of exile, the erection of a ziggurat meant in the eyes of J and his coreligionists substituting one temple for another, and one form of worship for another; cf. Dan 5:3. See Clifford, *The Cosmic Mountain in Canaan and the Old Testament*; Parrot, *The Tower of Babel*.

41. Adolf Hitler thought that the Third Reich would last a thousand years.

42. Ancient Rome's ambition was to universally impose the *Pax Romana*.

Babylonian striving to go ever higher cannot but recall the Greek myth of Icarus, to which we'll turn soon.[43]

Genesis 11 and Etiology

We saw above that etiology is one of the main elements in myths of origin, even to the point that anthropologists sometimes equate etiology and myth. This has been stressed by Edward B. Tylor, for instance, who is considered "one of the founders of modern anthropology,"[44] followed by Robin Horton. But all this is qualified by the social character of myth (i.e., the etiological explanation is not a private one). What is most important is that the etiology (whether in J's work, like Gen 3:20; 6:4; 10:9;[45] 11:9; or elsewhere in the Bible) is not meant just to be intellectually satisfying. Its purpose is to facilitate a collective participation in the "explained" phenomenon. Finishing Gen 11:1–9 readers are not expected to conclude, "Aha! That's why we have a plurality of languages in the world." Rather, the myth aims to elicit the following conclusion: "We are now using a confusing number of languages in the world because of our original/originary hubris that brought upon us a babble of languages and a physical dispersion, both in need of mending and healing."[46]

As a myth of origins, Genesis 11 has built, on the basis of a symbolization of "Babel," an archetype of universal history marked by the insatiable human desire of self-deification and immortality. Babel is Babylon and more. Historical Babylon becomes a microcosm in a very different way from the way she had thought of herself. Now she is the faithful mirror of a world that has become disoriented and is in dire need of re-creation.[47]

---

43. See the section on Icarus below in chap. 4.

44. So Oden, "Myth and Mythology," 950. See Tylor, *Primitive Culture,* 2 vols; Horton, "African Traditional and Western Science."

45. Genesis 10:8-9 belongs to J's inserts in the P work of Genesis 10. The association of Nimrod with the tower of Babel story as stated by Jewish tradition is thus established. This is further confirmed by J's using the verb *ḥll* in 4:26; 6:1; 9:20; and especially 10:8 and 11:6. John Milton also (in *Paradise Lost,* book xii) makes Nimrod the leader of the blaspheming builders.

46. Malinowski states that a myth is "not an intellectual explanation or an artistic imagery, but a pragmatic charter of primitive faith and moral wisdom" (*Magic,* 101; quoted in Oden, "Myth and Mythology," 952).

47. Walter Wink writes, "We are dealing with something fundamental to the spiritual journey itself, and not merely with etiological legends invented to 'explain' the origin of things" ("On Wrestling with God," 142).

Myths of origin, among which the story of Babel belongs, generally end on a note of contemporaneity with readers.[48] We shall be sensitive, however, to the difference in ethos between the Babel story (in which God thwarts the builders' quest for immortality) and the myth of Gilgamesh, for instance, in which Gilgamesh returns to Uruk to reign over his people *as if the adventurous quest for immortality had not occurred.* Genesis 11:9 closes the Babel story with a situation familiar to all: the human dispersion and the disturbing multiplication of languages. Both stories, of Gilgamesh and of Babel, are etiological, but their attitudes toward the aspiration of immortality are polar opposites.

In this respect, the story of Dedalus's labyrinth, for instance, warrants mention. In both the Mesopotamian and the Greek cases, there is a construction meant to rival the divine knowledge and the divinely prescribed fate. Human ingenuity and creativity are prominent. In both myths, the building proclaims the triumph of technology, but in both as well technology becomes fatal to those who have conceived it. Dedalus's curse of his own invention, when he discovers that his son Icarus died in the sea, could be shared by the dispersed Babelians at the end of J's story. In both stories, the creators have been guilty of immoderation.[49]

In contrast to mythology in general, Israel's myths are historically oriented and need not be part of a liturgy, for instance, that grounds their efficacy. Such an "intellectualizing" transformation of myth is remarkable and is properly unique, wherein myth remains myth only because of its paradigmatic character and its innate efficacy. Thus, when Gen 11:8 evokes the cessation of the city construction and, for all practical purposes, the end of Babylon, the myth becomes prophetic rather than wishful thinking.

My emphasis on the mythic dimension of the Babel tale opens the door to a text that is, in Robert Couffignal's words, "gorgé de symboles à portée mythique" (saturated with myth-oriented symbols).[50] Myth stems from a combination of primary symbols, such as we encountered in the philological section above: "valley," "Shinar," "city," "tower," "bricks," and so forth. All these—not to speak of the primary symbolism of evil in the form of human hubris—convey meanings whose intrinsic quality elevates

48. See Bost, *Babel*, 74.
49. See below, chap. 4, the section "Babel and the Dedalus-Icarus Myth."
50. Couffignal, "La Tour de Babel," 59.

the narrative to the plane of the metaphoric or the paradigmatic.[51] This
is the very condition for avoiding a misunderstanding common to Jewish
and non-Jewish commentators regarding the alleged lack of gravity in
the Babelians' sin. Often, the point of view is moralistic. Then, evil is
subversion of a specific rule, a pure transgression of a given prohibition.
Evidently, it is not the case in the myth of Babel. No commandment forbids building a city and a tower. Evil here is of another profundity, in
the human pretension to be autonomous and to rival the divine. Ever
since the myth of the fall, the *sicut Deus* of the serpent continues to offer the greatest challenge of all. Ricoeur says, "Evil 'abounds' wherever
man transcends himself in grandiose undertakings, wherein he sees the
culmination of his existence in the higher works of culture, in politics and
in religion . . . all forms of false worship."[52]

For if myth reveals "the most hidden modalities of being,"[53] in
the words of Eliade, it must be said that one of those modalities is the
camouflaged perversity and inclination to do evil (see Gen 6:5; 8:21). In
J's literary work, the issue of evil is the centerpiece. What is evil here?
Primarily the human desire to be like God, the desire for immortality, for
infinitude. It can also find expression in nostalgia for paradise. This latter
articulation is decisive in Genesis 11. When the text says about the tower
that it is meant to reach heaven, the Yahwistic context reminds readers
that "heaven" or "Eden" has been (temporarily) lost, thus becoming the
aspiration of humanity.

51. Reference should be made to the study of Paul Ricoeur in "Guilt, Ethics and
Religion." In *The Symbolism of Evil*, Ricoeur says about the symbols that, "their heteroge-
neity bears witness to the significant whole by its contingent outcroppings" (169; in the
French edition, 160).

52. Ricoeur, "Guilt, Ethics and Religion," 116. On Babylon's being a superb city, see
Isa 13:19; 14:12; Jer 50:42; 51:7, 41. Raschke speaks of "blinded Oedipus who has finally
seen clearly the meaning of his effort to play God, a decadent hypersensitivity or vacuous
narcissism which is the spur to incest in the first place" ("The Deconstruction of God,"
23). The fall of Babel after her bragging about her great name recalls the pattern of Greek
tragedy. In Sophocles's *Oedipus the King*, e.g., when the hero is close to discovering the
truth about himself, he adopts a triumphant tone in summoning the shepherd-witness
and proclaims himself the son of the goddess Chance, a claim that the chorus takes at
face value (see lines 997–1194 and 1195–1214). So Oedipus as a tragic hero is to fall from
greater heights.

53. Eliade, *Images and Symbols*, 12.

Prophetic Parallels to Genesis 11:1–9

Two major prophetic texts composed during the sixth-century exile in Babylon remarkably parallel some details of the J story. Isaiah 13–14 and Jeremiah 51 are fierce oracles against Babylon, and they forecast her total destruction. She is guilty of enormous hubris, and she will get a commensurable retribution for her crimes.

In both texts, it is clear that "Babel" is more than just the city or the province of Babylon. The prophets attribute to her mythic traits, so that what they vituperate against becomes an overblown picture of the divine indictment against "all the earth" and of God's consistent care for his people.

In what follows, I intend to briefly review these prophetic oracles and to show their striking kinship with J's tradition in Genesis 11 and their indirect influence on the Yahwist, or conversely from the Yahwist.

Isaiah 13–14

When we turn to Isaiah 13–14 (an oracle against Babylon, probably written in the sixth century BCE), it is clear that *Babylon* stands for a cosmic *topos*. Verse 11 makes it explicit: "I will requite to the world its evil, and to the wicked their iniquity; I will put an end to the pride of the arrogant and humble the haughtiness of tyrants" (JPS). What characterizes Babylon is pride and arrogance, insolence and hubris (see also Isa 14:14: "I mount the back of a cloud—I shall match the Most High [*'elyon*]"; see Jer 50:29, 31, 32; parallel with Gen 11:4, the making of a name), for Babylon is "the glory of kingdoms, the proud splendor of the Chaldeans" (Isa 13:19; cf. 14:9). Babylon's appetite for omnipotence is expressed especially in Isa 14:13–14, to which (although the oracle is addressed to the King of Tyre), Ezekiel 28 builds an uncanny parallel (see especially vv. 2, 6, 9, 13, and 14).

Babel had attracted all nations—either through forced migration or through its cultural and commercial allure (see Jer 51:44). It is even called "son of the dawn" or *Helal* (*helel*, "the shining one") in Isa 14:12; or again "Sheshak" (a cryptogram for Babylon) in Jer 25:26; 51:41. *Helal* is especially interesting as we find here again a word with two *lameds* as in *balal* of Gen 11:9 ("prattle") as a scornful etymology of the name Babel.[54]

---

54. Consistent with this, the fall of Babylon—like the later fall of Rome—provokes universal repercussions (see Isa 13:14; 14:7–8; Jer 50:46; 51:44, 48–49, 58, etc.).

This much corresponds to the first part of the J tale on Babel.
Comparable to the second part is the prophetic oracle of Babylon's being
"cut down to the ground" (Isa 14:12a; cf. 14:15, 19–20), for she is "fallen
from heaven" (14:12b). Didn't she say, "I shall ascend to heaven, higher
than the stars of God" (Isa 14:13, parallel to Gen 11:4; cf. Ps 139:8), and
"I will set my throne on high" (Isa 14:13)? In the mouth of God, the statement in Isa 14:21b is amazingly close to Gen 11:4: "lest they rise and pos-
sess the earth, and fill the surface of the world with [their] towns"—they
would then fill the earth in a demonstration of might, not by dispersion.
The opposition between "the mountain of the north" (Isa 14:13) and "the
bottom of the pit" (14:15) is also to be stressed. When the unavoidable catastrophe comes, the fragmentation and crumbling of the city is complete
(see Isa 47:15; Jer 51:9, 44).

Jeremiah 51

Jeremiah 51 is another exilic oracle of doom over Babylon, also delivered
in the sixth century BCE. The text is even richer in parallels with Gen
11:1–9 . I shall review the Jeremiah oracle almost verse by verse insofar as
the textual details evoke verbally or ideologically J's Babel story.

Verse 2 announces the dispersion of Babylon by strangers (or: its win-
nowing by winnowers, according to the wordplay here). See v. 9 below.

Verse 6 warns everyone to flee from Babylon and save their lives.
There is also the interesting exhortation not to remain silent, a motif we
tackle elsewhere. Babylon will get retribution commensurate with her
crimes, *middah keneged middah* ("measure for measure," "quid pro quo")
after the rabbinic principle. See the same idea in v. 13 and in Jer 16:18;
50:29; 51:56.

Verse 8: "Suddenly Babylon has fallen and is broken up!" (See also
Isa 21:9.)

Verse 9, besides repeating the motif of the Babelian dispersion encountered in v. 2, declares that the city's judgment "reaches up to heaven,
it is as high as the skies." Again we find the idea of a deserved quid pro
quo.

In vv. 11–1 2, we find the same motif of *mezimmah* ("plan, purpose")
that we saw in Gen 11:6 ("they purpose to make"); cf. Job 42:2 for the root
zmm.

About the unexpected expression "vengeance of His temple," I refer
to my study of the notion of space above, where I stress the idea that no

other place but Zion can legitimately claim centrality and sacrality. Babel is blasphemous and attracts the wrath from God's temple.

Jeremiah's oracle is interrupted by a hymn (vv. 15–19) that is not necessarily out of place here, but which interests us only indirectly at this point. Let us, however, note that in v. 15, it is God's intelligence that reaches to heaven, and that idolatry is scorned in vv. 17–18.

Within vv. 20–23, the verb *puṣ* appears no less than ten times, in parallel with Gen 11:4 (*pen naphuṣ* ["lest we be scattered"]). The primordial importance of this theme cannot be overstated. The kinship of J with the prophets of exile is evident.

Verse 25: Surprisingly, Babylon built on a plain or in a valley (Gen 11:2; archaeologically confirmed), is here twice called a mountain. From a *har hammaṣhith* ("mountain of the Destroyer"), she will become a *har śerephah* ("burnt-out mountain"). Calling Babel a mountain responds to a mythical or mystical demand, for the designation simply runs against geography. We find a similar transformation of the geographic reality in the shift from Zech 12:11 ("the valley of Megiddo[n]") to Rev 16:16, where Megiddo becomes a mountain ("Harmageddon")![55] It is hard in the Jeremiah text to bypass the probability that the allusion is to the Babylonian ziggurat or sham mountain. Then, the following locution ("the whole earth") is a further ideological echo of the same expression found in Gen 11:1, 4, 8, and 9 (twice). It appears again in Jer 51:49.

Verse 26 could be subtly alluding to the brick substitutes for the stones in Gen 11:3 (see also Jer 51:37), but more likely it refers to the competition between Babylon's gods and Jerusalem's God, YHWH (see Isa 28:16; Jer 51:52).

Verse 29: According to some Hebrew manuscripts and ancient versions, the verse is here again speaking of planning, as in vv. 11–12 above.

Verse 43 ("a land where no one lives" [see v. 44]) clashes with the statement in Gen 11:2 that all humanity settled in Shinar. The contrast between the beginnings of Babel and its end is just striking.

Verse 53 brings us again to the core of Genesis 11 (see Gen 11:4): Babylon strives to go ever higher, indeed to heaven, and her hostile intentions are clearly expressed with the mention of her fortresses.

---

55. On these texts, see LaCocque and Ricoeur, *Thinking Biblically*, especially my chapter on Zech 12:10: "Et aspicient ad me quem confixerunt," 401–21.

Verse 55 also clashes with an implied motif in Genesis 11, namely, the uncanny silence of the Babelians after God's judgment (11:8–9). In v. 55, Babylon has "a big voice" and sounds "a tumultuous voice."

Verse 58: What kind of work does "tire the peoples for naught and weary the nations for fire" (see also v. 64)? We are not told. Should we think of the construction of Babel and of its tower/ziggurat? The participation of "peoples" and "nations" in the great building enterprises in Babylon is beyond any doubt.[56] True, the Babylonians are not accused of enslaving the foreign exiles like the pharaoh of Egypt did during the time of the exodus, but it is clear that the aliens had no other recourse but to enroll in the local workforce.

---

56. See above (this chapter): King Nebuchadnezzar mentions in his inscriptions regarding the *Etemenanki* that he mobilized people from all corners of his empire.

CHAPTER FOUR

A Psychoanalytical Approach to Genesis 11:1–9

Psychological Biblical Criticism

BEFORE WE ENTER THIS new chapter in our exploration of the kerygma of Gen 11:1–9, a potential obstacle must be removed. I am referring to the objection by some that the psychoanalysis of a person is interactive while a text, allegedly, cannot reply to its interpretation. Such an argument is faulty. The text, any text, does not stand isolated and closed up. As Peter Rudnytsky, paraphrasing Robert Steele, states,

> In dealing with a text, the established procedure for checking an interpretation "is the test of the part against the whole; that is, seeing that each interpretation of a part fits with the emerging conception of the whole" ([Steele] 1979, 392). In addition the interpreter has an obligation to hearken to what can be gleaned from "investigating parallel texts by the same author, texts from the same tradition, and the historical period of the text's creation" ([Steele], 393), as well as from the history of the reception of the text. In all of these ways, the written text, like a person, "answers back" to the interpreter; and it is only the prejudice of the clinician against "applied analysis" that causes . . . to overlook that the interpretations of scholars in the humanities are no less interactive—and no more scientific—than [with a person].[1]

Indeed, the counterargument confuses two different aspects of psychoanalysis: one which is "the *art* of psychoanalytic therapy" and the

---

1. Rudnytsky, *Reading Psychoanalysis*, 236–37. See Steele, "Psychoanalysis and Hermeneutics."

other which is psychoanalysis as "natural *science*" dealing with "statistical probabilities."[2] Besides, Otto Rank has demonstrated the legitimate application of psychoanalysis to literature in *The Incest Theme in Literature and Legend: Fundamentals in a Psychology of Literary Creation* (1912). In this he was preceded by Freud's inroads in *Delusions and Dreams in Jensen's "Gradiva"* (1907) and in "Creative Writers and Day-Dreaming" (1908), and, of course, in his analysis of the Oedipus myth (see *The Interpretation of Dreams* [1900]).

A text, like a person, is multivocal, that is, both are endowed with a multiplicity of meanings (which Freud called "overdetermination" and Bakhtin "unfinalizability"). This has been our core principle in the present essay engaging the Babel myth from a multiplicity of critical viewpoints.

The terms used by J in his tale are not entirely negative, as we saw. J is too fine a psychologist not to leave open a free margin of interpretation in his choice of words and concepts. J's work is dialectical throughout:[3] God's care is never absent from the imposed punishment. Starting with Genesis 3, the divine chastisement goes along with high hopes after the human choice of autonomy. In Genesis 4 again, a margin of meaning is provided by the unexpected shield of protection around Cain the murderer. In Genesis 6–9, all of humanity is wiped out, but for a remnant, seed of a new world. Now, in Genesis 11, humanity is scattered and thus debilitated in its will to power, but this is the very condition for the rise of a new humanity with a diversified culture. As Ibn Ezra concluded, "God scattered the people for their own benefit."[4] Abravanel (fifteenth century), however, added that Ibn Ezra's comment must be understood as showing that a *punishment* may concomitantly be a blessing.[5]

The result of the divine intervention is thus paradoxical. True, the people of Shinar had not used their monoglossia to good purposes and thus deserved punishment, but now that human communication had become plural and the culture diversified, humans are scattered all over the world as they should be (see Gen 9:19; 10:32), although with the scattering comes a sense of isolation, of dislocation. The monoglossic humanity

2. Rudnytsky, *Reading Psychoanalysis*, 238 (italics added).
3. See LaCocque, *The Trial of Innocence*; and LaCocque, *Onslaught against Innocence*.
4. Ibn Ezra, *Genesis [Bereshit]*, 143. See below (in chapter 6) my excursus on Ibn Ezra.
5: *Ex malo bonum* ("out of bad something good [may] come"). The dictum's origin is unknown. It is claimed as a Christian saying by Georgette de Montenay in *Emblemes ou devises chrestiennes*, published in Lyons in 1571. Closer to us, it is mentioned several times in Griffin Dunne's movie *Fierce People* (2005). The relevance of this notion is evident: all punishment should be correctional, therapeutic—the opposite of vengeance.

of the beginning has truly become "the generation of the dispersion" (a traditional rabbinic designation). The primal cohesion is over, and it is to be expected that wars will erupt between ethnic and phonic entities.[6] We are evidently dealing with a paradigmatic description of the perennial human condition. That is why, in what follows, psychological biblical criticism and history-of-religion criticism will be used to read Gen 11:1–9. The fields of history of religion and of psychoanalysis are sometimes very close to each other; both are interested in myths as unveiling the depths of human soul. In the ancient Greek world, for example, the Oedipus complex (or effect), the Minotaur labyrinth, or again the flight of Icarus, have been shown to reflect a deep understanding of the human psyche and of the human spiritual dimension.[7]

Regarding the Bible, psychology and history of religion are of prime importance as far as narrative and tradition analyses are concerned. In the stories assembled in the early chapters of Genesis it is self-evident that the symbolic dimension is preponderant, whereby "something . . . represents something else."[8] The serpent in Genesis 3 is more than the speaking reptile of the story. The forbidden fruit represents a more general divine prohibition; the expulsion from the Garden overflows the reported episodic occurrence, etc. Rollins and Kille write, "as artifacts of human intention and reflections of human experience, biblical texts also demonstrate traces of deep psychological dynamics common to human beings."[9] They quote John A. Sanford, "A myth is the product of the unconscious mind; for this reason its full meaning goes beyond the present state of awareness not only of those who read the myth but of those who tell the myth."[10] The problem for psychological biblical criticism, therefore, is one of reference. If the tower of Babel is more than a simple tower, what does the symbol refer to?

6. So in *PRE* 24 (*in fine*), Rabbi Shimon's statement ("They will fight each other in frustration"). See also Hiebert, "The Tower of Babel," 48 n. 50.

7. They are generally referred to as building a "theory of personality."

8. Kille, *Psychological Biblical Criticism*, 142. Wayne Rollins's definition of the "psychological-critical approach to Scripture" is thought provoking: "The goal of a psychological approach is to examine texts, their origination, authorship, modes of expression, their construction, transmission, translation, reading, interpretation, their transposition into kindred and alien art forms and the history of their personal and cultural effect, as expressions of the structure, processes, and habits of the human psyche, both in individual and collective manifestations, past and present" (Rollins and Kille, *Psychological Insight into the Bible*, 17–18).

9. *Psychological Insight into the Bible*, 159.

10. Sanford, *The Man who Wrestled with God*, 116; quoted in ibid., 160–61.

Whatever may have been J's purpose in telling the Tower of Babel story, he clearly set it within the context of other tales of the primeval era. Now, like all that pertains to *Urzeit* (primordial times), the Genesis 1–11 stories set up archetypes[11] and a definite orientation to history. When St. Augustine, for instance, articulated the (misguided[12]) doctrine of the generational transmission of the original sin (Genesis 3), his referential methodology for doing so was nevertheless right.

Let us note here that speaking of Babel and its tower as symbolic is not another way of reading the biblical text as allegorical. In the ancient world, the symbol is one with the reality it represents. The city *is* the city *and* the carrier of femininity. The tower is itself and also a phallic emblem that stands in the closest possible relationship with the feminine city. Both of them, far from remaining mere objects are imbued with subjectivity.[13] Minimizing the importance of the tower—as some critics do, especially on the basis of the absence of its mention in Gen 11:8—is castrating J's image. The city is Babel *because* of its tower; and the tower without the city is like "personaggi in cerca d'autore" ("characters in search of an author" [Pirandello]).

About the nonmention of the tower in v. 8 (by hendiadys, as we saw above), psychoanalysis has more to say. Inasmuch as the tower is for the Babelians a Winnicottian "transitional object," standing symbolically "between the thumb and the teddy bear,"[14] the Babel tower is both inseparable from the subject *and a surrogate object for the mother.*

Now, the tower is evidently phallic, and its symbolizing motherly femininity is paradoxical. But Freud has explained this condition with his concept of the child's "phallic stage" during which there may be a fantasy of a "phallic woman" or "phallic mother."[15] In the J myth, the accent is on the (feminine) city (of Babylon). The tower plays an adjuvant role. This is

11. *Archetype*, of course, is also a Jungian concept. He believed that mythic motifs are inherited, universal, and collective (as originating from the "collective unconscious"). Biblical stories often reflect psychic archetypes (see *The Collected Works of Carl Jung*, 18:156; see also Jung, *Man and His Symbols*). The sacred mountain in Genesis 11 is such an archetypal image.

12. See LaCocque, *The Trial of Innocence.*

13. Cf. Jacobsen and Frankfort, et al., *Before Philosophy*, 144 (in the chapter called "The Mesopotamian Attitude toward the Phenomena of Nature").

14. See Winnicott, "Transitional Objects and Transitional Phenomena."

15. Freud, "The Infantile Genital Organization" (1923); "The Dissolution of the Oedipus Complex" (1924); and "Some Psychical Consequences of the Anatomical Distinction between the Sexes" (1925).

so much the case that some commentators further downgrade the mention of the tower in the text to a mere later redactional addition, as we saw. In fact, early humanity is building a feminine substitute, a projection and idealization of the mother figure. The construction of the city is a reconstruction of the initial blessed symbiotic relation with the mother. Within this complex, the tower is no later subsidiary compositional addition but is ambiguously the presence "in the picture" of the male (see the masc. used throughout) Babelian builders *and* the attribution to the mother of the "missing" phallus before, so to speak, her "castration." Therefore it fills a crucial role in the myth, but in a subordinate relation to the city. Furthermore, to the extent that the transitional object is inseparable from the subject, the demise of Babel/Babylon entails a fortiori the disappearance of the tower as well. Like the security blanket of the child, the tower as an external object loses its significance (and indeed its existence) with the broadening of the cultural field, namely, the scattering "over the face of all the earth."

Does such a psychoanalytical interpretation correspond to the Yahwist's inditing purpose? It behooves the critic to explore the relation of the sign to its referent, of the signifier to the signified, of the manifest to the latent. In the process, the critic realizes that the psychological reading may go beyond J's original intention. But the same situation is present as regards the stories of Oedipus or Icarus, among others, and of their need to be interpreted. The truth of the matter is that the author's subconscious is mediated by unconscious means—as body language, for instance, would do in other circumstances.[16] Did J intend Babel the city to represent femininity, and the tower as a phallus symbol? We do not know for sure, but we know that the authorial intent never exhausts the text's meanings.[17] The original author of the Oedipus story certainly did not fathom the enormous impact his tale would have later on modern theory of personality. But, notwithstanding, any warranted statement ever brought forth

16. In *The Incest Theme*, 224, Otto Rank writes: "The myth could never have been read off from the heavens in this human garb without there being a corresponding psychic idea . . . that may indeed already have been unconscious at the time the myth was formed" (quoted in Rudnytsky, *Reading Psychoanalysis*, 83).

17. Cf. Paul Ricoeur's "hermeneutic of suspicion." See also his concept of the "surplus of meaning." On this, see Rashkow, *The Phallacy of Genesis*. She notes the parallel between reading and psychoanalysis as both actions incorporate the *what* and *how* it is said (either by the analysand or the text [23]); Rashkow says, "a literary text, similar to an analyst, 'triggers' responses in a reader" (26).

by modern psychologists about Oedipus was already true *before* the tale took shape. The Oedipus myth is truth that found one expression of itself in the original tale and then in other versions of subsequent retellings. That truth is now embedded in the psychological dynamics of the written text. In other words, the semiotic (the symbolic image) of the Babel text corresponds to the "plain" understanding (the rabbinic *peshat*) while *independently of the author's intention*, the semantic meanings of the image correspond to its interpretation (the rabbinic *midrash*).[18] The pattern of repeating important words—especially in such a soberly worded story as is Gen 11:1–9—provides a code for understanding—"a 'subtext' which the work both conceals and reveals. A reader focuses simultaneously on the text itself (common rhetorical or stylistic features, its intertextuality) and the response to the text (transference) . . . [thus] expos[ing] the dynamic play of meaning behind what may seem to be a simple statement."[19]

The objective reality confirms the Tower of Babel symbolism. Historical Babylon deprived of its ziggurat loses its very identity.[20] And a ziggurat in the desert is nonsensical, an aberration. The conjunction of the one with the other shows again that Gen 11:8 was in no need to include both "city" and "tower." One of the two implied the other, like speaking of a vessel lost at sea, without necessarily adding "with the entire crew." J has the actual Babylon in mind, with its "tower" crowned by the Esagila shrine. But Babylon is in a broader reference to the "Babel" of human hubris and stupidity.

Wayne Rollins writes about "the universal presence of the *unconscious* in all we do, think, want, feel, create, remember and forget—in religion as well as in the rest of life."[21] This incontrovertible principle is, of course, of prime importance. Not only as regards a possible psychoanalysis of biblical personalities (such as Ezekiel or Jesus), but as regards the psychodynamics of J's narratives. All the more so as our analysis is applied to a text in which there are no identifiable characters to psychoanalyze, but only a narrative situation. True, it may be that J's personality

18. See Faur, *Golden Doves with Silver Dots*, 122 (also cited in Rashkow, *The Phallacy of Genesis*, 57–58).

19. Rashkow, *The Phallacy of Genesis*, 37; see also ibid., 40. The latent content of the image does "wish for recognition," says Paul Ricoeur (*Freud and Philosophy*, 573).

20. The ziggurat was seven cosmic stories high; these levels correspond to the seven planetary heavens. We find the same symbolism in the "seven steps" that take Buddha to the top of the world so that he transcends space and time.

21. Rollins and Kille, *Psychological Insight into the Bible*, 41.

becomes somewhat unveiled in the process, but my main interest at this point is the conscious and unconscious use by the author of symbols that transform the story from being "occasional and transitory into the realm of the ever-enduring," as Jung said.[22] He writes,

> Whoever speaks in primordial images speaks with a thousand voices; he enthralls and overpowers, while at the same time he lifts the idea he is seeking to express out of the occasional and transitory into the realm of the ever-enduring. He transmutes our personal destiny into the destiny of mankind, and evokes in us all those beneficent forces that ever and anon have enabled humanity to find a refuge from every peril and to outlive the longest night.[23]

Jung again would most probably treat Gen 11:1–9 as a *dream*, or at least as dream-like (for the story of Babel is too well structured not to be in the present stage the product of consciousness). As dream-like, that is as made with subliminal material, the tale is no less than ingenious. Jung said, "The ability to reach a rich vein of such material and to translate it effectively into philosophy, literature, music, or science discovery is one of the hallmarks of what is commonly called genius."[24] And it is really true that the spatio-chronological framework (Bakhtin's "chronotope") of the narrative is oneiric, something like "once upon a time," as we said, happening in an exotic, far-away oriental country. The presence of this dimension in the tale of Babel promotes it to what Jung calls a "cultural symbol" meant to "express 'eternal truth' . . . [that] can evoke a deep emotional response in some individuals."[25] The symbol is to be distinguished from a sign. We'll take Wayne Rollins's warning to heart: "Symbols don't send a single, simple, instant message. Symbols, unlike signs, are 'alive' and somehow carry with them a piece of the living reality they represent."[26] As we saw above, there is a certain reading of the Babel myth that is content with a word picture deprived of emotion and of the numinous. In contrast to such a reading, the Jungian definition of archetypes as primordial images of the collective unconscious is of special interest to us.

22. Jung, *The Spirit of Man, Art, and Literature*, par. 129, quoted in Rollins and Kille, *Psychological Insight into the Bible*, 47.

23. Jung, *The Spirit of Man, Art, and Literature*, quoted in ibid., 47–48.

24. Jung, "Approaching the Unconscious," 38.

25. Ibid., 95.

26. Rollins and Kille, *Psychological Insight into the Bible*, 100. Elsewhere Rollins says pointedly, "Symbols function as the native language of the psyche" (Rollins, *Soul and Psyche*, 116).

Psychoanalysis has discovered that there are things like "unconscious ideas," or, in Norman O. Brown's parlance, "involuntary purposes."[27] This, I would argue, is not only true of the (implied) author of a text (here J), but of the reader, who no less than the author opposes a strong defense mechanism (the Freudian "repression"[28]) to the meanings embedded in the unconscious. After all, J's interest in the primeval incipience of humanity and of its history must respond to a deep-felt intuition of what Freud will later call "the content of the unconscious . . . [being] collective anyhow"[29] (= Jung's "the collective unconscious"), adding that the child must "cover the enormous distance of development from primitive man of the Stone Age to civilized man of today."[30] This is the price to pay for the stories in Genesis 1–11 not to be gratuitous and just entertaining.

So, rather than to psychoanalyze J through his text on the tower of Babel and to conclude, for instance, that he was unconsciously moved to tell his story as a cover-up for his inner hostility toward his father (here represented by a phallic tower,)[31] what is more interesting is to psychoanalyze the symbolism he displays. Admittedly such research is not purely psychological but at the crossroads of psychology and history of religion, indeed of psychology and structural analysis. For a psychological approach to the biblical text—or to any text for that matter—is not to be used in isolation from other critical methods, which will prevent the psychological reading from becoming psychologism.[32]

But before we leave the personality and the motivation of J in Genesis 11, we shall note with Jung the compensatory function of unconscious manifestations for one-sided or faulty elements of consciousness.[33] Reading Genesis 11 as myth—that is, as a manifestation of the unconscious—

27. Brown, *Life against Death*, 4. When James Barr, e.g., polemicizes against the full semantic horizon of Hebrew words (like *dabar* or *berith*) because, in their practical use no one ascribed such etymological richness to them, he ignores the role of the unconscious.

28. See in particular Freud, "The Ego and the Id," 12.

29. Freud, *The Basic Writings of Sigmund Freud*, 588 and note.

30. Freud, *A General Introduction to Psychanalysis*, 332.

31. So the absence of mention of the tower in 11:8 would be "telling" on that score as well!

32. In one of John A. Sanford's contributions to Rollins and Kille, *Psychological Insight into the Bible*, we read, "Psychological perspectives can (and should) be used in conjunction with other methods" (160). As N. O. Brown says, "What is needed is a synthesis of psychoanalysis, anthropology, and history" (*Life against Death*, xi).

33. Jung, "Approaching the Unconscious," passim.

unveils, at least in part, J's rationale for telling it. While the confusion of tongues and the scattering of people "all over the earth" are here proposed as a negative outcome of human hubris, the very telling of the myth is a compensatory and healing act, an illocutionary utterance. The myth of the Babel's construction is J's story, and thus he at a minimum participates in the narrated events, which, as we shall see below, he transforms into facts.[34] What can be said, for instance, of the author's "complicity in the crime" of Jephthah's daughter in Judges 11,[35] is also true, but this time positively, of J in Genesis 11. The event described escapes the realm of chance and randomness to become a creative occurrence. The Yahwist and his audience do engage the powers represented by and embodied in Babylon. They actually work toward the collapse of the wicked city. But the collapse of the empire entails a *catastrophê* (*Jub.* 10:26), that is, a cosmic tearing that begs to be mended. And, indeed, the resulting confusion and dispersion of Babylon's fall are not one dimensional. They paradoxically already fulfill God's purpose and design for a new beginning.

Within this context, storytelling is endowed with an exceptional importance. According to Israel's vision, the human problem is not one of climbing up to the sky, but of coming within the closest possible proximity to God's Word, with a truth that best reveals God's Truth.[36] In Gen 11:1–9, the Babelian context is starkly spatial and the aim is to "assault heaven," as Jewish tradition has it. Words are not center stage—the Babelians are oddly silent while building; technique is central.[37] Now, word, language is "immaterial." It can be bent to express technical means and practice, but veritable human discourse is an ongoing attempt at uttering the ultimate. It is therefore temporal as it is teleological. Its historical evolution belies the immobility of the pyramid/ziggurat.

Within the spatiality of Babel, time is reintroduced by the myth-telling itself. The tale is about the divinely operated shift from concentrated space to its diffusion and hence to human becoming (from stasis to dynamism). Space itself is transformed. It ceases to be the somewhat otherworldly and hence time-impervious "Shinar," that is, a country hardly

34. See below chapter 6, the section called "'Babel und Bible'?"

35. See Exum, *Fragmented Women*, 20, 41 (on Judges 11).

36. Paul Ricoeur speaks of "the discrepancy between the purely symbolic plenitude and the finiteness of the experience that furnishes man with 'analogues' of that which is signified" (*The Symbolism of Evil*, 169 [French, *La Symbolique du mal*, 160]).

37. This could be a chronicle of our own times.

more precise than the Garden of Eden in Genesis 2–3. In the Israelite myth, mythic Shinar knows a historical incarnation. It is identified with Babel, or Babylon, and becomes a chronotope. Thus, at the outset, telling the story of the demise of Babel becomes a watershed in the history of humanity—especially when it is realized that Babylon is at that point of the sixth century still standing and thriving. But the very recitation of the myth contributes to Babel/Babylon's fading on the horizon and leaving room for historical time: the time of nonrepeatable events, such as the beginning of the multiplicity of languages and the diversity of nations with their particular *Versuch* ("experiment, exploration"), as von Humboldt said.[38]

For Alberto Manguel also, the end of the Babel tale is "the reflection of the story told about it."[39] He calls attention to the end of the Gilgamesh legend. Gilgamesh writes the story and restores the glory of Uruk, his city, as we saw above. "Both tasks," says Manguel, "are complementary: both speak of the ultimate connection between building a city of walls and building a story of words, and both require, in order to be accomplished, the existence of the other."[40] Strikingly, the one who provides the "story of words" (we could say, the "city of words"), is the very Israelite author who helps, by his writing, the destruction of Babel and the dispersion of its wall builders! Such dialectic dimension of J's narrative will not surprise the reader of Genesis 2–3 and Genesis 4. A good part of J's genius lies in his multifaceted approach to his task as a poet. Things here are never just black and white. No one could accuse J of Manichaeism. The Mesopotamian Babel was in need of a builder of a story/city of words—which the Jew eventually provided for it. J as interpreter is metamorphoser.

So, myth (and mythmaking) reenters the contemporary scene with an amazing relevance, thanks to psychoanalysis and the history of religion. The modern social sciences cannot exist independently of myths. Neither does theology. What brings these two fields together is the inexpressibility of the human soul and of the divine holiness. In both cases, only approximations will do.[41] Psychoanalysis and history-of-religion

38. See, above, chap. 2 n. 95.

39. Manguel, *The City of Words*, 16.

40. Ibid., 46.

41. Jung writes, "We cannot define either the psyche or nature. We can merely state what we believe them to be and describe, as best we can, how they function" ("Approaching the Unconscious," 23).

criticism have revived a keen interest in ancient and modern folkloric tales. No one today can read J's narratives while ignoring these valuable tools. What the eighteenth and nineteenth centuries had thought to have disposed of as irrelevant and primitive has proven to be a golden key to theology and anthropology. From this point of view, the story of the Tower of Babel has never been more pertinent than today, as it brings its reader "to understand oneself in front of the text."[42]

Once Again, on the Myth of the Center (We vs. All Others)

In the beginning, says our text, people were on the move and looking for a place to settle down. We wonder, of course, from where humanity is migrating. The tale does not give any clue, but, at any rate, "from [to] the east" is a clear allusion to the exile from Eden (Gen 3:23–24). Commentators have done little about this initial theme of the story. The fact that the "heroes" of the tale are associated with the east and settle in a selected place points to a first uprooting of sorts. The crowds are leaving behind a former existence, so that an anticipated parallel is set with Abraham's departure from Ur in Chaldea in the next chapter. In both cases—but with vastly different motivations—there is rejection of a past and of a "parental" superego. As regards Abraham, the renunciation of the past occurs in order to follow the star of a demanding ascetic ideal; the arrival place is unknown to him and independent of his choice or liking. As to the generation of Babel, by contrast, the "unknown" is readily denied, and there is a deliberate choice of settlement. There is no leap of faith in their settling down (in spite of the Babelians' religious motivation), just the blotting out of a background that has become a black hole.[43] The openly declared Oedipal goal is to become *causa sui*, the father of oneself: the builders won't be named by any name but by the one they'll make for themselves.

Genesis 11 concerns humanity at large (vv. 1–2, 5) before it becomes chronotopologically the Babelians (on the way to being the Babylonians). The mythic paradigm of the primal horde coming from the east illustrates Freud's idea of an original patricide.[44] Their existence starts after that, in the ruins—"on their journey," says v. 2—of another culture, which remains

---

42. Ricoeur, "The Hermeneutical Function of Distanciation," 88.
43. Abraham's past is acknowledged and protected by his ancestral genealogy.
44. See Freud, *Totem and Taboo.*

unknown to us, but not to them. Their nonidentifying it is a cover-up that is repressed into their subconscious.[45] We are not surprised, therefore, that they decide in common accord to become their own superego. They ventriloquistically find a voice of their own whose commands they uniformly follow. There is no outer voice, no vocation, only an externalization of their phantasms onto a crafted totem of sorts. In advance they submit to the demands of this fetish object, an immense projection of the immense vacuum of their souls.

The other side of the coin is shown at the end of the story, when the same people are scattered. The "totem" falls into ruins and the quest for immortality is unveiled for the sham that it is. Then, surprisingly, the Babelians return to a prior situation, when they still were in "the east." They are migrating again. Babel was just an impasse. When the throngs give up on their failed project, the story stops openended. We are not told how they will henceforth tackle reality—surely in very different ways, as they have become diverse and other. Will they abandon their foolish desire to be their own fathers? No; Genesis 12 comes within this context as the great exception, the miraculous "otherness" that is both judgment and relief for "all the families of the earth." Then for the first time, history does not find its springboard in a patricide or a fratricide, but in the acknowledgment of the divine superego. But that is another story, as Rudyard Kipling would say.

The Babel throngs want to create a concentrative phalanstery. So, there will be a center of the world, and they will be *šam*, "right there." To be sure, the Copernican demonstration of an *absence* of center was more than an astronomic revolution. Already in the sixteenth century, it questioned humans' centeredness, so dear to their ego. But if the universe is without a center, this strikingly resembles the infinity of God himself. Jean Laplanche cites Hermes Trismegistus's expression of the divine infinity as "a sphere whose center is everywhere and whose circumference is nowhere."[46] Pascal adopted the formula and applied it to "the infinite vastness of things," although, for him, the two infinities are of different

---

45. The 1789 French revolutionaries, after they killed the "father," began counting the years from the starting point of the Revolution. Such an attempt was doomed. On the regicide of the French Revolution, see Raschke, "The Deconstruction of God," 23–24.

46. Laplanche, *Essays on Otherness*, 56 n. 10 (French: *Le Primat de l'autre en psychanalyse*).

orders.[47] In this respect, the conclusion of the Tower of Babel story, with its decisive decentering of humanity comes as an amazing precursor of modern astronomy. For the physical scattering of the Babel crowd, with the dispersing of their languages, and consequently of their respective projects, is purposely—see 11:7—initiating a centrifugal epistemology (11:9). This, adds Jean Laplanche, is "hard to accept."[48] Indeed, all anti-pluralisms and fundamentalisms, let alone historical dictatorships, attempt to reverse God's move and are definitely centripetal.

So, although "from (or) to the east" is a rather vague topos, the main point is that the humans proceed right away with putting their imprint on it: they start building with bricks and bitumen. Their motivation is clear: they fear being (again?) dispersed. They will build themselves a center, an *axis mundi*, a universal magnet for all human beings, a gate to the divine.[49] Their center will snug a still more central point, an umbilicus or, rather, an erected phallus pinpointing the center of centers, and more or less a threat to heaven if it does not "behave." In this contextual imagery, the heavens become a belly that the phallus wants to penetrate, that is, a mother that must be protected from incest by the father God.[50]

Such a myth of the center is universal. Every nation, tribe, or clan under the sun has always considered itself the center of the world.[51] If anything, the history of cartography would illustrate the point. This conviction amounts eventually to an individual or collective self-centeredness that considers the others at best aliens, at worst enemies. The notion draws a sharp distinction between "us" and "them." With an appalling frequency, it leads to so-called ethnic cleansing.

The tale in Genesis 11, however, displays a striking uniqueness; for, at the dawn of time, humanity wants to constitute a "we" without a "they." The absence of "they" means the absence of otherness (by absorption), and also the absence of the Other. *Homo erectus*, in whose image the tower is built, stands alone in the immensity of space and the emptiness of heaven.

47. Pascal, *Pensées*, 1:112.

48. Laplanche, *Essays on Otherness*, 57.

49. With the *axis*, says Mircea Eliade, God provides a bridge, a link with himself, to establish *closer, clearer* communication. When this function is not properly deciphered, God must *descend* to speak in words (*Patterns in Comparative Religion*, chap. 7).

50. The French poet Pierre Emmanuel said, "Babel fut une érection du genre humain" (*Jacob*, 103).

51. The Greeks, for instance, believed that the world was flat and circular, with Greece at the center around the Mount Olympus, abode of the gods.

Where he stands is emphatically *šam* ("there"), repeated five times, twice
in alliteration with *šem* ["name"]), besides which there is nothing. In no
other preceding chapter of the J saga had we come to such a quintessence
of human hubris and blasphemy.

We must emphasize the concentricity of the city and its tower. They
are, as it were, an oasis in the desert, an island in the ocean. Quite a center
of order, of organized space, in surroundings that are chaotic and threatening ("east" of Eden). This, by the way, explains why the people of Babel
fear so much to be dispersed (Gen 11:4). In this regard, the thrice-repeated
expression "over the whole surface of the earth" (vv. 4, 8, 9) is less neutral
than meets the eye. For the earth is here uninhabited and disorganized,
a desert unknown and dangerous, seat of ghosts and demons.[52] Isaiah
13:21–22 pictures the desert that Babylon will become. Consequently, the
eventual dispersion is a sending into the wild, a centrifugal move fraught
with danger and tremendous challenge.

The Babelian Neurosis

Often missed by the exegetes of Genesis 11 is the psychological effect of
fear (anxiety, terror) at the root of the building project. The apprehen-
sion of a possible lack of success or of danger can evidently turn easily
into dread or what Freud calls "anxiety neurosis."[53] Most relevant here is
so-called separation anxiety, which designates the fear of being separated
from the mother or from a familiar environment. The attachment of the
Babelians to their own production expresses itself in a significant way
through their angst to be dispersed. From this point of view, the situation
described in Gen 11:1–5 is one of infancy and immaturity. As the city they
build and wall in is symbol of the mother, and as the tower they erect and
idealize signifies the father, the eventual dispersion is a forced weaning,
unless (and this is more plausible) it be a dismantling of a sham mother-
and-father substitute (a subrogation construct). Freud spoke of people
huddling together for fear of "separation and expulsion from the horde,"[54]
or, in the words of Géza Róheim, of "being left alone in the dark."[55]

52. See Deut 8:15; Job 12:24; Jer 33:10. Time and again, the desert is said to be "the
dwelling of jackals"; see, e.g., Jer 49:33.
53. Freud, "On the Grounds of Detaching a Particular Syndrome from Neurasthenia,"
315–44.
54. Freud, *Inhibitions, Symptoms and Anxiety*, 93–95, 104–12.
55. Róheim, *The Origin and Function of Culture*, 77–79, 98. Recall that Isa 47:5 reads,
"Sit in silence, and go into darkness, daughter of Chaldea" (NRSV)!

Indeed, the verb *puṣ* used in our story means "to be scattered or dispersed" and belongs to the semantic field of *separation*. The Babelians fear to be separated, a traumatic angst at the root of the psychological fantasy of becoming the father of oneself. The wish to avoid separation amounts to a striving to indefinitely prolong infancy. To achieve this fantasy, it may be necessary to have recourse to patricide and incest by way of constructing, and hence generating, substitutes to the father and the mother, namely, a phallic tower and an all-embracing city controlled by the builders.

The reluctance of the Babelians to be separated parallels the child's reluctance to be weaned.[56] The Babelians demonstrate similar reluctance and anxiety by building city and tower. They live in a society in the grips of anxiety and doubt. In short, the Babelians are paranoid, and a paralyzing sentiment is conducive to its opposite: to hyperactivity as reassurance, a recourse to mass consciousness; to a discourse crammed with clichés and slogans; to an ideology all the more inept as it is conceived to flatter base, vulgar instincts. There is a direct relation between paranoia and hubris. Feeling powerless and disenfranchised—in Gen 11:2 during the metaphorical "migrating from the east"—the delusional personality camouflages its complex of inferiority into bullying others (as Cain does in Genesis 4), or at least into constructing a false reality (as the Babelians do). Feeling void and anonymous, humans sense no more urgent a desire than to "make a name for ourselves."

The city and its tower are the projection of inner demons they are objectifying and camouflaging into a *thing*, rather than facing the inner deficiency it really is. This, of course, is in psychology the habitual defense mechanism of externalization. The construction of the tower detracts from the construction of a life-meaning environment. The desire to build one's ego and to erect a protective wall against the intrusion of the reality principle ("lest we be scattered") so that the selected object and the ego cannot be any longer distinguished—without the Babel building, the Babelians are simply nonexistent—is characteristic of infancy/immaturity, we said. This idea allows us to return to the seeming pleonasm of Gen 11:1: The Babelians had one language for them all. But what does *debarim* *ʾaḥadim* add to the picture? Are we to understand the locution as referring perhaps to the limited vocabulary of the child? Did they have one

---

56. Couffignal ("La Tour de Babel") speaks of a "*regressus ad uterum*" ("return to the womb").

language because of their limited vocabulary, marked by mere repetitions ("to brick bricks, to flame in the flame . . ." v. 3)?[57] This contemplated possibility is at least plausible.

In the first volume of the present trilogy, on Adam and Eve,[58] we dealt with an inner opposition between the tree of life and the tree of knowledge—unless we see them as one double-faced tree. Now, from a psychoanalytical point of view, tasting of the tree of life represents the free reign of libido experienced during the stage of infancy. The tree of knowledge is the repression exerted by the "reality principle" (Freud) of adult life. Transposed into the myth of the tower of Babel, and keeping in mind that "ontogeny recapitulates phylogeny,"[59] humanity's piling up construction blocks evidently demonstrates a sign of its stagnant infancy stage. It is a stage of primitive undifferentiating, when even language and ideas feel no obstacle or repression, and belong to a naïveté that is primal, naked.[60] The Freudian "reality principle" then erupts in the form of a universal acculturation through diversity. From one stage to the next, the shift is painful, as is puberty in the individual's life. Confusion and dispersion are expressive of the hard collective and the individual rite of passage.

This interpretation of the Babel story is only one ring of the textual "onion," however. But the fact of its concurrence with the literary, the sociological, and the historical "rings" further buttresses our general approach. The truth embedded in the myths is anthropological; it is psychological.

A second aspect of the Babelians' fear is an implicit confession of guilt. Innocence and naïveté have disappeared. Rather than being, they have

57. Freud observes, "Children cannot have their pleasurable experiences repeated often enough and they are inexorable in their insistence that the repetition shall be an identical one" (*Beyond the Pleasure Principle*, 45). Lévi-Strauss states that a myth's diachronical sequence must be read synchronically; this is encouraged by the inner process of repetition (*Structural Anthropology 2*, 231).

58. LaCocque, *The Trial of Innocence*.

59. See Brown, *Life against Death*, 13.

60. Paul Ricoeur calls mature naïveté "second naïveté," that is, after coming to terms with the reality principle. It is the opposite of infantilism. (We recall that Friedrich Nietzsche spoke of a "second innocence" [*The Philosophy of Nietzsche*. 709].) At the stage of infancy, the individual/collectivity relates to the father (here the tower of Babel) by "identification," and to the mother (here, the city) by "narcissistic object choice." Both terms are Freudian (see *Group Psychology and the Analysis of the Ego*, 60–62; and *New Introductory Lectures on Psychoanalysis*, 86; both also cited in Brown, *Life against Death*, 41, and 327 n. 1).

opted for having. The human project is economic: storing up, possessing, amassing power. The group has chosen a totemic ownership. Salvation ("not being scattered") is obtained by hoarding goods and investing one's soul in them. From the (infantile) biological body to the (sublimated) social body. The covered-up goal is the escape from death. Babel is the time-defying projection in bricks and cement of the decaying body of the builders. Such a swapping of being and having is perhaps childish, but it is so universally repeated that we must recognize in it a common human trait, "since the inclination of the human heart is evil from youth" (Gen 8:21 [NRSV]). For psychoanalysis, it is the ever-recurring Oedipal drive toward immortality.[61]

As Norman Brown states, "Every city is an eternal city: civilized money lasts forever." He cites Oswald Spengler, "the gigantic megalopolis, the *city-as-world* . . . suffers nothing beside itself and sets about *annihilating* the country picture."[62] Brown adds, "The city is a deposit of accumulated sublimation, and by the same token a deposit of accumulated guilt. The temple buildings which dominate the first cities are monuments of accumulated guilt and expiation" (283). Anticipating that much (Gen 11:4), Babel traces around itself a boundary, a threshold separating two worlds, deemed inimical to each other. It makes the center sacred, and rejects the periphery as part of the profane.[63] The very name *Babel* ("Gate of the Divine") stresses the dangerous passage from the latter to the former.[64]

In fact, the people of Genesis 11 cross the threshold twice: the first time, when coming eastward to Shinar (11:1), that is, from a zone they consider profane to a zone they consecrate to the gods with a ziggurat. The second time: when eventually they are compelled to leave the sacred and are dispersed again into the profane realm. True, the first passage was a

61. Again and always the Oedipus complex? Yes, for as our story shows again, "in the last resort, the Oedipus complex exists only in its cultural derivatives; it exists only as long as the life in culture in the present perpetuates the infantile flight from death" (Brown, *Life against Death*, 155).

62. Spengler, *The Decline of the West* 2:94 (see also below n. 131), in Brown, *Life against Death*, 282–83. See the abridged English edition of *The Decline of the West*, translated by Atkinson and Helps.

63. See Eliade, *Images and Symbols*, 39–40: "Every microcosm, every inhabited region, has what may be called a 'Centre'; that is to say, a place that is sacred above all . . . literally called the 'Centre of the world,'" and "manifested with the hiero-cosmic symbols (the Pillar of the World, the Cosmic Tree, etc.)."

64. Joseph Campbell says, "The passage of the threshold is a form of self-annihilation" (*Creative Mythology*, 91).

jubilant "homecoming" of sorts. They said, "Come, let us build" (11:3–4), and "We'll make a name for ourselves" (11:4). But on their second and involuntary crossing of the threshold, with their idiom scattered into six thousand languages, that is, six thousand ways to utter their feelings, they said—nothing.[65]

Let us develop this point further. The people coming from the east are said to find a plain or a valley that is not designated offhand and naturally to be central. On the contrary, they deliberate among themselves and they *decide* to build the Center of the World right where they are. Such a building of the center amounts to a cosmogony. The human endeavor repeats the act of creation we saw. It does it anew, with new materials (bricks instead of stones, tar instead of mortar) and with another demiurgic pattern (a city, not a Garden, with a tower in the middle, not a tree of life).

Told by an Israelite, the poem in prose reflects an ideological conflict with the Hebrew tradition around Zion as the *omphalos* (see Judg 9:37; Ezek 38:12; *Jubilees* 8:19). The difference is that Jerusalem is designated by God without Israel's construction or artificiality. Texts insist on the construction not made by Israelite hands (see Josh 24:13; Jer 45:4; and especially Heb 9:11). It is built by others with purposes and means that Israel does not condone. In comparison, Babylon is a parody. Its mountain is a ziggurat. It belongs to magic and partakes in the quality of magic. As a matter of fact, if scaling the heights of the ziggurat may be interpreted as just symbolic of the spiritual absorption into the divine; the very ritual at the top of the tower is more than symbolic. The king eats of the plant of life and drinks from the water of life. He also engages into a *hieros gamos* ("holy marriage") with the divine. These acts are sympathetic (imitative) magic. They convey a "sacrament" of immortality to the king, and through him to the people.

The Babelians are moved by a magic mentality. As long as they are erecting the tower/ziggurat, they share in what their construction represents. Hence they indulge in "fetishism" or obsessive fixation with the tower,[66] a characterization to which its phallic aspect contributes. In psy-

---

65. See chapter 2 above (the close reading of Gen 11:1). As was noted earlier, six thousand is the approximate number of languages and dialects in the world.

66. The word "fetish," incidentally, comes from Portuguese *fetiço*, ("magic") and from Latin *facticious* ("artificial"). In the denunciation of the Babylonian hubris and quest for self-divinity in Isaiah 47, v. 12, reads, "Stand fast in your enchantments and your many sorceries, with which you have labored from your youth . . . Let those who study the heavens stand up and save you, those who gaze at the stars, and at each new moon predict

choanalysis, this is called "obsessive compulsive disorder." Significantly, the disorder involves at least some magic action meant for protection against an evil fate. The construction of a tower that will reach heaven is by definition endless—unless the constructors decide at some point to give up their repetitive quest for alibis. Then the city of Babel and its tower are left unfinished.[67]

According to J, the magic of Babel was short lived. Now, such a conclusion may contradict the reality of the Babylonian ziggurat (let alone the city of Babylon itself), which, architecturally speaking was duly completed and did endure a long time. J's statement must therefore be understood as tolling the death knell for the magic that the tower and the city represent. Realistically speaking, their demise reveals their intrinsic impotence, the vanity of their claim. This prophetic thinking on the part of J is one more warrant to read the text of Genesis 11 symbolically. Babel is Babylon of sorts; there is one Babylon but a multitude of Babels![68]

From this perspective, collapsing the ostensible sequential chronology of the story, as we did above when we suggested a concomitant temporality, is psychologically illuminating. Indeed, there is a textual coincidence between the time of building the tower and the time of the builders' feeling confused due to mutual incomprehension. The fetishists are in fact fundamentally insecure as to their chosen identification with the object. Their inner emptiness cannot be filled by the fetish's inanity.

---

what shall befall you" (NRSV); see esp. Jer 50:38 "a land of idols," cf. 50:2). Brown writes, "The infantile conflict between actual impotence and dreams of omnipotence is also the basic theme of the universal history of mankind" (*Life against Death*, 25). Saint Augustine calls the dream of omnipotence *libido dominandi* (freely translated as "the obsession inherent in the will of power" (*De civitate Dei* 14, chap. 28). Above we noted that the tower may be seen as a Winnicottian "transitional object," whose possible fate is to become fetishistic.

67. The classic study of "obsessive-compulsive disorder" is, of course, Sigmund Freud's "Notes upon a Case of Obsessional Neurosis" ("The Rat-Man"). See also the fine analysis by Mahony, *Freud and the Rat Man*. The fact that the builders construct then deconstruct Babel evokes Freud's statement about the Rat-Man: "Compulsive acts like this, in two successive stages, of which the second neutralizes the first, are a typical occurrence in obsessional neuroses" (192). The comparison with the Rat-Man case would even shed new light on Babelian boasting about the tower's reaching up to heaven. The tone of the statement might be one of self-derision, "a derisive affirmation attached to an absurd condition which could never be fulfilled" (218).

68. Jacques Derrida's article is typically titled, "Des Tours de Babel" (see below, chap. 6, on deconstruction).

In J's tale, God scrambles all the data, and the fetish is revealed for what it actually is: an illusion.

Magic is essentially a denial of limits. The tower must not just be tall; it must reach heaven. Human discourse must not just be in one single language, it must uniformly have the same content, so that listening to one speaker is listening to all.[69] There is no difference of opinion and no room for interpretation. The negation of limits amounts of course to the denial of death, that is, at bottom, the denial of life. For, in order to be truly human, we need limits. The limits create meaning. Paradoxically, without death, everything becomes insignificant. Rabbi Meïr read Gen 1:31 as saying, "behold, death is good."[70]

The tower of Babel challenges death with a monstrous denial of it. The tower is erected defiantly, and it celebrates its own triumph. Sex has disengaged itself from being interwoven with death. It proclaims creation without destruction, ultimation without finitude, orgasm without cessation. Elsewhere, I have elaborated on the theme of love and death.[71] Suffice it here to mention the names of Viktor Frankl, Abraham Maslow, Rollo May, Ernest Becker, and Mikhail Bakhtin, who all judiciously insist on the "goodness" of death, that is, the felicitousness of cessation, when God tells his servant, "Well done, . . . enter into the joy of your master" (Matt 25:21, 23).

As we know, Jewish tradition has often stumbled on the fact that Gen 11:8–9 does not spell out a specific crime deserving the expressed punishment. But while Adam and Eve could have ignored the serpent's enticement, and Cain could have refrained from blind rage, and the generation of the flood could have renounced violence, no human being can resist the urge to search for immortality.[72] Passivity in the face of the necessity

69. The paucity of vocabulary is not proper to Babel. In a region of the U.S. where I lived for a while, the local population's glossary was severely limited in words pertaining to hunting.

70. Wordplay on m'od and moth.

71. See my Romance, She Wrote.

72. No one can escape the fact that "the human's essential quality is vanity and self-overvaluation," as said Georg Groddeck. He also wrote, "I am I. That is a fundamental sentence of our life. My assertion that this sentence, in which the human ego-feeling expresses itself, is an error will not shatter the world, as it would if one believed the assertion. One will not believe it, cannot believe it; I myself don't believe it, and yet it is true"

of death is itself a grave mental illness. In other words, we are all neurotic, both energized and deceived by our desires. True, some of us die like Abraham, "satisfied with his days" (Gen 25:7), or like Moses, "at the LORD's command" (Deut 34:5; literally, "on the mouth of the LORD"); but many die before their time, internally so to speak, confused and "scattered," understanding nothing.

The Babelians leave off the construction of the city and, therefore, encounter the very death they had denied all along. Their imposed rest is also their "R.I.P." It is their Black Sabbath. Genesis 11:8 describes much more than unemployment. The builders have received a black slip. Suddenly death extends its sway to "the surface of the whole earth." There is no escape, and all the calls for help are useless, for no one "hears" (11:7, literally). They are scattered like the dry bones in the valley that Ezekiel saw (Ezek 37:1–2). The J myth ends—and with it the stories of the primeval era—on this apocalyptic note.

But Babel's sin is too general and actually too ingrained in human nature to be eradicated by divine punishment without killing the culprit (cf. Gen 8:21). This is why, with regard to the generation of the dispersion, the chastisement is in terms of *limitations*—exactly what the Babel builders were trying so hard to avoid. All things considered, the punishment exactly fits the crime, as is usual in the biblical conception of divine justice.[73] This perfect equilibrium or commensurability is indicative of the self-defeating nature of the human attempt to be like God. The worm is always already in the fruit, and death is in the fruit eating.[74] The ultimate barrier erected by God is the *moth tamuth* ("you shall certainly die" [and any striving to reach immortality is futile]) of Gen 2:17. In a striking way, J sees in the division into six thousand languages the premonitory symptom of hubris's defeat.

True, as we have already stressed, it is not unwarranted to interpret the multiplication of languages as progress for humanity at large, multi-

---

(*Das Buch vom Es*, 263, 279, quoted in Rudnytsky, *Reading Psychoanalysis*, 206 [I have rendered *Mensch* "the human"]). In 1926, Groddeck also wrote, "Every man is and was before Abraham was" ("The Id in Everyday Life," 49).

73. The rabbis call it *middah keneged middah*, "measure for measure," "tit for tat," as we saw above. Some modern readers have a minimalist understanding of Genesis 2–11 (see, e.g., Fewell, "Building Babel," 6), but there is nothing childish in disobeying a commandment, in killing one's brother, in filling the earth with violence, and in being morbidly desirous to kill God and take his place.

74. As the inventors of the atomic bomb themselves confessed, it was only after the completion of their devilish creation that they realized what they had done.

plex access to a diversified culture (as in Gen 1:28 and Genesis 10, both
from **P**), but this is only one face of the Janus-like reality. The point is
important because **J** is preparing the ground for Abraham's call *in deserto*
(in the wilderness). When Abraham's vocation is sounded in Genesis 12,
the bell also tolls for the quest of humans to assert themselves as *causa sui*,
their own First Cause. They have tried deception in Genesis 3, eradication
of the other in Genesis 4, angelicalness in Genesis 6,[75] violence and cor-
ruption in Genesis 6–8, and religious and political exclusivism in Genesis
11. Only with Abraham are those manifestations of arrogance and self-
divinization abandoned and redeemed. Abraham inaugurates an entirely
different humanity, marked by faith rather than hubris, by humility rather
than arrogance.[76]

Systemic arrogance is intrinsically fragile. If—or when (for there is
always an appointed time, a *kairos*)—the "tower" cracks, a catastrophic
breaking up happens. Hence from its being erected, the tower, or its innumerable substitutes, must never show signs of weakness. The tower is
meant to be without fissures; the dictator's health is to be always proclaimed perfect; confronted with hard reality, the ideology is to be always
flawless.[77] For, as Mircea Eliade said, the center is the zone of absolute
reality; it is a taste of immortality, a passage from death to eternity, from
humanness to divinity.[78]

The disillusionment is not far off. The culture hatching the notion
of the Center tends to inflate itself to monstrous proportions . . . and to
burst like the fabled frog that wished to make herself as big as an ox.[79] La
Fontaine brought this recurrent happening to the level of a paradigm of
human pride (*superbia*). As for Freud, he stressed the culture's dialectical
nature. In the words of Charles Winquist, "In Freud, the scene of origina-

75. Note in Genesis 6 the striking reversal of direction in the violation of the boundaries between the divine and the human realms. Here, the *benei Elohim* envy the humans
and invade their world. In the story of Babel, of course, it is the humans who assault
heavens.

76. This is also said of Moses, "more humble than anyone on earth" (Num 12:3).

77. If something goes wrong in the tower-city, it can never be the system's fault, but
the fault of "anarchists," "deviationists," or foreign powers, who viciously prevent the
system from functioning. Popular readiness to blame a scapegoat for their own failures
made it incredibly easy for Hitler to convince his people that the Jews were the corrup-
tive element gnawing the life forces of the German body. Since then, the hoax has been
multiplied a thousandfold elsewhere in the world.

78. Cf. Eliade, *The Myth of the Eternal Return*, 18.

79. La Fontaine, *Fables*, Book I, fable 3.

tion, the primal scene, is a repression that creates and compromises culture at the same time."[80] Now, culture is language, and the amazing thing is that, in the sixth century BCE, J already understood the intrinsic relationship of the phenomenon with its inscription. When Babel is in crisis, what "ensues is usually thought to be a crisis of meaning or values . . . when, in fact, what we are experiencing is a larger crisis in our relationship with language."[81]

In Gen 11:9, language comes first and the human dispersion second, as a consequence of the "larger crisis" of language. The Babel myth starts with language and ends with language. For there is no meaning but the one its "text" creates. Without language, nothing has meaning. Language is not just a practical and conventional channel of communication; it is world.[82]

In this context again, the divine judgment is a perfect fit for the Babelian neurosis. Genesis 11 tells us that the Babelians "left off building the city" (11:8), they are scattered into the beyondness of the "surface of the earth," and their language is now cacophonic. Initially, they spoke "one language,"[83] but if you came closer, within earshot, you realized that their tongue was but sound and fury. Their dispersion is meant to make them confront reality and truth away from Babel, but history shows that they never ceased building the tower or the empire. Parallel with Job 38:8, where God sets a limit to the raging sea (without taming it), so in Genesis 11 God thwarts human ambitions with an act of decentering (without eradicating humans).

Interestingly enough, modern psychoanalysis substantiates the notion of the subject's decentering and provides a better understanding of the role of otherness in the formation of the ego.[84] This anti-Ptolemaic process of decentering recognizes the "break-in"[85] from the other (in Genesis 11, namely, the divine intervention). Decentering the subject is painful, often traumatic, but is the very condition for healing, for sanity. We meet again in Gen 11:8–9 the ambivalence of the *pharmakon*.[86]

80. Winquist, "Body, Text, and Imagination," 44.

81. Ibid., 46–47.

82. Ellen van Wolde titled one of her books *Words Become Worlds*. See chap. 1 n. 10, for a citation to an essay in this book.

83. In J's tale, the oneness of language is in reference to an exclusive purpose and its technology (Gen 11:3–4). It also pointedly refers to *logos* in contradistinction to *mythos*.

84. See Laplanche, *Essays on Otherness*.

85. Laplanche, *Vie et mort en psychanalyse*.

86. See above, chap. 2 n. 2.

Now, where there is denial of death and escape from history, care for others is tragically absent. "As Aristotle somewhere put it," says Becker, "luck is when the guy next to you gets hit with the arrow."[87] Cain, for one, makes sure that the arrow hits his brother rather than himself. As for the builders in Genesis 11, nothing is said in the text proper of their disregard for one another, but we probably do not err in inferring, with rabbinic tradition, callousness on the part of the Babelians. Chances are that there is something of it in the seemingly objective and neutral indication that they used bricks and tar instead of stones and mortar. Artificiality is a fabricated "truth" that camouflages pathetic human finitude. The tower with its head in heaven is the very image of the builders' self-consciousness.[88]

Disregard for others is rooted in hatred for otherness and, more deeply, for *the* Other and his Name.[89] "Let us make a name for ourselves" is the Babelian program. But we remember J's conviction, expressed in Gen 4:26, that already Seth and Enoch realized that the Name proclaimed is YHWH's. By contrast, in Genesis 11 the object of all human endeavors is condensed into making a name for humans themselves, unavoidably in competition with YHWH's name.

Šem ("name"), twice present in the narrative, has become the trophy worthy to fight for. In Genesis 12, which follows, another name is put in bas-relief. God says to Abram, "I shall make your name great" (Gen 12:2). Here divine agency is decisive; otherwise the name becomes self-referential and has no other substance than the one the self attributes to it.

Otherness is conspicuously absent in the first part of the Babel story. Our myth starts by stating that humanity is huddled up in one place, and that they based their cohesion on the unicity of language and a conceptual uniformity (11:1). What this means is that they chose a way of life where no *translation* is necessary. In psychoanalytical terms this implies a total absence of the subconscious, since the other's "break-in" does not occur, which would demand a (more-or-less delayed) reinterpretation or translation. Freud spoke of repression as a failure of translation of signi-

87. Becker, *The Denial of Death*, 2. In a previous publication, this evasion of life responsibility has been called the Jonah Complex (after Abraham Maslow's "Jonah Syndrome"): see LaCocque and LaCocque, *Jonah*. Maslow describes neurosis as the fear "of being shattered and disintegrated" ("Neurosis as a Failure of Personal Growth," 163).

88. Becker says, "In other words, men use the fabrications of culture, in whatever form, as charms with which to transcend natural reality" (*The Denial of Death*, 141).

89. In *The Brothers Karamazov*, Dostoevsky states that if there is no God, *everything* becomes permissible.

fiers (always enigmatic). But to the Babelians, there is repression already at the level of the signifiers. Everyone thinks the same, talks the same, and acts the same. The individuals are interchangeable.[90] They have no "id" and no collective memory, for everyone and everything is viewed and understood the same way, without need for interpretation.[91]

That is why, when the splitting of language into languages occurs, no one at first is equipped for proceeding to translation. For all concerned the sudden diversity of languages is sheer cacophony, an "idiot's story. Full of noise and passion. Meaning nothing."[92] So, strikingly, what started as an absence of meaning in the builders' endeavor ends as meaningless also, in the absence of translation.

Absence of translation, but not of death angst. The unique aim of the undifferentiated humanity is to "make a name for ourselves" (11:4a), that is, to reach immortality, as we said. This is the very cement (or, ominously, the bitumen) that binds them all together: fear and denial of death. They associate death with disintegration (11:4b) and metaphorically with dispersion. In an earlier context, Cain's commuted death sentence had made him rove around as "a fugitive and a wanderer" (4:14), that is, as a "scattered" personality. In contrast with the rest of their fellow humans, Noah and his family are saved by gathering together in an ark. The rabbis of old said that the tower of Babel was built with the aim of being high enough to escape the rising waters of a potential second deluge.[93] The image is powerful. The midrashic interpretation here appears to be without textual support, but it translates an important dimension of the story, namely, the Babelians' fear of disintegration (see b. *Sanhedrin* 109a). Note that Jer 51:42 mentions such a rising sea against Babylon. The very conception of microcosmic Babel surrounded by an ocean of formlessness called for the rabbinic suggestion.[94] Furthermore, all the Center of the World symbols imply a geological highpoint beyond the reach of the waters of a deluge—quite an interesting twist of an alleged God-commissioned instrument of life into a peak of death denial!

90. The closest modern model is provided by the stupefied populace of North Korea.

91. The "id" alienates us from ourselves and thus "puts a virtually definitive seal on this recognition of our fundamental decenteredness" (Laplanche, *Essays on Otherness*, 120).

92. Shakespeare, *Macbeth*, act 5, sc. 5.

93. See Josephus *Ant.* 1.113–14; cf. *PRE* 24. Catastrophic flooding was frequent in Mesopotamia (see the myth of *Atrahasis* [= Utnapishtim], *ANET*, 104–6; and "The Epic of Gilgamesh" (*ANET*, 95).

94. Babylon is the powerhouse among all the nations contemporary with it.

The repeated motto here of "denial of death" unmistakably recalls Ernest Becker's famous study with the same title. Under his leadership, the following development will, I hope, prove helpful.

The urge to secure the unification of human purposes is called Eros. It is also an urge to heroism, which itself is the outcome of narcissism. As William James stated, "Mankind's common instinct for reality . . . has always held the world to be essentially a theatre for heroism."[95] Everyone struggles to gain what Becker calls a "cosmic significance." This goes side by side with reaching out to timelessness. The construction of a pyramid or of a ziggurat is a tangible testimony to this existential quest. The first McCormick Center in Chicago, which burned to the ground some years later, would, according to a dedication speaker, outlive the pyramids! The aspiration remains strikingly unchanged, a clear symptom of the terror of death and of the terror of history. To wit, the builders' endeavor is starkly ahistorical, as we saw. Space is especially an interest of theirs (five times the word "there" appears in the tale), but time is irrelevant (at most an evocation of times past, cf. vv. 1 and 6).

True, a new humanity was born after the flood, but, J says, nothing really had changed in the human heart. Apart from Noah and his family, no one learned the lesson of the deluge. Arrogance still plagues human character, and what one could not individually achieve earlier, one tries now to build up by mobilizing throngs in the construction of a single edifice erected for the glory of humanity. In short, a standardizing ideology transforms them into an ant swarm, something a long way indeed from a voluntary association of free minds.[96]

For the favored way to escape history and death is by the Authority's fiat. When the established power decides to freeze the status quo and proclaims a thousand-year-long *Reich*, history becomes not only a retrograded concern but an arena for a ferment of subversion. From this perspective, the Mesopotamian Babel and the Israelite bard are pitted against each other. Babylon represents Authority and the Yahwist represents Desire. Desire, libido, confronts all the powers that psychoanalysis identifies as destruction and death. Insofar as J and his people are threatened by mighty Babylon, the Yahwistic myth is a critique of the empire.

---

95. James, *The Varieties of Religious Experience*, 281.

96. Surely no one will find it difficult to identify modern parallels to Babel's "standardizing ideology."

But Babel is not just the Babylonian Reich; it is also a terrible inner enemy, the *Thanatos* instinct, and this instinct is exacerbated by the empire. For no one is really immune to the formidable power of the empire and its ideology. The empire suffers no dissent. It builds Bastille-like dungeons and Pentagon-like weapon arsenals. Power expresses itself in various ways, the supreme one of which is the wielding of violence and death: "The strongest is always right," said La Fontaine in a fable about the wolf devouring the lamb.[97] There is an uncanny connivance between power and death, and the connivance exists at the level not only of empire, but also of the individual instinct. Here it is still more surprising, for the will to power is promiscuously mixed with a self-destructive impulse that associates sadism and masochism. It is against this background that the divine commandment spells out the deadly outcome of self-deification. The temptation to be like God is almost irresistible—and all-powerful Babylon is this ultimate temptation. With its demise, the nations' claimed raison d'être collapses. This is a traumatic international event, although with a silver lining: the coercive centripetal movement becomes a liberating, centrifugal one.

Theodore Hiebert is particularly irked by the use liberation theologians make of Genesis 11. But the very name of the place (*Babel*) admittedly evokes the empire, even an insatiable empire. In this respect, the initial centripetal movement of gathering must not deceive us. The aim is to concentrate power in one locale (see v. 4): the throng *comes* to the valley of Shinar. They settle there on purpose. Fearing their explosion, they implode. Verse 4 says, "so that we will not be scattered," and the LXX reads "*before* we are scattered," thus implying resistance to God's plans.[98]

By opposing mighty Babel, J makes an excruciating choice in favor of weakness. Now, weakness would cease to be weakness if it eventually occupied the place of the deconstructed power. The sad reality is that the individual or collective J can become in his turn "Babel." Instead, J's itinerary goes through the vocation of Abraham, an insignificant former idol worshipper of Ur in Chaldea. Abraham leaves behind his institutional moorings because of their claim to incontestable authority. In psychoanalytical terms, this is surrendering to the Superego (*Über-Ich*).[99] The Yahwist emerges wounded from the wrangle with Babel, like his later

97. La Fontaine, book I, fable 10 (conclusion).
98. See Hiebert, "The Tower of Babel," 36 n. 19.
99. See Freud, "The Ego and the Id."

character Jacob at the ford of Jabbok (Gen 32:23–32). It is the price to pay for acknowledging YHWH as the legitimate Superego.

By contrast, when human beings are one single people, have only one language, and are uniformly sharing the same concepts, that is, when they are soulless robots without substance, how could they make for themselves something out of nothing? What kind of name will they be able to make for themselves? How in the world will they cease to be anonymous?[100]

Characteristically, they decide to construct something. A tangible object seems more reliable than discourse or theory. Aladdin's lamp is ready whenever you need it and, correctly rubbed, guarantees the fulfillment of your desires. The Egyptians had their pyramids, the Mesopotamians their ziggurats, the Stone-Age folks their dolmens, and the nations in general have their altars, statues, monuments, and flags. Immortality, however, does not reside in a *thing*—a plant perhaps, golden apples, a fleece, a tower. The Bible promises eternal life not to those who have but to those who are, to the innocent ones (as against the violent, the arrogant, and the wicked).[101] In sum, there would have been nothing wrong with building Babel and the tower, provided that the builders, like Penelope, had destroyed at night what they had built during the day! As Laplanche writes, "Mourning, as a work of unweaving . . . can also be conceived as the very model of psychoanalysis: unweaving so that the new fabric can be woven"[102] But the builders in Genesis 11 have no patience for unweaving and reweaving. What they want is a solid, indestructible, nondeconstructible *axis mundi,* forcing the gates of heaven. Using different symbolism, J repeats in Genesis 11 what the myth of "the sons of God" copulating with "the daughters of man" had said in Genesis 6. J's story in Genesis 11 is no less terrifying a story. It comes as the culmination of human degeneration since the fall.

100. Several Jewish traditions, on the basis of Gen 10:8–10, where Shinar is associated with Babel and with Nimrod, make of the latter the initiator and the leader of the building of Babel. Does not his name mean "Rebellion"? (See Philo, *Questions and Answers in Genesis*, 2.82; Josephus, *Ant.* 1.113–14). According to Josephus, Nimrod became the builders' tyrant "bringing them into a constant dependence upon his power." We recall, Mic 5:5 says that Assyria is the land of Nimrod. J, however, has carefully kept his human characters nameless.

101. See Matt 19:29; 25:46; John 3:15, 36.

102. Laplanche, *Essays on Otherness*, 253–54 .

Ernest Becker writes, "This is [Otto] Rank's devastating Kierke-gaardian conclusion: if neurosis is sin, and not disease, then the only thing which can 'cure' it is a world-view."[103] The divine intervention in Gen 11:8–9 provides the necessary environment for the advent of the new worldview. As long as the builders shared the same ideology, no cure was possible. They were cultivating their malady to death. Their neurosis/sin, as we saw above, shows itself in their will to artificially create an *axis mundi*, a piv-ot—an objectified reflection of their souls—around which reality would swirl and be enthralled. Their tower would consolidate heaven, earth, and hell into a composition under their control. This is the very definition of neurosis. Unfortunately, there comes a time when the "patients" will be unable to disengage themselves from their addiction to power; then the addiction must be broken from the outside, and the break occurs in the form of a deconstruction.[104]

I realize that some people might think that I am too harsh with the build-ers in Genesis 11, while the text seems to say close to nothing about their frame of mind. But a group, like an individual, is moved by psychological motivations, as Freud brilliantly demonstrated in *Group Psychology and the Analysis of the Ego.*[105] He states that in a group people return to the state of dependent children, blindly following the hypnotic spell of the leader. The leader of course, whether he understands or not the mechanism, does cultivate this type of relationship. In the book of Esther, for instance, the Persian monarch may not be seen face-to-face without the "culprit" risking being put to death (Esth 4:11). The crowd willingly and gratefully bows before him, even before his image (see Daniel 2–3).[106] Such unity in obedience is described in Genesis 11 as "one language with unanimous purposes." The Babelians will do anything to remain enslaved in their one language and purpose. "And so," says Ernest Becker, "we understand the terrifying sadism of group activity."[107]

103. Becker, *The Denial of Death*, 198.
104. See chap. 6, below, on deconstruction.
105. Freud, *Group Psychology and the Analysis of the Ego*.
106. It is still the case in North Korea today. Besides, a leader like David Koresh can lead his flock uncoerced to poison themselves.
107. Becker, *The Denial of Death*, 133. My Lai and Abu Ghraib come to mind.

Once the group has a fixed obsession (that is, making a name for itself by building an immense city with its tower, for example), we saw that this transference becomes fetishism, all the more easily here since the tower is a temple, a gate to the divine. The whole world disappears behind the screen of the "tower"; the tower is the world. This is what justifies a monoglossic, monologic, monodeistic purpose. Imagination is out. So is interpretation. The vacuum is ready to be filled with the fundamental- ist dictation of inerrancy. Rather than "fetish," Erich Fromm says "idol." And indeed the idolization of Babel is what the story of Genesis 11 is all about. All energies cannot be dedicated to a single project without provoking a *religious* feverish fervor.[108] The ultimate purpose is to climb up to heaven and to prevent the human dispersion. The unity of action is a crucial means to that purpose. On a positive plane, it could have been instrumental to constructing a cohesive social unit (11:4). Now, such con- ceptual imagination on the part of an Israelite living (or who used to live) within the narrow confines of Jerusalem and its surroundings, warrants mention. The idea of a universal history and the unity of humankind is highly unusual—we note the blatant absence of anything "Israelite" but for the Name of God in the tale. In the ancient world, it can be found again in Greek philosophical speculation. We find an echo of this in the Qoheleth—influenced as he was by Hellenism in the Ptolemaic time—for which there is only one universal God of all humanity. J's distinction is to have intuited a world-historical consciousness. This is indeed a distinc- tion, because when the world horizon is open, one better understands one's own culture and identity.

The Tower as Phallus

In our story, the crowd's construction is dual: a city and a tower. The tower is evidently phallic; the city, Carl Jung says, "is a maternal symbol . . . The Old Testament treats the cities of Jerusalem, Babylon, etc., just as if they were women (cf. Isaiah 47:1ff.; Jeremiah 50:12; and Isaiah 1:21; 23:16 . . .)."[109] In Gen 11:1–9, the symbols for masculinity and femininity are combined. The name given to *her* (*šemah*, v. 9, i.e., Babylon) is Babel, understood ironically as meaning "confusion." As a maternal symbol (as

108. Even the Manson "family" spoke of their "holy mission"; so did the Nazis and later the Serbs.

109. Jung, et al., *Man and His Symbols*, 208. (See also especially the use of the term *mother* in Jer 50:12.)

in the book of Jeremiah), she parallels the life-preserving ark of Noah. But it is a parallel of contrasts. The ark was built on the instructions of God, and for the purpose of selecting Noah and his family from the rest of the people to become the seed of a new humanity. True, the ark is a concentrated space, like Babel in Genesis 11, but it is a *moving center*. By contrast, Babel is static. It is built to rob God of divinity, and humanity of mobility (see 11:4). The ark is intimately embedded in a time frame (40 days, 120 days) and is therefore transient. Babel is built to last forever; it negates time like an Egyptian pyramid, pitting eternity against the passing of time and against history.[110]

The feminine and masculine symbolism in the raising of two structures at Babel will be determinative in our assessment of the deconstruction of Babel. Meantime, we turn to a *Zohar*'s intriguing reflection on male circumcision. Circumcision, it says, symbolically feminizes the male Israelites;[111] but then all the ancient Near Eastern circumcised (feminized) males are pushed back to the margin of the picture in Genesis 11, and the tower of Babel becomes the arrogant competitor to God as *the* phallus, the sole "opener of the womb."[112] For, while the mythic goddess—Tiamat, Persephone—belongs to the underworld (recall the settlement in Genesis 11 in a depression), the masculine principle of heaven is symbol of an ever-higher ascension, and the tower is erected toward it. As Winnicott said, "rising has a phallic, that is, erection significance, as is obvious."[113]

In my earlier study of Cain and Abel—*Onslaught against Innocence*— I exposed a similar situation where with the fading presence of Adam and the violent elimination of Abel, Cain remains the sole phallic character facing God.[114] Now Cain is dead and the generation of the flood has disappeared; so that God, apparently, is filling the horizon. But the reality principle reappears with a vengeance. In lieu of Cain, Lamech, Nimrod, . . . the tower of Babel is thrust up toward the sky and challenges God as impregnator. "This is what they have started to make, so that henceforth no(thing) will be inaccessible to them (in) all that they will plot to make,"

---

110. "You [Babylon] said, 'I shall be mistress for ever'" (Isa 47:7 [NRSV]).

111. *Zohar* 2:36a on Exod 12:23, as cited in Rashkow, *The Phallacy of Genesis*, 93–94; she adds Ezek 16:6 as a backup text.

112. Cf. Gen 29:31; 30:22; Exod 13:2; 1 Sam 1:5, 6; Isa 66:9.

113. Winnicott, *Through Paediatrics to Psycho-Analysis*, 136.

114. See LaCocque, *Onslaught against Innocence*, 47–51.

God declares (v. 6). Babel is erected as the ultimate alternative to God's lordship. It is now an "either-or," in Kierkegaard's phrase.

Eventually Babylon, the great melting pot of all nations, breaks into shards in the image of the cacophonous medley of languages. The name/ fame they wanted to make for themselves (*šem*) is now punned into the "from there" (*miššam*) of their dispersion. The all-ingathering "mother" is incapable of harboring her children. And the erected *axis mundi,* whose foundation was in the netherworld and the crown in the heaven, is now a vestige of a lost illusion: its verticality is cancelled into a flat horizontality: ʿ*al penei kol ha-ʾareṣ,* "on the surface of all the earth." *Post coitum triste animal est.* ("After sex, the animal is sad.")

Meaning and innocence will, however, resurface, but not from the Babel populace. Ironically, God's prescribed *pharmakon* to the human mass culture is the vocation in Genesis 12 of an obscure individual—not a throng—from the very country of Babel. He will reintroduce innocence, and will initiate not only a new *Weltanschauung* ("worldview") but a new world. Abraham, a living closure to the primal couple's hubris, to the fratricidal Cain's isolation, to the culture of violence, and to the neurotic self-aggrandizement of empire builders, abandons city and tower and makes the leap of faith that will transform history and humanity.

That is how Abraham becomes a blessing for all humanity (Gen 12:2–3). In Abraham's person, a new history and economy emerge under the sign of a covenantal relationship with God—a dynamic covenant, not a static forced-open "gate."

Babel and the Myth of Dedalus and Icarus

Although syntactically different from the J myth of Babel, the Greek myth of Dedalus and Icarus comes thematically close to it.[115] Icarus's father, Dedalus, the inventor of the Knossos labyrinth, served King Minos of Crete, but fell into disfavor for helping Theseus, Minos's foe. Dedalus and his son Icarus are imprisoned in the labyrinth, but Dedalus fashions two pairs of wings made of wood and feathers glued with wax. (Note the technical nature and the artificiality of the materials.) With those wings, father and son can fly away from the fortress, but Icarus is instructed not to fly too high or too low, not to be guided by the stars, and not to

115. On the Greek myth, see Ovid *Metamorphoses,* book 8 lines 183–235 in Young-husband, *Classic Mythology.* 52–53.

trust anything but his father's lead. Icarus, however, becomes quickly enthralled with the technical powers of the contraption that carries him, and at a certain time starts to soar upward toward heaven, thus disobeying the orders of his father.[116] As he nears it, the sun melts the wax holding together the feathers, and Icarus plunges to his death into the Aegean Sea. Such is the gist of this impressive paradigm. At this point, the following statement of mythologist Mircea Eliade is very useful: "In the majority of archaic religions, flight signifies access to superhuman mode of being . . . in the last analysis, freedom to go wherever one wills, hence an appropriation of the condition of the spirit."[117]

Strikingly, the disobedience and death of Icarus make him miss the flight's significance as "intelligence, the understanding of secret things and metaphysical truths."[118]

True, the builders of the Tower of Babel story are not flying like Icarus, and their useful invention of bricks and bitumen is not for the sake of escaping a tower-dungeon, but the symbols in the two stories invite transposition. In both cases, there is present an obsession with "an ontological mutation of the human beings," a "transcending [of] this world of ours [so that] one re-enters into a primordial situation." [119] Icarus is not only the image of Crete's decline; he is an epitome of "everyman." Like the primal couple in Genesis 2, he is not left without instruction and warning. Like the human being ("the son of Adam") of Psalm 8, Icarus is at the outset "a little less than Elohim," and concomitantly "the worm" of Psalm 22.[120] Disaster befalls him the very moment he forgets this second aspect of his being. He should not have flown too high or too low. Too low he'd be snapped by the sea waves and drowned; too high, he'd be burned by the sun. Icarus indeed confirms both omens in the reverse order: he is burned and he drowns.

The Babel builders' aim is also taking them way beyond their human limitations, both in height and in depth. They intend to reach up to no less than heaven and to become thereby world famous, while what they have ultimately at heart is somewhat trifling: not to be dispersed. So much

116. A Phoenician myth introduces a hubristic hero named (as if he were Greek) Phaeton, who attempts to fly to heaven, an act that provoked the coming of the flood.

117. Eliade, *The Sacred and the Profane*, 176.

118. Eliade, *Myths, Dreams, and Mysteries*, 105.

119. Ibid., 108, 115.

120. See also Job 17:14; 25:6. Recall that bold, vaulting ambition can be described as *Icarian*.

for so little! Well, with so flimsy a foundation, not surprisingly the tower crumbles and the arrogant city lies in ruins. Humanity has brought upon itself its demise—as usual.

In the Hebrew myth, there is a spectacular consequence to the Babylonian hubris: not only is the forced communication with the divine thwarted, but human dialogue explodes into six thousand fragments. The magnet-city of Babylon is no gate to the divine, but the usher of chaos. Authentic dialogue with God and between humans occurs when God "descends" (Gen 11:5, 7). This naively anthropomorphic motif must be set in the context of humanity's attempting to climb up to heaven and to steal the divine power.[121] Another Greek parallel comes to mind: the myth of Prometheus.

Prometheus, we recall, steals from heaven the fire hidden by the gods, and brings it down to the humans. The background of the Greek myth differs vastly from Hebrew mentality. Prometheus lights his torch with the sun and carries the fire back to earth. His enmity with Zeus temporarily gets the better of the highest god. For in general, the gift of the Greek gods has been poisoned; the name of the gift is Pandora, the seductive female created by Hephaestus at the order of Zeus, with an evil intention toward humans. Pandora is forbidden to open the jar she has received in trust, but like Icarus, she disobeys, and from the jar escapes a multitude of evils. "The earth is full of evils and the sea is also full," Hesiod says.[122]

This is only one aspect of the myth. The parallel with Genesis 11 stops here, for Prometheus's act benefits humanity, and does not merely satisfy Prometheus's own hubris. Here Zeus rather than human hubris is the tyrannical power.

Evoking those well-known Greek myths leads to the incontrovertible conclusion that they, like the story of Babel in the Bible, uncover what Ernest Becker used to call "the denial of death." In the valley of Shinar, in Crete, or in the Caucasus Mountains, the quest for immortality begins anew. It starts in Eden (Gen 3:4) and has never abated since (see Gen 4:8; 6:5, 11–13). Inwardly the realization of human finitude gnaws at our

121. God's anthropomorphisms and anthropopathy in the Bible are based on the Israelite conviction that God has created the human in his own image. Ezekiel 1:26, for example, reverses the representation and shows God as a human-like figure. (This early conception of the kinship of God and the human gave rise to the fiction of the "soul" as *speculum mundi*, mirror of both the universe and its Creator.)

122. Hesiod, *Works and Days*, lines 1–275.

existence. Nothing is more urgently felt than the need to overcome death, and this by any means: murder/fratricide, violence, self-corruption, magic, technological artifices, enforced standards of uniformity for humans, pyramids/ziggurats, insatiable conquests, artificial changes to geography and demography, so-called ethnic cleansing, slavery, rape, and so forth. Humans are avid to inflict upon others what they fear themselves, thus magically deflecting the arrows of death.[123]

When the throngs in Genesis 11 voice their fear of being scattered, what they express, in terms of the Icarus's myth, is their desire to break with the trifling generality of the human condition, with "the way of the world," as the rabbis said. To be scattered stands for human contingency. The opposite is "to make a name for ourselves," whereby space is transcended or at least shrunk to the restricted area of the tower (*šam*, "there"), and time to the immediacy of a construction. City and tower are concrete things, undeniable possessions, a magnet for power, a nucleus for the growth of the empire. Babel constitutes a foil to Abraham, to whom the following statement of Erich Fromm applies: "The willingness to let go of all 'certainties' and illusions—requires *courage* and *faith*. Courage to let go of certainties, courage to be different and to stand isolation; courage, as the Bible puts it in the story of Abraham, to leave one's own land and family and to go to a land yet unknown."[124]

Certainties are also what Faust is after. We shall come back to Faust in the following section, but it is remarkable that Goethe in his play about that character mentions again the wish to fly and to follow the sun on its eternal, life-giving journey and to "drink its eternal light, the day always before me and the night behind, the heavens above me and the waves beneath."[125] And again in the same play, in "High Mountains,"[126] the child of Faust and Helen of Troy, Euphorion, longs to fly: "I long to

123 At the other end of the spectrum, love humbly accepts being the target of arrows, like St. Sebastian. In extreme cases, the lover sets himself as the willing substitute victim, like Father Maximilian Kolbe in Auschwitz.

124. Fromm, "The Creative Attitude," 53 (italics original). See John Keats's concept of "negative capability": "At once it struck me what quality went to form a man of achievement, especially in literature, and which Shakespeare possessed so enormously—I mean Negative Capability, that is, when a man is capable of being in uncertainties, mysteries, doubts, without any irritable reaching after fact and reason" (Forman, *The Letters of John Keats* [letter to George and Thomas Keats, December 1817], 57).

125. Fairley, *A Study of Goethe,* 17 (Goethe, "Faust to Wagner" in *Faust* part 1, act 2, scene 2).

126. Ibid.,165 ("High Mountains," *Faust,* part 2, act 4, scene 1).

fly up into the sky. I can't wait." To which Faust responds, as did Dedalus to Icarus, "Careful, careful. Don't be rash, lest you meet with disaster and ruin us all."

But the throngs in Babel would rather reach up to the sun or (in the terms of Gen 11:4) to heaven. They are moved by what Eliade calls "the nostalgia of paradise"[127] or the "myth of the land of Eden," "mythical geography."[128] Eliade also notes: "The progressive elevation, terrace by terrace, up to the 'pure land' at the highest level of the temple. . . . This desire, so deeply rooted in man, to find himself at the very heart of the real—at the Center of the World, the place of communication with Heaven—explains the ubiquitous use of 'Centers of the World.'"[129]

The general pattern of the Babel story parallels the recurrent cycles of the calendar and the life seasons—birth, growth, maturity, and decay— at the basis of other myths. Suffice it to recall here the widespread myth of the hero: his humble origin, his progressive victory over major enemies, his inclination to the sin of hubris, and his death. The key for interpreting this common scheme is the feverish human quest for individual or collective identity. In the case illustrated by the myth of Icarus, a tragic denouement occurs of the hero's attempt, here again, "to climb up to heaven." Icarus and the Babel builders have chosen a false heroism.

Icarus falls into the sea; Babel is left behind as an incomplete and deceptive project. Icarus is masculine, the city of Babel is feminine. The scattering of the people of Babel looks like a weaning "from an enticing devouring aspect of the mother image."[130] Incidentally, along this line of reasoning, the purpose behind the exclusive mention of the city (without the masculine tower) in Gen 11:8 becomes clearer with the dispersion: Babel disposed of an enticing voice and language, but at the root this voice of unity was a very confusing one indeed.

---

127. Eliade, *Images and Symbols*, 448.

128. Eliade, *Patterns*, 432–33.

129. Eliade, *Images and Symbols*, 53–54. The plural number of "Centers" is eloquent, for indeed there are as many centers as there are endeavors to reach the apex of power ("heaven"). André Gide, in *Theseus*, says that everyone wants "to lose himself . . . in a labyrinth of his own devising" (76). Our attachment to our discrete "towers" renders any different reality "charmless and one no longer has any wish to return to it. And that—that above all—is what keeps one inside the labyrinth" (77).

130. See Henderson, "Ancient Myths and Modern Man," 125.

Babel and the Myth of Faust

To see human history and particularly the Western mentality as being Faustian sounds rather Spenglerian.[131] It is a fact that the modern populace (in the image of the ancient one) constantly strives toward the unattainable. So the worm is in the fruit and the "decline" is unavoidable. Spengler says, "World history is the history of the great Cultures, and peoples are but the symbolic forms and vessels in which the people of these Cultures fulfill their Destinies." Interestingly enough, about the identity of nations Spengler also states: "Neither the unity of speech nor physical descent is decisive . . . Peoples are neither linguistic nor political nor zoological, but spiritual units." A people's general evolution starts with culture (Babylonian, Egyptian, Greek . . .) and fades into what he calls civilization when its original creativity wanes away. Then remain only the ruins of the ancient glory. Humanity's history shows a Faustian restlessness in not being able to identify its real desires. It is, by false compensation, engulfed in a whirlwind striving to surpass all human capability, investing all its energies, for instance, in constructions like the tower of Babel. But then, when their project does not yield the desired outcome, humanity abandons the "tower" and sinks into despair when not into violence. In the prologue to *Faust* (285–86) Goethe writes, "[The human] calls it reason and employs it, resolute / To be more brutish than is any brute."[132]

To conclude this foray into the Faustian character of the Babelian enterprise, it is proper to contrast again the two "gates" Jesus is reported to have mentioned in Matt 7:13–14: "Enter through the narrow gate; for the gate is wide and the road is easy that leads to destruction, and there are many who take it. For the gate is narrow and the road is hard that leads to life, and there are few who find it" (NRSV).

Norman Brown evokes Marx, who "attributes to man a psychological-physiological structure such that the act of satisfying a need, and making an instrument to satisfy a need, provokes a new need. Such an assumption makes man eternally Faustian and restless and therefore precludes happiness."[133]

---

131. See Spengler, *Der Untergang des Abendlandes*, 2 vols, 1918 and 1922 (*The Decline of the West*). The revised second volume is subtitled, *Perspectives of World History* [1923]. Spengler was strongly influenced by Goethe.

132. Goethe, *The Tragedy of Faust, Part 1*, lines 285–86.

133. Brown, *Life against Death*, 259.

At the other end of the spectrum from such "Faustian restlessness," the Bible proclaims the human rulership over creation, to be sure; but the good ruler remains humble, knowing that he or she is only a steward.[134] As a result of this, St. Paul saw the church as reversing Gen 11:9, and he spoke of the church's retrieved unity in diversity (1 Corinthians 12).

---

134. See 1 Cor 4:1; 1 Pet 4:10.

Chapter Five

Translation

1. *It so happened that all the earth was of one language and with a limited vocabulary.*
2. *And on their move to the east, they found a depression in the land of Shinar.*
   There they settled.
3. *Each said to the other, "Come! Let's brick bricks that we'll flame in flame."*
   So, brick was to them for stone, and tar was to them for mortar.
4. *They said, "Come! Let's build us a city with a tower. Its head be in heaven. Let's make us a name,*
   lest we be scattered over the surface of all the earth."
5. *YHWH descended to see the city and the tower that the Adamites were building.*
6. *YHWH said, "As (this is) one nation with one language for all, and that's how they started to act, henceforth no action of theirs that they plot will be impossible.*
7. *Come! Let us descend and confound (right) there their language, so that they will not hear the language of one another."*
8. *YHWH scattered them from there over the surface of all the earth,*
   and they ceased building the city.
9. *This is why He called its name Babel ["babble"],*
   because there YHWH confounded the language of all the earth,
   and from there He scattered them over the surface of all the earth.

Part Two

CHAPTER SIX

Deconstruction

A Deconstructive Approach

IN THE "CONSTRUCTION" PART of the present study (chapter 2), the text of J's narrative has been presented as an integral unity in which all elements are harmoniously integrated into the whole. Both the impressive balance of the two halves of the text and the impeccable patterning of the piece have contributed to an impression of a well-wrought text without cracks.

Such a "perfection" in the composition is nonetheless more vulnerable to criticism than it seems at first. As we shall show in what follows, the Tower of Babel tale is opened to deconstruction—like the city and its tower that the myth wants to deconstruct.

Now, deconstruction is not demolition. When a text is deconstructed, it remains standing. This new part in our inquiry on Gen 11:1–9 will not render the first part obsolete, but it will certainly subvert the "roundedness" of what we have discovered in part 1 of this book.

Deconstruction explores the "subconscious" of the text, so to speak.[1] It demonstrates the latent complexities that may amount to inconsistencies and to an authorial inner conflict. Subconscious features, or rather subtextual clues, as the underpinning of the narrative, are not necessarily totally unconscious on the part of the author. Intentional irony, for instance, is a potent subverting literary device; so are, of course, metaphor and other tropes, and they all may reveal some pent-up sentiments. The composer works on several levels at once, with the surface level throwing a

---

1. Moore says that postmodern criticism is the "id" of historical criticism (*Poststructuralism and the New Testament*, 117).

veil upon the deeper ones. The situation she describes may be ambiguous and its message self-critical, even self-deconstructing. For instance, much could be said along this line about many a story about the patriarch Jacob or about Abraham's and Ephron's attitude in Genesis 23. Deconstruction is thus able "to bring to the centre of analysis observations that have long been repressed in margins and footnotes," as Yvonne Sherwood says.[2]

When we turn to Gen 11:1–9, the story introduces two protagonists: YHWH and the Babelians. One of the two is patently superior to the other, and Babel doesn't have a chance. But once we realize that Babel is not destroyed (only deconstructed), its survival becomes ominous, like the persistence of evil, and the vastly superior power of YHWH is, as it were, relativized!

It is certainly not insignificant that Jacques Derrida "seizes on the two most iconically disruptive and aporetic biblical texts for his most overtly biblical meditations to date," namely, the Tower of Babel story and Genesis 22 (Abraham's near sacrifice of Isaac). For Genesis 11 is "the quintessential narrative of dispersal and confusion, the interruption of the structure by the God who proclaims himself 'I am the one I am' and who pronounces confusion in the midst of the imperialism dream of the universal idiom, one people and one lip (Gen. 11:6)."[3]

Indeed, from a deconstructive point of view, several elements of the Babel text, besides the evident deconstructionist conclusion in vv. 8–9, must be emphasized. I shall start by highlighting three of them, namely, *debarim ʾaḥadim*, *šam*, and *babel*.

First, let us remember that the Babelian discourse as reported in vv. 3–4 is singularly poor in vocabulary. These are really *debarim ʾaḥadim*! No wonder that they belong to a *śaphah ʾaḥath* ("a single language"). But more needs to be said of this expression. Without the specificity of being composed with *debarim*, the "one language" of v. 1 would remain a mere abstraction. The language, as Scharlemann says, has a "close connection . . . with the being of human beings for, like Dasein, a word is itself ontological; it is a perceptible thing that is also a meaning and a meaning

2. Sherwood, *The Prostitute and the Prophet*, 328.
3. Sherwood, "Derrida" (in reference to Jacques Derrida, "Des Tours de Babel" ["Towers of Babel"]), 73.

that is also a perceptible thing."[4] An illustration of this is afforded by the Hebrew *dabar*, which means variously "word," "thing," and "event." To say that the primeval people were using one *language* means that they were producing the same *things* and making the same *events* uniformly happen. What things? What events? Things and events that were *ᵓaḥadim*, that is, few in number and restricted in scope. Hence, what they came up with was a transient construction that they believed eternal, so that their *debarim* also would remain unassailable concepts, words without end.

Šam ("There")

This overdetermined lexeme evokes a popular deep implantation as well as a contingency of happening. "There," repeated five times, reflects an inner compulsion within the myth to be actual and concrete. Thanks to "there," this is not a "once upon a time in an indeterminate country" story: Babel is Babylon in the land of Mesopotamia, where one can actually find clay and bitumen in abundance, where there are big cities built around their central ziggurats, and where, most important, J's Judean audience or readership has been exiled.

But if "there," is it also everywhere? For if it is not also elsewhere, it would single out Babel as exceptional and unique. Now, Babel is surely that, as the universal center of idolatry. "There" in this sense, means there and nowhere else (at least not to a comparable degree of depravity). But, on the other hand, what is so concentrated "there" is also about to be dispersed "from there." That is, the uniqueness of Babylon is unable to maintain its arrogant isolation. "There" becomes everywhere one can point to a human conglomeration; everywhere human beings are building *des tours de Babel*. In this latter case, *there* has lost none of its specificity, for the erection of any tower will forever recall *the* tower of Babel. And, conversely, all towers forever will evoke confusion, disorientation, and folly.

Babel

Babel is a chronotope, that is, an alloy of time and space, not only a locus but a concentrate of cultural markers: historical, economic, political, social, religious, and the like.[5] In conformity with other biblical stories focusing on places outside the national framework (Joseph in Egypt, Jonah

---

4. Scharlemann, "The Being of God," 87.
5. See Bakhtin, "Response to a Question from *Novy Mir*."

in Nineveh, Daniel in Babylon), J proceeds to draw ever-narrowing concentric circles from "all the earth" to Shinar and, eventually, to Babel and to its tower. By contrast, the broadening of Israel's world vision, especially as regards Babylon, found its springboard with the sixth-century exile in Babylonia. There the exiles of all conquered nations were amazed with the dimension and splendor of the megalopolis of Babylon and its immense ziggurat. The space axis became overwhelmingly present. Babylon was commensurate with the tremendous expanse of the empire.

Israel until then had been much more interested in the historical axis—a history viewed from a subjective standpoint—than in architecture: ancient Israel left behind no pyramids, no ziggurats, and hardly any temple buildings and palaces. But with the triumph of "the nations," space grew more important in the Israelite imagination.[6] To this "intrusion" of sorts we owe the first eleven chapters of the Bible, as well as other literary witnesses such as the book of Esther, for instance.[7] With the events of the sixth century BCE, it had become evident to Judah that no real national future could be envisaged independently from a spatial resolution. It would be either Babylon or Zion (later, either Athens or Jerusalem). Space and time, if ever ideologically considered discrete entities, became inseparable in Israel's consciousness. A mystique of the land of Israel developed that would take center staged until today.

J's dealing with Babel as a chronotope, and more so with the Valley of Shinar as representing all of Mesopotamia, underscores his universalistic vision (explicated in Gen 11:9). For that matter, even the focalization on the individual Abraham in Genesis 12 does not detract from the concept of universalism. Abraham comes from a "foreign" country, and the worldwide dimension of his call and covenant is immediately underlined (see Gen 12:3). Undoubtedly, this broad perception of the narrator corresponds to a preoccupation with the world at large. When Israel saw itself being absorbed (by force) into "the nations," a most pressing issue arose about the lordship of God.[8] Did it extend to the confines of the whole earth? If so, was it so broad and unlimited as to lose sight of tiny Judah? J addresses both issues squarely in Genesis 2–12* and beyond. Methodologically, he proceeds from the most extensive generalities

6. See chap. 2, above, especially the section offering "A Close Reading of Verses 1–3."
7. See LaCocque, *Esther Regina*, esp. 22–25.
8. So during the European Middle Ages, the Crusades did open minds in the Latin world to the size of the non-Christian expanse.

(Eden and the universal flood) to the narrowest particularity (Abraham). Along the way, Gen 11:1–9 is the transitional bridge that straddles both standpoints. Ever since J's work, universalism and particularism are the two sides of the same coin. The particular Israel is in the universe like the bridgehead of God in his reconquest of the world.

All of this underscores foreign influence as considerable, and this always has been a contentious issue in Israelite religious milieus. Babel, for one, claimed universal centrality and sovereignty over "all the earth." The city was architecturally, politically, administratively, the most impressive realization the world had ever seen. Entire captive populations were forcibly displaced to the "Gate of the Divine." Against this background, Genesis 11 is a polemical piece scoffing at (and prophesying) the incompletion and the ruin of Babel's most significant endeavor. The narrative sees in the dispersion of the nations—the very opposite of the Babylonian myth of the magnetic center—the divine intervention that thwarts the accomplishment of the "pagan," idolatrous purposes. Babel in truth is Confusion.

But is it not true that *Babel* as another name for "confusion" is incoherent in any other language and philosophy than the Hebrew tongue and the Hebrew philosophy? Does not the Hebrew language, therefore, entail a severe limitation of the universality proposed by the mythic association of the two terms? Harping on this theme, Derrida reflects on the confused use of a proper name as a common noun. A proper name is by definition untranslatable and must, therefore, be rendered in any recipient language only in transliteration. "Babel-Confusion" is paraphrastic, not a translation, just as *Londres* is no translation of *London*. In Genesis 11, however, God, in giving "his name, a name of his choice, in giving all names, the father would be at the origin of language."[9] In fact, "Babel" as "Confusion" is, on the part of J, an interpretation of an interpretation: to the extent that Babel-Confusion is a divine sentence, it is uttered by J as such.[10] But to the Babylonians, among others, it is worthless. It is even a word of blasphemy, for Babel is the sublime expression of the divine/human contact. J's interpretation deconstructs the Babylonian interpretation as utterly wrong. Deconstruction does not deny the possibility of a divine/human contact at Babel (deconstruction is not annihilation; it is disassembly[11]), but then the contact exposes the human religious manipulation of the divine to

9. Derrida, "Des Tours de Babel," 105.
10. See ibid., 105, 109–10.
11. See Odell-Scott, "Deconstruction," 55.

its own deification. Interpretation versus interpretation, Gen 11:8–9 is a summary of the entire biblical "antireligious" kerygma. By deconstructing the Tower of Babel story, we can demonstrate that Babylon and its claim to be the navel of the world is the epitome of religion torn to shreds. With "all the earth" witnessing, Babel reveals the originary Confusion of its being. Although ominously built with bricks and bitumen, it was supposed to make a name/fame for its inhabitants—but the only name it made is Confusion. The ziggurat mountain gave birth to a mouse. This also is paradigmatic: all mountains painfully accumulated by a Babelian humanity ("all the earth") will always give birth to a mouse. On that score, Gen 11:1–9 within the primeval history combines prophecy and wisdom, archaeology and eschatology.

The dissemination of languages at the end of the tale is strikingly illustrating the deconstructionist dialectic of presence and absence.[12] It is only in its absence—that is, in the disengagement from its own identity— that the presence becomes real. The unity, univocity, and uniformity, of language mentioned in Gen 11:1 was a monolithic presence—in need of deconstruction. Language was *used* to express things always desperately the same, *debarim ʾaḥadim*, ("sameness"). Only through its imposed absence, its scattering, does sameness become difference. Self-identity is now dead, and so it fulfills the very condition for life to spring forth. Mikhail Bakhtin said that death "is the necessary link in the process of people's growth and renewal. It is the 'other side' of birth."[13] He shows that the Carnival's pattern alternates death and rebirth, and he speaks of "the image of pregnant death" or "death pregnant with life." He states, "Everything is reborn and renewed through death." "Carnival is the festival of all-annihilating and all-renewing time."[14]

J ends his series of primeval tales with an "image of pregnant death." In order for life in the person of Abraham to spring forth, there must earlier be some kind of *tabula rasa*. (The Hebrews who enter the Promised

---

12. See Taylor, "Text as Victim," 72: "The dissemination of the Word is its reincorporation, reincarnation, or reinscription." To recall, "Derrida uses dissemination as a play on *Shem* and the language of the name, and on *semen* and the sowing (or scattering) of the seed of the father" (Sherwood, *The Prostitute and the Prophet*, 206). The unlimited multiplicity of peoples and languages contributes, of course, to the attribution of a sexual connotation to the dispersion.

13. Bakhtin, *Rabelais and His World*, 407.

14. Bakhtin, *Problems of Dostoevsky's Poetics*, 126, 127, 124.

Land tread, as it were, on the dead generation of their parents in the Sinai desert.)[15]

What do the dead in the tale of Babel represent? Along with their tower, the Babelians had first erected their one language to the stature of the universal. They wanted their language also to have its head in heaven. This philosophical identification of language and factuality is precisely what the deconstruction movement is deconstructing! Language ruins itself by passing from spirit to letter, from intention to communication. In building an object that would appropriate otherness and transform it into sameness, the Babelians were sterilizing their discourse and ultimately closing themselves into a state of noncommunication. But the object could never be constructed and the language could never be identified with the object. Once the reference failed, language itself was emptied of all content; it became a "babbling," and the object could be called "Babel," because from the outset it was misconceived. Babel is the symbol of all human constructions or devices of reassurance and of certainty.[16]

There is thus at the origin of language(s) a divine violence. God founds language on his name that he gives—the foundation and limit of all language. The divine name must necessarily be said, but it is ineffable. On its model, all translation is necessary and impossible. The story of the Tower of Babel ends with the confusion of human languages, but also with speakers of separate languages unable to communicate with one another. In addition, not only are languages confused, but inside each language there is confusion of speech itself. For better or for worse, before the deconstruction of Babel, all humanity shared the same tongue, with referents designating the same signifieds for all. After the deconstruction, the human tongue splits into a multiplicity of idioms, and *langue* becomes confused.

Hence, although readers must suspend their disbelief in order to understand the text, readers need not suspend the critique of systemic principles touted by any system as valid for all people and for all times.[17] The divine violence in Gen 11:8–9 shatters the implicit violence of

15. See Num 32:11–1 3; Deut 2:14–15; cf. Exod 1:6.

16. Carl Raschke states, "Meaning is pure movement, the overflowing self-effacement of language." "The Deconstruction of God," 9.

17. Here reference to Jean-François Lyotard is appropriate. He recommends "incredulity toward metanarrative" (MacIntyre, *After Virtue*, xxiv). The very compositional brevity and the subversion inherent in the myth of Babel bring to mind the "little stories" that Lyotard speaks about, which question the powers that be.

monoglossic ideology (the Babelianism that speaks one language with uniform referents). Plurivocity and pluralism summarize postmodern deconstruction.

It is not the first time, of course, that J imagines a divine violence snuffing out a previous (human) violence. The best example is the flood. As regards the Tower of Babel, the tale ends on a note of confusion—a confusion that defeats a preceding confusion, for Babel has always been confusion. This concept of evil overcome by evil recalls the ambiguous nature of the *pharmakon*, simultaneously medicine and poison[18]—so that, in a sense, all remedies are homeopathic. There is no neutralization of evil but through evil; the sole exception is the miracle.[19] The divine recourse to dispersion at the end of the myth implies renunciation of the miracle and, once again, underscores the uncanny weakness of God. For violence is not a sign of power but rather of despair. When violence has reached its goal—and Babelian humanity has been scattered "over the face of the whole earth"—nothing is really accomplished. The problem has only shifted: What will scattered humanity do that it did not do before, and not do that it did do before? The story's end is no end. Babel itself had demonstrated "the impossibility of finishing, of totalizing, of saturating, of completing something of the order of edification, architectural construction, system and architectonics."[20] After Gen 11:9, there is nonetheless only a pause, a caesura, a void that demands to be filled by the Mesopotamian Abraham.

Although it is not forbidden to see the linguistic and ethnological outcome of Genesis 11 (v. 9) as fulfilling the spreading of nations and tongues in Genesis 10, it remains that "confusion" resides at its core. In the light of Gen 11:8–9, we face an unbearably paradoxical situation regarding human speech (language and *langue*): something like, the more words we use, the more remote the Word appears to be, the Name that would render all other words and names obsolete. That is why Gen 11:8–9 is not definitive but rather striving toward its own deconstruction.

Did J himself deconstruct his text? The story of Babel has no closure. It ends on an absence. Language is shattered; humanity is scattered; then what? Whither does this lead? The text remains in suspension.

18. "The pharmakon is neither the cure nor the poison, neither good nor evil, neither the inside nor the outside, neither speech nor writing" (Derrida, "Positions," 36).

19. Conceivably, God could have set Babel on fire like Sodom and Gomorrah.

20. Derrida, "Des Tours de Babel," 3–4.

After Gen 11:9 and the cacophony of human languages comes silence, a silence that indeed deconstructs the din of the logorrhea. The text of the myth does not satisfy the "metaphysical gesture" (Derrida) that expects the thought pattern to conclude with a reprieve, a return to the original purity. Nothing of this occurs here (in the same way that it did not occur in Genesis 3 or 4). Therefore, the situation is one of deconstruction without reconstruction. In order that God's intent be fulfilled, there must be a human transgression, just as the divine call back to the original purity of Israel happens through Hosea's marrying a harlot.[21] The origin is transgressed, but it was itself impure from the outset: true, the whole of humanity spoke a single language, but they were coming *miqqedem*, and they expressed their intention not to be dispersed but to make a name for themselves. So as the worm is in the apple, deconstruction was already in the construction. Nothing here is pure and ideal. Yvonne Sherwood observes, "The collision of redemption and punishment in the undecideables [i.e. whether positive or negative; here, the scattering of language and people] . . . suggests that Yhwh himself turns into an undecideable, who nurtures and abuses [in a stance of nonintervention, but only when it is "too late"], strips and restores, seduces and deprives."[22]

Isn't it the real motive of the reader's embarrassment with the notion of God's descent to see, as if God were nearsighted or had misplaced his glasses? Wasn't there an implied possibility that after looking closer, God would be content with what he saw and return appeased to heaven? More disturbingly, the justification for his negative decision to dismantle the house of cards that is Babel in v. 6 ("As [this is] one nation with one language for all, and that's how they started to act, henceforth no action that they plot to do will be impossible"), which so closely restates the ambiguous Gen 3:22, appears to make a so-far unfounded accusation against the Babelians (a *procès d'intention*). This, to be sure, does not reflect favorably on the judge.

Are these just weaknesses of the narrative, or do they reveal something deeper, a failure of theology perhaps? Then the survival of Babylon beyond the "prophecy" of J affords a situation in which both YHWH and Babylon are in a constant confrontation, neither able to crush the other in a "violent hierarchy" (Derrida). This inability "produces a sense of indefi-

---

21. See Sherwood, *The Prostitute and the Prophet*, 209.
22. Ibid., 214.

nite fluctuation between the two possibilities."[23] At the end of the story, Babylon is wounded, *and* YHWH is far from being unscarred. Against his better judgment (see Gen 1:28), he had to use violence in order to obtain only a partial realization of his own *mezimmah* ("purpose," see 11:6) for humanity. There is here no clue to an alleged divine omnipotence so dear to Western and Eastern Christianity.[24] To be sure, YHWH will be vindicated, not thanks to his power but to a mutual choice/espousal between God and a man of flesh and blood, Abraham. In order to be powerful, God needed the intervention of human weakness! The whole of the concept of "incarnation" is already here in embryonic form.

We need to further investigate the clash between J's wishful "prophecy" and the "reality principle" of Babylon's survival. This we do by noticing that, under the pen of J, the Tower of Babel story has become an object of art. It is as an object of art that "Babel" is erected and eventually deconstructed. As a concrete monument built by human hands, Babylon with its ziggurat is not symbolic, except of itself; it is self-referential. But as a poetic creation, Babel becomes a web of significations carefully elaborated by the poet.

This distanciation between the crude object and its interpretation is crucial. Mikhail Bakhtin, more than anyone else, has insisted on that necessary distance, the "non-coinciding with itself" of the subject.[25] As a monolith "coinciding with itself," Babel is "monoglossic"; as a poetic creation, it has a thousand voices. The colossal mistake of the Babel builders was to confine themselves to having "one lip" for all (Gen 11:1, literally): what a powerful image of monoglossia! The outcome of such an introverted discourse could only be a mausoleum, like an Egyptian pyramid. Babel is a gigantic mass grave for "all humanity" (Gen 11:1).

Babylon as witnessed by J continued to exist as a necessary presence in an era when innocence is shockingly in captivity. The untimely eradication of Babylon would render the Judean exile senseless, an empty parenthesis in Israel's history.[26] True, in the absolute, Jerusalem is in no

23. Derrida, *Dissemination*, 225 (quoted in Sherwood, *The Prostitute and the Prophet*, 211).

24. See my article "Justice for the Innocent Job!"

25. Also called by Bakhtin "transgredience" or "outsideness" (see *Art and Answerability*. I refer readers to my *Esther Regina*, 58–63 ["Outsideness"]). Ricoeur's insistence on distanciation falls in full agreement with Bakhtin's. The title "The Hermeneutical Function of Distanciation" in *From Text to Action* says it well.

26. This is, *mutatis mutandis*, the spark of truth in Jean-Paul Sartre's statement about

need of Babylon to be herself; but the captivity of Jerusalem shows that Babylon belongs to her historical identity.[27]

When all is said and the balance sheet has been drawn up negative, the unavoidable question is: was all this colossal effort called Babel for naught? Babylon is now (proleptically) turned into a desert where hyenas and ostriches roam, but no humans (Isa 13:20–22; Jer 51:39).

The heavy silence of the desert calls for a *vox clamans in deserto* ("voice crying in the wilderness"), and therefore Gen 11:9 is decisively opening up to something that follows and is capable either of confirming the outcome of the Babelian rebellion, or of transcending it toward the recovery of a—"second"—"one language with an economy of words." After Gen 11:9, the next sentence from the Yahwist reads, "And YHWH said to Abram . . ." (Gen 12:1). The silence is torn apart, on the heels of a dramatic deconstruction, which, in J's work on the primeval era, has come as the last stroke in a series of deconstructions of the human will to power (cf. Isa 14:14).

In Genesis 12 and the vocation of Abraham, *God* speaks, and thus the confused language of "all the earth" retrieves its glorious function of divine discourse. As confused monoglossia, language used to express hubris, arrogance, "sound and fury." Now language becomes a divine call to cooperate, and a promise of a "name" to Abraham that will be a blessing for "all the families of the earth." What is starting with the "little stories" (Lyotard) of Abraham is a sort of *evangelium continuum* that, "yet for a little while" (Heb 10:37) runs parallel with the confused language of the throngs of the Babel builders.

Furthermore, the very pun on the name *Babel* as being a babbling close to cacophony does not obliterate the initial message intended by the city's name, that is, the "Gate of the Divine." The name has become dialectical. The arrogance of the Babelians and their quest for fame is turned into a shame-full babbling "signifying nothing." But the name that came initially, the first one chronologically and originary, is intrinsically a promise: the city *can* become the Gate of the Divine, and a highway can be opened "from Egypt to Assyria" (Isa 19:23).

---

anti-Semitism creating Jewish identity: Jews are constrained to be Jews by anti-Semites. See Sartre, *Anti-Semite and Jew.*

27. It is up to the following generations after the Shoah to "add a barb" (Elie Wiesel) to the barbed wire, or to eliminate one at a time. The whole of (Israel's) history is the perpetual confrontation with the "Babels" erected against innocence by "the wicked."

The Tower of Babel and Freud's "Fort-da" Child

Charles Winquist reminds us of Freud's experience with the little so-called Fort-da child.[28] To the child, the disappearance or reappearance of the mother found a substitutive materiality in a reel with a string attached. Throwing away the reel (*fort/*"disappearance") was compensated by retrieving it (*da/*"reappearance") thanks to the string. The "Fort-da" child had thus a device for controlling the mother's feared absences.[29]

Analyzing Freud's report on his grandson Ernst, Jacques Derrida notes "that what in the child's 'game' appears and disappears does indeed include the child himself or his image. He is part of his *Spielzeug*."[30] In transposition, by splitting language, that is, a "unity of a dispersible multiplicity" (125), God himself or his image is also appearing and disappearing. What happens to humanity in Gen 11:8–9 ricochets upon the divine author of the occurrence. Genesis 11:8–9 is as much an act of power as a sign of weakness. "Power is made perfect in weakness" (2 Cor 12:9, NRSV), said St. Paul—a truth that applies here if only because the end of the Tower of Babel story is not an end, but a beginning.

A further parallelism with the story of Babel can be drawn. Freud had come to the conclusion about the child's behavior that "it was a game." Derrida observes that here Freud "interpreted—and *named*" a phenomenon that reminds us of something similar in J's story.[31] What is called "Confusion" in Gen 11:9 corresponds to "game" in the "Fort-da" case. The crucial difference, however, is that in the latter: "What's involved is the *re-* in general, returning in general, and disappearance/ reappearance . . . in other words the self-presentation of re-presentation . . . the disappearance and reappearance of *oneself*, the object coming back into *his own*, himself."[32]

But the fate of Babel in J's story does not involve a *re-*, unless perhaps eschatologically. For the duration of history, Babel's disappearance is without return (but not without an ominous presence hidden behind absence). Nonetheless, there is still something of a parallel with our story in the "Fort-da" Freudian report, for in the end and somewhat regretfully,

28. Winquist, "Body, Text, and Imagination," 42.

29. Freud's analysis of the "Fort-da" episode is found in chap. 2 of *Beyond the Pleasure Principle*.

30. Derrida, "Coming into One's Own," 125–26.

31. Ibid., 126.

32. Ibid., 132.

Freud adds that the *Fortgehen* ("going away") was more often repeated by the child and "was staged as a game in itself," as Derrida says,[33] thus reaching completeness in itself. Furthermore, in "still another interpretation," Freud envisages the sending away (of father and mother) as a way for the child "to revenge himself," an interpretation that invites us to wonder whether the divine chastisement of the Babelians, like the *Fortgehen*, can be construed as a revenge (see Gen 11:6).

Why does J evoke such a fundamental "discontent" at all? Freud accounts for the discontentment by claiming that it arises from an impulse to repeat a situation of displeasure in order to master it and, consequently, to convert into pleasure. In transposition, the Yahwist imagines the origins of Babylon as a distressful event, which, characteristically, he disguises into a myth of cosmic origin while furnishing the clues necessary for identification: *Babel*, ziggurat, human dispersion, and plurality of languages.

Exilic prophets straightforwardly confronted sixth-century Babylon and forecasted its total destruction. As for the Yahwist, he makes a detour by means of the mythization of Babel and its "tower," just as the dreamer proceeds in dreaming. In this particular case, the prophets represent the Cs (conscious), and J the Ucs (unconscious). J's camouflage allowed him to present a universalizing paradigm for human hubris and its unavoidable destruction.

We can speculate that the break of the string, that is to say the demise of Babel—would occasion a loss of meaning and create a deep frustration as the deconstruction of the materiality of the game would ricochet upon what the game stood for. With the interruption of Babel, the loss is much more than of a city and its tower (see Isa 13:20–22; Jer 50:13, 23, 39–40; 51:26, 29, 37, 43, 62). Babylon now means dispersion and confusion: any dispersion and any confusion. The "mother" has disappeared for good, and no string will ever be able to bring her back. The mother was after all a bad and untrustworthy mother; her dissipation shows that she was a whore (cf. Jer 50:12; Rev 17:1, 5, 15; 19:2).

In this case (potentially, for the "Fort-da" child; actually, for the Babelians), the child is orphaned; humanity leaves in all directions, for it has lost the Shinar anchorage and feels disoriented.[34] Former sham com-

---

33. Ibid., 137.

34. Winquist is right to broaden the scope. He draws a parallel, an "uncomfortable one," he says, between the failure to control the mother's disappearance when the string

munication crumbles; no one understands anyone else. Jean-Paul Sartre would call this an accident, but it is much more than an accident. It is a revelation. The human logorrhea communicates nothing; it means nothing, short of spelling out the Name of God.

Now that the human languages have become an archipelago of tongues, how will the name of God be spelled? By whom? Where? How? When?—*we-'im lo' 'aršayw 'eymathay*? (If not now, then when?) J's response is Abraham. The history of Israel is the history of a people whose "babbling," instead of "signifying nothing," dramatically attempts to invoke the name (cf. Gen 4:26). They are the Semites, the carriers of the name. To that extent, the deconstruction of their theological and anthropological constructions shows that they are *innocent*. In Babylon, they did not prostrate at the top of the ziggurat; they were coerced into the Babylonian captivity, but they did not allow themselves to be made captives of imperial illusions. They alone, as *personae non gratae*, were thrown into the furnaces erected by a brainwashed and brainwashing empire, but they outlived the fire, for there was with them a presence that no power could reduce to an absence (Daniel 3).

In contrast to the innocent ones emerging from the furnace alive and vindicated, Babel's iron wall crumbles, and the guilty Babelians are burned, like Nebuchadnezzar's henchmen in Dan 3:22 (cf. Isa 14:3–23; Jer 50:32; 51:32, 35, 58).

The Quest for the Beginning/End

In what precedes, I have made frequent references to psychoanalysis, whose characteristic is the quest for the analysand's beginnings. In a similar vein, the Tower of Babel myth is a retrieval of "events" that belong with the narratives about the primeval era. All attempts at sundering Genesis 11 from this context are ill advised. Here as in J's other exploratory inroads into the originary (Genesis 2–11*), the problem par excellence is a quest for the beginning. Now, the analysand is as much J himself as every one in his audience. Actually, the redundant "all the earth" in the narrative is a clear indication of the universal dimension of the analysis. The "beginning" concerns the whole earth, not just a selected tribe or

---

breaks, on one hand, and, on the other, the scramble of theology's game "mastering the disappearance of God" when realizing that its language is unconnected ("Body, Text, and Imagination," 49). J's choice of a myth as the vessel of language is thus felicitous since myth is essentially metaphorical, as all theological language should be.

nation. We cannot overemphasize the remarkable literary and ideological phenomenon of the biblical revelation starting so powerfully with an *in illo tempore* when not only was "there . . . no shrub of the field and no grass, no rain and no man to till the ground" (Gen 2:4–5), but no people of Israel!

A bard of his people, the Israelite J explores a domain that predates the conscious identity of Israel. He uncovers their unconscious, that is, according to a dictionary of psychology: "a part of the mind containing repressed instincts and their representative wishes, ideas, and images that are not accessible to direct examination, its functions being governed by the mechanisms of the primary process, especially condensation and displacement."[35]

So, J is looking for himself, and we as his readers are looking for ourselves.[36] Using the psychoanalytical model further, it must be said that the beginning is essentially elusive and already loaded with meanings of its own. Thus our mentor J takes us first to the Garden of Eden and its problematic trial of innocence, then to another starting point with a rivalry between brothers that eventuates in a fratricidal onslaught against innocence. Sequentially, J strikes our imagination with such a collective human wickedness that only a general flood of water can cleanse (Genesis 6–9). Eventually, the "beginning" takes the form of an imperial megalomania, boasting about its primordial importance . . . The series could have not ended here, and could have continued ad infinitum, for the unconscious is never fully unveiled; but in each unit, a beginning is decoded. What the human religious, philosophical, scientific, physical, and psychological constructions wanted to conceal by repression are revealed for what they actually are, and they are deconstructed. They all have been epitomized in the Gen 3:5 formula, *sicut Deus* ("like God"). This "sickness to death" (Kierkegaard), of course, takes a thousand and one forms, from competing with God's wisdom to murdering to systemic violence to totalitarian hubris . . . This apparently bottomless pit is endlessly filled by the Danaides' bottomless vessels, as punishment for the murders of their husbands.

The central Freudian principle of repression also takes a thousand and one forms; it always finds a new possible disguise for wrapping up the beginning. One of its favorite ways is to pretend that the beginning

35. Colman, *Dictionary of Psychology*, 766.
36. "To understand oneself in front of the text," said Paul Ricoeur in "The Hermeneutical Function of Distanciation," 88.

is but a trifling thing, unworthy of mention and certainly of recall. The Yahwist did not accept this cop-out. At the origin of humanity (hence of Israel among its peers), there are unconscionable and indelible acts, sort of originary spots that characterize "all the earth" and each individual as being in need of purification and redemption (see Gen 8:21). Freud thought of an originary massacre of the father by his sons.[37] This is not part of J's primeval stories, but the principle remains the same: humanity's origin and atavism (so to speak) is shameful and makes us all guilty, if only by idleness and indifference. For the ethical is not natural. What is natural in humanity is neurosis.[38] Morality is an option that runs counter to the innate human propensity for sluggishness and self-gratification. The saint is the living demonstration that the others are inexcusable not to be saints with him or her.[39]

Not surprisingly, what psychoanalysis discovers in each analysand is a repressed guilt, an individual desire to build a "tower" so aloof as to be incomparable and unassailable. Now, what psychoanalysis uncovers in the individual, the Yahwist has decoded at the level of "all the earth."[40]

Within such "reminiscences" of the origin, there is always a *before* the beginning, as we recalled above with the quotation of Gen 2:4–5.[41] For Freud, the *before* is when the father was alive and well, and the sons were not (yet) in competition with him. Because this precedes the beginning, it designates an ahistorical ideal that escapes the paradigmatic quality of the tale "from the beginning." It constitutes the indispensable background, and proleptically the ultimate foreground. The latter occurs when the history of the human guilt is over. Then the father and his sons are reconciled (see Mal 4:6 on the turning of the hearts of parents to their children and the hearts of children to their parents), and scattered humanity is reunited with their disorganized speech healed into one language again. See Zeph 3:9 on God's purifying the speech of all peoples so that they spell out the

37. See Freud, *Totem and Taboo.*

38. Characteristically, a symptom of schizophrenia is disorganized speech, a phenomenon that is not foreign to Babel's outcome.

39. That is why the saint unwillingly unleashes nauseous "Cainic" forces like Auschwitz. Richard L. Rubenstein has sensed this correctly, although he comes to unwarranted conclusions (see *After Auschwitz;* and *The Religious Imagination*).

40. Lévi-Strauss insists on the parallel between psychoanalysis and ethnology; see *Structural Anthropology.*

41. As the story of Babel starts with a *waw* ("and") in the very first word *wayyehi,* while purporting to report a beginning/origin, it invites one to think of the possibility to place another beginning before the beginning.

divine Name and serve him in a unified effort (note this last term, "effort"; cf. also Mal 1:11).

The Priestly composer (another "psychoanalyst") said that before all beginning is God, a declaration about incipience that the Gospel of John adopts under the form of the divine *logos*. But what looks like a metaphysical construct, hence in need of being deconstructed, from the Priestly or the Johannine *logos* is the opposite of it. For the *logos* here is *life*, life with a name, an identity; so that Word—or "language," as in Gen 11:1—is *rhema* ("flow"). Within the context of the alternation of J and P,[42] P does not detract from but rather contributes to J's vision. Both the Priestly liturgical statement about origins and the Yahwistic myths about the primeval era are less attempts at mirroring the beginning than they are plunges into the flow. For, once the liturgy is over and the myth is told, nothing is definitively told. The only real telling is only announced. The authentic telling starts with the life of Abraham, which itself is properly unutterable and unfinalizable (Bakhtin; the "short stories" about Abraham do not amount to a biography). I am unable to tell my biography, although *graph* tells us that there is *bio* only when it is *graphed*. A fortiori, Abraham's biography— or Jesus's—is impossible. The writing of the cycle of Abraham leaves *traces* of a presence of Abraham, which is also an absence.

In terms of the Tower of Babel story with its backdrop of the one language spoken by all, the *trace* becomes conspicuous with the actual multiplicity of languages in the world. Outlined against the cacophony of languages, as a kind of watermark, the one language is both present and absent. Babel is the hollow side of a trace, for its claim to be the beginning is only a hoax. The Babel beginning starts with the conjunction "and" (11:1, "And it happened that . . .)! When the monolith of Babel goes eventually through its deconstruction, the emperor's nakedness is exposed. The truth is that the great technological achievements of Babylon hid a ghost town. Now, if even "the most beautiful kingdom" of Babylon (Isa 13:19) is a smokescreen, what will be said of all the other constructions of ours? J shows that at the universal level, humanity as a whole repeats the individual flight from the truth, as charged by psychoanalysis. From repression to repression, from camouflage to camouflage, from delusion to delusion, we build impressive towers behind which to hide our pitiful nudity (see Gen 3:8).

---

42. See above chap. 1 ("Introductory Remarks").

In the preceding volumes of the present trilogy, I have strongly advanced the idea that J is building an anthropology. Anthropology, I said, is the other face of theology. It is the essential viewpoint to speak about God, because the human being—any human being, but especially the one called "Son of Man"—is a trace of the divine presence/absence. *Qua* God's images, women and men are theophanic, and each ethical move of theirs is an epiphany. Such is the glory of those "You have made a little less than divine, adorned with glory and majesty" (Ps 8:6). But then, within this context, any derogation from the inner *imago* becomes deicidal. Genesis says that ever since the expulsion from the Garden of Eden, humanity has more and more gravely stumbled, to the point that the Creator himself came to despair about his creation.

No one more than J has been conscious of this. As we arrive at the end of this chapter in our exploration of the Yahwistic work, it must be said that J went even one step further in Genesis 11. He deconstructed his own anthropology, showing that the greatest human achievements and even the language for their inscription are like many escapes, denials, and repressions. "Vanity of vanities," there is no valid anthropology and consequently no valid theology. In Gen 11:1–9 "theology" is epitomized in a divine move from above to below—in stark contrast with the Babelians' plot to build up to heaven on high. The divine descent is completed by Babel's deconstruction, that is, by the dethronement of "majestic" humanity.

Theologically and anthropologically, this picture leaves nonetheless much to be desired. Certainly a God who comes down from heaven to look at human vanity is no valid theology; and a scattered humanity incapable of "translation" is no valid anthropology. Did the Yahwist write this with a smirk? The trait is so mundane in the midst of the deadly serious situation of the Judean exile that we are left to wonder. On this score, again, the theology of Gen 11:1–9 is about an absence after a former presence that left a trace of its passage. The only undeniable statement about God here is the people scattered and the language fragmented. The divine descent was a provisory reconstruction; it is destined to be dismissed—and replaced by another construction, to be replaced ad infinitum.

J's "meager" theology in Genesis 11 is surprising, for the Yahwist had accustomed us to a more sophisticated way of speaking of God: say, as Creator, Judge and Dispenser of justice, Exterminator, and Care-Taker . . . Here, by contrast, YHWH appears rather puny, and his deliberation with himself in 11:6–7 does not help to shore up his greatness. Given J's poetic mastery, J could have displayed a much more adroit skill at this point. It is to be wondered indeed whether J is using here an irony folding upon itself before addressing it bitterly to Babel. At any rate, both protagonists, the divine and the human, come out bruised from the confrontation.[43]

But this is only scratching the surface. We must realize that the reading process is an interpretation of an interpretation, namely, the reader's interpretation of J's interpretation. As we said above, "The myth of the Babel's construction is J's story, and thus he at a minimum participates in the narrated events, which . . . he transforms into facts." In doing so, J appears as omniscient (see 11:6!). He "knows" about God's descent as a *deus ex machina,* because he has witnessed (prophetically?) a miraculous reversal of fortune in the fate of Babylon. God has mixed up the Babylonian data; he did (or he will) disperse the Babelians and confuse their means of communication. Indirectly, J proclaims the innocence of the exiles and restores their hopes.

For his myth making, J works inductively. From empirical data on the planes of space and history, J proceeds to retrieve their origin through an imaginative reconstruction. This, of course, is true of any myth, as any myth is interpretation. Now, in the terms of Freud, the interpretation of interpretation resembles a translation from one language to another more intelligible.[44] We could also say that the interpreter is substituting a text for a preexisting text. Both "texts" are justifiably deconstructible because the "facts" they report are inevitably distorted (the Freudian *Entstellung*). I am referring to the *Traumdeutung* (*The Interpretation of Dreams*) because like dreams that resuscitate our childhood and desires, myth intends to uncover our collective drives.[45]

Now in both dream work and mythmaking, the most puzzling element is the intrinsic *censorship*. The J myth came into its final composition through a censorship. Decoding the latter is of utmost importance. Thus, it seems clear that the mythmaker proceeds from a preconceived negative judgment against Babel/Babylon. The standpoint is one of a gravely frustrated Judean in exile, vexed by the problem of YHWH's *impotence,*

43. But see above Lévi-Strauss's statement about naïve elements in myths (cited in chap. 2, above n. 125). On God and J's bruising, as in Genesis 32, see above in chap. 4 the text around n. 99.

44. Freud, *The Interpretation of Dreams*, 277.

45. The individual's dream is his/her private mythology, while the myth is the daydream of the whole people, so that Sophocles's *Oedipus* or Shakespeare's *Hamlet* demand to be interpreted like dreams.

whether temporary or essential. Babylon is a locked gate, a "*bab*," barring the way to the understanding of God, "*el.*" By sheer historical accident, the understanding of YHWH henceforth comes through an understanding of Babel, but then Babel's gate is flung open.

J's myth is thus the opposite of impartiality. It is heavily charged with its author's bias and even hatred.[46] According to the "reality principle," Babylon appears as indestructible and its construction as unstoppable. But the worm is in the fruit—at least that much is wished by the Yahwist, whose story comes as a curse on Babel. Babel's construction will be interrupted by a divine intervention (the Freudian *Wunscherfüllung*). So is the assurance of faith, for if God would not come down from heaven, who knows how far human schemes would take them (11:6)? Up to the dethronement of God (11:4a)? Would they inflate their hubris to the point of substituting their own name for the Name of glory (11:4b)? God will assuredly stop them. He will give them a name, but it is a name of shame and of confusion. He will disperse them across the whole earth (11:9).

The Yahwistic curse on Babel is also a prayer on behalf of Israel. History is not engulfed in Babylon; after Babel, after the deluge, comes Abraham.

Because Gen 11:1–9 is the expression of a desire, a retrospective light is shed on our earlier decoding of its symbolization. As we saw, it partly refers to sexuality: a feminine city penetrated by a phallic tower. The city of Babylon is essentially a display of power, and power (especially wielded violently) is but an aspect of the sexual drive. Whether or not the "tower" stands at the compositional center of Genesis 11, it is not irrelevant to note that the myth has impressed all of its readers as "the Tower of Babel." What characterizes Babylon is this immense erected phallus, emblem of its hubristic might. But, soon it will be castrated to impotence. Miming his Lord's response in Ps 37:13 (see also 2:4; 59:9), J "laughs at the wicked, for he sees that their day is coming" (NRSV).

Where J is certainly ironic in Gen 11:9 is when he comes with a "palaeonymy" (Derrida) on the name *Babel*, putting it "under erasure" so that the hinted sense of "Confusion" emerges. Were it not said sarcastically, the pun would pretend to be science and, consequently, would discredit the myth as of little value. It remains, however, that the very dénouement of

---

46. For if true spiritual love is able to apprehend the loved one's *entelechy*, as Frankl says (*The Doctor and the Soul*, 120), spiritual hatred is also able to discern the enemy's waning and dissolution.

the story is built on the shaky ground of a misnomer. J's Judean audience or readership in Babylon felt a pleasurable relief to share in the mocking the oppressive empire, but they knew also their powerlessness against the "real world." Innocence was well and truly in captivity.

The deconstruction of the palaeonymy on Babel stresses the use of irony as a weapon of resistance—sometimes the last one left to the victim—facing the tormentors.[47] The Yahwist, as a fine pedagogue, has created a myth to galvanize the exiles' resistance and to shape hope in the coming restoration.

The trace left by the myth of Babel is indelible. It has struck the imagination of innumerable people ever since it was composed. In spite of or thanks to its intrinsic humility and self-deconstruction, the tower of Babel story has imposed itself as one of the major myths of humanity. Whether known superficially or in depth, it has spurred the feeling that in this story we face a profound wisdom about our souls.

Babel und Bibel?

Some contemporary scholars invite us to read Gen 11:1–9 from a Babylonian standpoint. According to them (I mean Bernhard Anderson, Ellen van Wolde, Theodor Hiebert, and others), the Babel story is a celebration of Babylon as the cradle of universal civilizations. In their exegetical stance, we can detect a remnant of the now-obsolete *Babel und Bibel* School. Between 1880 and 1890 Hermann Gunkel, with Albert Eichhorn, William Wrede, and Wilhelm Bousset, founded a new approach to biblical study: *Die Religionsgeschichtliche Schule* or the "history of religion school." Of particular importance for our discussion here is Gunkel's conception of the biblical text as a point of arrival after a long evolution going back to prebiblical times and peoples. Although Gunkel demanded a more balanced approach than the pan-Babylonian advocates,[48] the task of the exegete is to retrieve the primeval meaning of the traditions developed further by Israel and consigned now in the Bible. In all this, the blatant absence of the text's foreground will have to be dealt with.

47. True, not every exile felt tormented in Babylon, only those who were religiously frustrated after being uprooted from the "holy city" and its temple—the very opposite of the unholy city of Babylon and its ziggurat. From my own experience of growing up in Belgium, I can say that during the dark years of the Nazi occupation of Europe, the invaders were the butt of our sarcasm.

48. See Gunkel, *Israel and Babylon*.

As regards the Babel story, its topographical setting in "Shinar" directs our investigation toward Mesopotamia—to the satisfaction of the history of religion school. This *Sitz im Leben*, it is true, is of crucial importance, as even Israel's acknowledged patriarchs and matriarchs come originally from that region of the world. Hiebert, for one, draws from this datum an argument in favor of his interpretation. But Mesopotamia is a country *from which* the forebears of Israel depart, *westward*. When the movement is reversed and Babylon becomes the place *to which* "all the earth" and particularly the Judeans go, it is historically a land of exile, not a return to the "native land" (Gen 11:28; 24:7). Such a dialectical conception of the country of Mesopotamia parallels the view of the land of Egypt in the Joseph tradition, for example.[49] Israel, squeezed between the tremendous powers of the one and the other, claimed to get a footing in each of them. Typically, Genesis 10 mentions Shinar and Egypt in succession (vv. 8–12 [Nimrod], and 13ff. [Mizraïm, then the Philistines, Canaan, Sidon]). Nevertheless here in **P**, the perspective is entirely different, displaying a partly taxonomic, nonparadigmatic composition.

Much of the history of religion approach to Gen 11:1–9 depends upon its understanding of the first part of the tale as *positive*. Then the "one language with similar words [for all]," the plan to build a city with a high tower, the building of Babel itself as the grand settlement of early humanity, and the cultural "bricks and bitumen" replacing the natural stone and mortar are considered as describing a pure origin, a la Jean-Jacques Rousseau. It is such a pristine beginning that a later redactor perverted, and he described the dismantling of the city on the model of the fall.

Jacques Derrida, for one, polemicizes against this so-called "violent hierarchy," which privileges one term over another (like pure over impure, original over derivative)—a characteristic of Western metaphysics, that is, a Manichaean binary philosophy, that Derrida aims to subvert.[50] Along a deconstructive line of thought, Derrida sees the dispersion as an act of God that "interrupts also the colonial violence or the linguistic

49. There is nothing to redeem Egypt in the fact that Joseph married an Egyptian, the daughter of a priest of On, and sired through her Manasseh and Ephraim (Gen 41:45, 50–52). But Isaiah prophesies that there will eventually be a highway joining Assyria and Egypt (19:23).

50. Western metaphysics "asserts a distinction between the origin and the deviation, the proper and the regression," dichotomies that deconstruction opposes (Sherwood, *The Prostitute and the Prophet*, 161). Derrida speaks of "the lost or impossible presence of the absent origin" ("Structure, Sign and Play," 292).

imperialism"[51] present in part 1 of the story. YHWH is the "deconstructor of the Tower of Babel."[52]

So the dispersion of the humans and their languages is to be seen first and foremost as a punishment; the text emphasizes the lack of mutual understanding—rather a tomb than a womb! Again, we find the same conclusion under the pen of P in Genesis 10 (see vv. 5, 20, 31). In other words, viewing the story retrospectively, an initially common language did not denote a unity transcending diversity, but a unity without diversity.[53] What will be hoped for in the history of religion (*Religionsgeschichte*) is a unity that goes beyond diversity, a "second" unique language (see, e.g., Acts 2:6); that is how *Endzeit* ("end time") is no mere duplication of *Urzeit* ("primeval time").[54]

Another pillar of the *Religionsgeschichtliche Schule* reading of our tale is interpreting the "tower with its top in heaven" as mere hyperbole. We shall note the neutralization of the symbolic meaning(s) and consequently of the very relevance of the tower. We have seen above several textual elements that militate against such a minimization process. The evacuation of the symbolic function is also the evacuation of the readers of the text. The symbol or the poetic image, says Gaston Bachelard, "nous exprime en nous faisant ce qu'elle exprime" ("expresses us by shaping us according to its expression").[55] Ricoeur adds, "le mouvement qui m' entraîne vers le sens second m'*assimile* à ce qui est dit, me rend participant de ce qui m' est annoncé" ("the movement that drives me towards the second meaning does *assimilate* me to what is said; it makes me a participant of what is announced to me.")[56] "Le symbole donne à penser" ("The symbol gives food to the thought"), said Kant, followed by Ricoeur.

I now turn to the deconstructionist quarters for further arguments. Deconstructive reading stresses the "otherness" of the tower. The Babel tower *is* a tower and *is not* what towers generally are; in that sense, it *is not*

51. Derrida, "Des Tours de Babel," 253.

52. Derrida, *The Ear of the Other*, 102.

53. Bakhtin—who knew experientially what he was speaking about—mentions the "system of unitary language" as "an expression of the centripetal forces of language . . . opposed to the realities of heteroglossia" (*The Dialogic Imagination*, 269–70).

54. Hiebert's contentment with the dispersion as creative of cultures and civilizations must be tempered by the fact that such had already started with Cain's fratricide and errantry. Cain and the Cainites build cities and develop industries—but they are not exonerated!

55. Bachelard, *La poétique de l'espace*, 7.

56. Ricoeur, *De l'interprétation: essai sur Freud*, 40 [= *Freud and Philosophy* 32].

a tower, as the height of this one is in heaven. As Scharlemann says, "This depiction of the unity of being and non-being in the [tower description] is the way in which the narrative speaks of the otherness that is the real referent."[57] If so, the otherness of the Tower of Babel is first real before it is mythic. That is, the myth of Babel originates in a nonmythic experience of otherness that can be divine or demonic. So, in the episode of the burning bush—to take an example after Scharlemann—the otherness was God's. In the case of the tower of Babel, the otherness is of a humanity-that-wants-to-be-god. In their attempt to get rid of the Living God, humans have no other choice but to ape God. It is their way to be other.[58]

The basic experience of otherness, instead of pointing to a possible foreign background for the tale (say, to Mesopotamian traditions), does point to the ongoing-ness of the human experience. Hence, otherness becomes the foreground of the text. The history of religion school simply bypasses this crucial aspect. The historical interpretations of the Tower of Babel story in both Judaism and Christianity are ignored in favor of an alleged and speculative original meaning of the tradition reported in Gen 11:1–9.[59] In other words, the stream of signifiers is blocked at some early, indeed so-called original, point, when the signified Babylon was filling the horizon by its presence. But deconstructionism[60] shows the absence of such absolute presence.[61] The sign is never anything else but the sign of a sign, ad infinitum. "There is nothing outside of the text," writes Odell-Scott. "Interpretation yields interpretation."

Indeed, we must—with Burnett, for instance—distinguish between event and fact.[62] "Events happen; facts are constituted by linguistic description."[63] J, on the basis of events in the sixth century, has constructed facts, that is, interpretations without which the events would evaporate. The facts of the Babel tower started to exist under the pen of J. They are J's vision of the events (that is, of the existence of Babylon, of its ziggurat, of its grandiosity, of its imperialism, and the like). There were in existence competitive historiographies of Babel. It is, as a matter of

57. Scharlemann, "The Being of God," 104.

58. The profession of atheism comes to mind. The definition of *atheism* must necessarily be theological!

59. Let us note also that the sarcastic and polemical accent of the J text is entirely missed.

60. Odell-Scott, "Deconstruction," 59.

61. Or rather, in Derrida's parlance, the "erasure of presence" (*Of Grammatology*, 139).

62. Burnett, "Historiography," 111.

63. White, "'Figuring the Nature of the Times Deceased,'" 35.

fact, historiographically possible to look at Babel as being, for instance, the cradle of civilization in the ancient Near East and beyond. Then the chronicler is dealing with another set of facts, *not* the one created by J. The legitimacy of this other set of facts is not in question. To another game, its proper rules. To another game, these facts are the proper rules. In the comparison between J's and the non-J's interpretations of the events, the ethical criterion is important: which one is able to become paradigmatic and change lives?[64]

The voluntary ignorance of the foreground of a biblical text denotes a misunderstanding of that text. For text is never "in-itself," but becomes text through interpretation. "Interpretation is not secondary to a more primary original, but is always an interpretation of what itself is already an interpretation."[65] Already in 1985, Hubert Bost stated, "Le texte *s'effectue*, il se réalise dans la lecture . . . il *est* l'histoire de sa lecture."[66]

Excursus on Ibn Ezra's Commentary (Twelfth Century)

The matter of a work's author has become a major issue in psychoanalysis, deconstruction, and postmodern thinking in general. This is especially true since the 1968 article of Roland Barthes called "The Death of the Author."[67] It now belongs to general consciousness that any text both reveals much of the author's sociopolitical and psychoreligious milieu and biases, and distances itself from the author by transcending his or her original intention. An author's consciousness never fully realizes this about him- or herself. Their text, therefore, is somewhat autonomous in the image of the individual's subconscious or unconscious.[68]

This awareness must be paramount in our inquiry about Abraham ben Meïr Ibn Ezra's approach to the Bible and particularly to the Tower of Babel story. This excursus finds its motivation in the fact that some scholars have touted Ibn Ezra's commentary on Gen 11:1–9 as heralding their own history of religion reading of the text. As a matter of fact, the

64. On this, see Adam, *What Is Postmodern Biblical Criticism?* 45–60.

65. Taylor, "Text as Victim", 67.

66. Bost, *Babel*, 118. ("The text *is a process of effectuation*. It realizes itself by being read . . . It *is* the history of its reading.") Speaking of Bernhard Anderson's position, Bost says that it is "plus un souci d' éthique raciale qu'une mise à l' écoute authentique du texte" (that "it reflects his concern regarding racial ethics rather than an authentic attention to the text itself" [83 n. 90]).

67. Barthes, *Image, Music, Text*, 142–49.

68. See chap. 4 above, especially the first section.

Jewish commentator's withholding judgment regarding the relative absence of divine punishment of the Babelians in Gen 11:8–9 is noticeable. He writes, "God scattered the people for their own benefit." But, as we saw above, Abravanel (fifteenth century) added that Ibn Ezra's comment must be understood as showing that a *punishment* may concomitantly be a blessing.[69]

Let us further analyze Ibn Ezra as an author. In his entire career, Ibn Ezra remained faithful to his proclaimed anti-allegorical, anti-midrashic, and anti-rabbinic method of interpretation. He is a grammarian. Anything the biblical text does not say *expressis verbis* is looked at with suspicion. The Bible is no cryptic document. He tends to ignore even obvious allusions. Now to understand Ibn Ezra's reaction to former (midrashic) readings of Genesis 11, we must remember his logic that in the absence of the law, the Babel builders can be seen as if "they did not know [God's will for humanity's dispersion]."[70] God, however, felt he had to stop the construction on the ground that nothing would be impossible for humanity to do (see 11:6).[71]

Ibn Ezra's inclusion of Noah and Abraham among the builders of Babel runs clearly against the grain of his grammatical method. There is no clue in the text that suggests such a patriarchal contribution to the construction. The rabbinic view of Nimrod as the leader of the Babelians would have found more solid ground after Gen 10:8–12.[72] Unwittingly Ibn Ezra unveils therewith his hidden agenda, namely, his intent to declare innocent his only surviving son who converted to Islam: He was like them "who did not know [God's will]"; even Noah and Abraham were blind enough to be counted among the builders of Babel!

But eventually Ibn Ezra must surrender to the obvious and confess that the dispersion is (also) negative: "Different religions create jealousy and hatred among people. The same is true regarding the different languages."[73] So, in the end, the conclusion of his reading of Gen 11:1–9 is similar to the rabbinic one.

---

69. See Ibn Ezra, *Genesis*. For a dialectical conception of punishment and blessing, see *b. Sanhedrin* 71b.

70. Ibn Ezra, *Genesis*, 140.

71. Ibid., 141.

72. On the Jewish traditional view of Nimrod (alternatively, Nebuchadnezzar) and Babel, see *Gen. Rab.* 11:3, in parallel with *3 Bar.* 3:5 (cf. Isa 14:3–6; 47:6); *PRE* 24; Josephus *Ant.* 1.113–14; *Tg. Neof.* Gen 11:4; *b. Ḥullin* 89a.

73. Ibn Ezra, *Genesis*, 141.

CHAPTER SEVEN

Conclusion

THE STORY OF THE Tower of Babel concludes the Yahwist's series of mythic narratives on the primeval era. Such a privileged setting into the protohistorical fresco is itself already emphatic. It compares with the initial setting of the myth of creation in Genesis 2–3.

Several aspects of the Tower of Babel composition are readily imposing themselves upon the reader. For one thing, the tale is extremely short (nine verses) and this trimness is a warning to the interpreter: all unnecessary ornaments have been sternly pruned out, so that the resulting text is a radical condensation and is highly charged. Second, this parable of sorts is strictly balanced with two parts in mutual contrasted correspondence, a kind of construction followed by a deconstruction. Third, the rhetorical structure here has reached a summit of perfection. J's mastery of language becomes the general thesis of the myth as expressed in Gen 11:1 ("one language") and in v. 9 ("YHWH confounded [their] speech"). Fourth, the subject matter concerns a well-known city of the ancient Near East, Babel/Babylon, and the author's sarcasm is unmistakable: Babel/Confusion.

This latter point raises an important problem: Is Babylon the "setting in life" of the composition? In spite of the "classic" historical criticism that dates the Yahwist's work in the time of King Solomon (ninth century BCE), the answer is yes. Starting with the story of Adam and Eve, and continuing with Cain and Abel, I have stressed, after other contemporary scholars, a (post)exilic date for J. Genesis 11:1–9 is written in reaction to the profound impression the city of Babylon and its ziggurat made on the Yahwist and his people in exile. Babylon is "the east" that reappears so significantly in the primeval stories. It happens to be an immense empire, a universal power of which the physical and linguistic concentration (see vv. 1, 2, 4) is an overwhelming wonder but also a threat for a Judean uprooted, whose city and temple have been destroyed by Babylon. This constitutes the sociopolitical setting of the J myth.

The Tower of Babel is a myth; it was mostly created by J, although there were extant ancient Near Eastern mythic elements that J may have used. The story fulfills the four main criteria of myth making. First, it takes its audience to the *in illo tempore*, dear to Mircea Eliade. Second, it presents a divine intervention in human affairs. Third, its function is in part etiological. And fourth, the tale is highly symbolic, even paradigmatic. Furthermore, that the Babel centerpiece here is a historical reality poses no problem. The Mesopotamian city plays a similar mythic role in Babylonian myths.

To start with the fourth criterion of the mythic, namely, its symbolic dimension, there are throughout the story of Babel signifiers that orient readers to the paradigmatic quality of the myth. Babel is Babylon and more on axes of both space and time; so the "tower" is a particular temple-ziggurat and, beyond, a token of the human attempt to snatch immortality and self-deification from "heaven." The original one language says something about an original innocence of sorts, but also about an imperialistic, linguistic imposition on "all the earth": a fact illustrated historically in the insatiable expansionism of the Babylonian empire. In short, mythic meaning is overflowing, and the eventual deconstruction of the human hubristic constructions speaks volumes about the endless human endeavors that never reach their goal, expressed in Genesis 3 as becoming like God. The Babelians' hidden agenda is to supersede God's Name with their name (11:4).

On the etiological level (the third criterion), the story has two purposes. It "explains" the origin of the multiple human languages as well as the human dispersion "over the face of the whole earth" (v. 9), but also, in a sarcastic vein, the deeper meaning of the city's identity.[1] Babylon is not the "Gate to the Divine" it claims to be, but a gateway to confusion/chaos. On both these scores, J does not pretend to be "scientific" (or even historical). His etiologies are presented tongue in cheek—something we should not confuse with a joke, for the ultimate aim is dead serious.

As to the divine intervention in human affairs (the second criterion above), we may be surprised by its present naïve form. We were accus-

---

1. The word "explanation" must be used with a caveat. See above p. 66 n. 128 (with Jean-Jacques Rousseau's statement) and p. 82 n. 46 (with Malinowski's).

tomed to a more sophisticated theology in the J literary source. But the feature fits perfectly the mythic genre of the story. Here God comes down to earth from heaven (the desired point of the tower's completion: v. 4). He then makes a more or less ambiguous declaration that amounts to a *procès d'intention* (a so-far ungrounded accusation). Rather than anticlimactic, vv. 5–6 are a further manifestation of J's irony. Note the divine countermovement reversing the Babelians' climbing up to heaven (v. 4).

Self-evidently, the story is set in the ostensible temporality of *in illo tempore*, that is, in a time before time, in a proto-historical era that belongs more to imagination than to history proper. We now meet the first criterion enunciated above. True, there actually was a Babel/Babylon with a huge ziggurat. There was also historically a megalomaniac ambition to subdue the whole world to its imperial dictation. True also, at some point of the human evolution, there happened a geographical dispersion and an explosion of regional languages. But all this fades in comparison with J's purpose to offer a *paradigmatic* symbolism; "des tours de Babel," as Jacques Derrida says. Inasmuch as Babel stands for a manifestation of evil (as it does in the whole Bible), the empire's survival—Babel is deconstructed but not destroyed in Genesis 11—demonstrates the historic "persistence of evil" (Jon Levenson). After denouncing the manifestation of evil by means of representative individuals, such as Adam and Eve, Cain and Lamech, Ham and Canaan, J tackles here collective evil (as he had earlier in the story of the flood). Individually or collectively, humans are building shrines (sometimes cities) in celebration of their own names (v. 4), and towers to dupe their own mortality. Babel/Babylon is not only "confusion"; its complex is also emblematic of perniciousness.

Thus time is allegedly transcended. The other axis, space, plays an amazingly central role in the J myth. The emphasis of the text on "there" or "from there," as well as on settlement and dispersion (feared and actualized), indicates J's keen interest in the spatial. This was already clear from the outset, with the Garden of Eden and its closing up, with Cain's aimless wandering and his building of cities, with the ark of Noah, with Mount Ararat, and now with Shinar and Babel. Evidently the very immensity of the Babylonian Empire imposed that concern with the spatial, even on someone from Israel more historically oriented than were the Babylonians. But more important, the Judean deportation to a "goyish" country could not but deeply brand Jewish consciousness with an indelible scar. The sixth-century exile is the great watershed in Israel's ancient history, followed by numberless other displacements until our own time.

Stressing the mythic nature of the Tower of Babel story has opened the way to a psychoanalytical approach to the text. From this point of view, the tower is a transparent phallic symbol, and the femininity of the city (especially in Hebrew[2]) comes to the fore. As is well known, the power game usually entails a sex game. The individual or collective claim to be the navel of the world—that the myth of the center illustrates—must translate into tangibility, be it armaments, oppression of others, gold, sex, or booty (animate and inanimate). Other myths and numerous theater plays, beside the Yahwist's stories, have unveiled the congenital hubris of humankind. From the Dedalus and Icarus failure to the Faust tragedy (not to mention Sophocles or Shakespeare), mythmakers have reflected on the destructive and fatal propensity to play god (the genial *sicut Deus* of Gen 3:5).

A large part of the Yahwist's success is due to his psychological penetration. After meeting his "actors" and reading their "adventures," no one can forget Adam and Eve, Cain and Abel, Noah and family . . . the Babelians and their constructions. These are so strikingly human and "soulful" as to leave an enduring impression on us all. Adam is every man and Eve every woman. In each of us there is a Cain and (hopefully) an Abel. And as I said above, there is between all of us and the Babelians an uncanny kinship. "Des tours de Babel," that is what every human being is busy building—even, we should add, knowing in advance that they will crumble like houses of cards. Vanity of vanities, indeed.

At any rate, by broadening the scope of the myth to enclose humanity J is able to avoid a Manichaean judgment on the Babelians as others. The rebellious and hubristic builders of Babel include the narrator himself and his audience! The paradigm allows no exception.[3] Abraham must extract himself from the Mesopotamian crowd (as Noah had earlier from his contemporaries). The Babelian is *homo communis* (universal humanity) while Abraham becomes a *homo insignis* (extraordinary humanity) not so much by intrinsic virtues as by an existential *choice*.

---

2. But also in many other languages, such as Greek (*hè polis*), Latin (*civitas*), French (*la ville*), German (*die Stadt*), Spanish (*la ciudad*), and Italian (*la citta*).

3. That is why, as we saw above, a Jewish tradition had Abraham counted among the builders.

This brings us to the second part of this essay: deconstruction. I shall not summarize here the deconstructive process of the biblical text under consideration. A few additional remarks will suffice. J has brilliantly dismantled the Babelian grandiosity. The ("zigguratic") hill gave birth to a mouse. The dictatorial linguistic uniformity became a cacophony. All the allegedly undisputable categories have sunk in confusion. But the very report of the catastrophe itself needs be deconstructed. YHWH and Babel are not mutually as incommensurate as appears at first. The divine Child of Genesis 11 holds the string of the reel and is so powerful as to be able to send away (*fortgehen*) Babylon—but the feat is hanging by a thread. First, God's power is paradoxical: his success in scattering humanity is gained through violence, and this is certainly a sign of weakness (that P in Genesis 10 carefully avoided mentioning, even contemplating). Second, that God did not resort to destruction (as God did in the case of Sodom and Gomorrah) leaves Babylon wounded but not dead (like the serpent trampled underfoot but still biting, in Gen 3:15). The persistence of Babylon is ominous. The string that holds it in check may break (like it actually did at the Shoah), and then the monster is on the loose.

It is paradoxical, creatively paradoxical though, that J as an artist in communication, that is, as someone seeking the audience's understanding and approval, would end his narrative on an indictment: After Babel, there is a general absence of mutual comprehension, a total lack of communication. Paradox but also logical conclusion to the extent that art puzzles reason and gives a voice to the unconscious. "The poet dreams being awake," said Charles Lamb, cited by Lionel Trilling.[4] It is here that we find the very root of J's criticism of the city, both in Genesis 4 and Genesis 11. The city stands for the human effort to organize civilization (see especially Gen 4:17–22, and remember what Spengler said of culture when its original creativity wanes away to the level of civilization; see above, chap. 4, n.131). "Art," says Norman O. Brown, "if its object is to undo repressions, and if civilization is essentially repressive, is in this sense subversive of civilization."[5] He echoes J, the artist, for whom civilization is just a stuttered "tale told by an idiot." According to scholars, J's offered etymology of *Babel* is unscientific. On this they were preceded by the artist himself, who used his wit rather than the expected critical judgment.

4. Trilling, *The Liberal Imagination*, 53.
5. Brown, *Life against Death*, 63.

The Babelians wanted homeostasis, that is, stability—a tower like a rock—including homomorphism and heterophobia. Their dispersion destroys homeostasis and introduces dynamism and heterotopy (see Genesis 12). This is why, even though the last note in Gen 11:9 is negative, telling the myth as well as being receptive to it gathers back together composer and audience from their dispersion and exile. They feel united in their opposition to Babel, in their life option opposite the Babelians', united in dreaming in what they believe to be the original language before its having been shattered. Telling and retelling the myth is thus therapeutic. If building Babel leads to fragmentation and alienation, rejecting Babel is the surest way toward restoration and cohesion.

And finally, this book of mine also needs be deconstructed, but I leave this to the care of my readers. They will certainly not deprive themselves of such a pleasurable exercise.

Bibliography

Adam, A. K. M., editor. *Handbook of Postmodern Biblical Interpretation*. St. Louis: Chalice, 2000.

———, editor. *Postmodern Interpretations of the Bible: A Reader*. St. Louis: Chalice, 2001.

———. *What Is Postmodern Biblical Criticism?* GBS. New Testament Series. Minneapolis: Fortress, 1995.

Alster, Bendt. "An Aspect of 'Enmerkar and the Lord of Arappa.'" *Revue d'Assyriologie* 67 (1973) 101–9.

———. *Wisdom of Ancient Sumer*. Bethesda, MD: CDL, 2005.

Alt, Albrecht. "The God of the Fathers." In *Essays on Old Testament History and Religion*, 1–77. Biblical Seminar. Sheffield: JSOT Press, 1989.

Alter, Robert. *Genesis, Translation and Commentary*. New York: Norton, 1996.

Altizer, Thomas J. J. "History as Apocalypse." In *Deconstruction and Theology*, edited by Thomas J. J. Aitizer, et al., 147–77. New York: Crossroad, 1982.

Altizer Thomas J. J., et al., editors. *Deconstruction and Theology*. New York: Crossroad, 1982.

Anderson, Bernhard W. *From Creation to New Creation: Old Testament Perspectives*. OBT. Minneapolis: Fortress, 1995.

———. "Le récit de Babel: Paradigme de l'unité et de la diversité humaines" *Concilium* 121 (1977) 89–97.

Anderson, Harold H., editor. *Creativity and Its Cultivation*. New York: Harper, 1959.

Armstrong, Karen. *A Short History of Myth*. Edinburgh: Canongate, 2005.

Auffret, Pierre. *La Sagesse a bâti sa maison: études de structures littéraires dans l'Ancien Testament et spécialement dans les Psaumes*. OBO 49. Fribourg: Editions Universitaires, 1982.

Augustine. *Concerning the City of God: Against the Pagans*. Translated by Henry Bettenson. Middlesex: Penguin, 1984.

Bachelard, Gaston. *La poétique de l'espace*. Paris: Presses Universitaires de France, 1978.

Baden, Joel S. "The Tower of Babel: A Case Study in the Competing Methods of Historical and Modern Literary Criticism." *JBL* 128 (2009) 209–24.

Bakhtin, Mikhail. *Art and Answerability: Early Philosophical Essays*. Edited by Michael Holquist and Vadim Liapunov. University of Texas Press Slavic Studies Series 9. Austin: University of Texas Press, 1990.

———. *The Dialogic Imagination: Four Essays*. Edited by Michael Holquist. Translated by Caryl Emerson and Michael Holquist. University of Texas Press Slavic Series 1. Austin: University of Texas Press, 1981.

————. *Problems of Dostoevsky's Poetics.* Translated and edited by Caryl Emerson. Theory and History of Literature 8. Minneapolis: University of Minnesota Press, 1984.

————. *Rabelais and His World.* Translated by Helene Iswolsky. Cambridge: MIT Press, 1968.

————. "Response to a Question from the *Novy Mir* Editorial Staff." In *Speech Genres and Other Late Essays,* edited by Caryl Emerson and Michael Holquist, 1–9. Translated by Vern W. McGee. University of Texas Press Slavic Series 9. Austin: University of Texas Press, 1986.

Banon, David. "Babel ou l'idolâtrie embusquée." *Bulletin du Centre Protestant d'Etudes Genève* 6 (1980) 3–30.

Barth, Karl. *Church Dogmatics.* Vol. 1/2, *The Doctrine of the Word of God.* Edited by Geoffrey W. Bromiley and T. F. Torrance. Translated by G. T. Thomson and Harold Knight. Edinburgh: T. & T. Clark, 1956.

Barthes, Roland. *Image, Music, Text.* Translated by Stephen Heath. New York: Hill and Wang, 1977.

Becker, Ernest. *The Denial of Death.* New York: Free Press, 1973.

Benjamin, Walter. *Illuminations.* Edited and with an introduction by Hannah Arendt. Translated by Harry Zohn. New York: Schocken, 1969.

Blenkinsopp, Joseph. "Theme and Motif in the Succession History (2 Sam xi 2ff) and the Jahwist Corpus." In *Volume du Congrès: Genève, 1965,* 44–57. VTSup 15. Leiden: Brill, 1966.

Bloom Harold, with the Hebrew text translated by David Rosenberg. *The Book of J.* New York: Vintage, 1991.

Boman, Thorleif. *Das hebräische Denken im Vergleich mit dem Griechischen.* Göttingen: Vandenhoeck & Ruprecht, 1952.

————. *Hebrew Thought Compared with Greek.* Translated by Jules L. Moreau. Library of History and Doctrine. Philadelphia: Westminster, 1960.

Bost, Hubert. *Babel: Du texte au symbole.* Le Monde de la Bible. Geneva: Labor et Fides, 1985.

Britt, Brian. *Walter Benjamin and the Bible.* New York: Continuum, 1996.

Bromiley G. W. and T. F. Torrance, editors. *Church Dogmatics,* by Karl Barth. 4 vols. New York: Scribner, 1956–1975.

Brongers, H. A. "Bemerkungen zum Gebrauch des Adverbialen weʾattāh im Alten Testament (Ein Lexikologischer Beitrag)."*VT* 15 (1965) 289–99.

Brown, Norman O. *Life against Death: The Psychoanalytical Meaning of History.* Middletown, CT: Wesleyan University Press, 1959.

Brueggemann, Walter. *Genesis.* Interpretation: A Commentary for Teaching and Preaching. Atlanta, John Knox, 1982.

————. "Yahwist." In *Interpreter Dictionary of the Bible Supplementary Volume,* edited by Keith Crim, et al., 971–75. Nashville: Abingdon, 1976.

Budde, Karl. *Die biblische Urgeschichte (Genesis 1—12,5).* Giessen: Ricker, 1883.

Burnett, Fred W. "Historiography." In *Handbook of Postmodern Biblical Interpretation,* edited by A. K. M. Adam, 106–12. St. Louis: Chalice, 2000.

Burrows, Eric. "Some Cosmological Patterns in Babylonian Religion." In *The Labyrinth: Further Studies in the Relation between Myth and Ritual in the Ancient World,* edited by S. H. Hooke, 43–70. London: SPCK, 1935.

Calvin, John. *Commentaire de Jean.*

———. *Le livre de la Genèse*. Commentaire de Jean Calvin sur l'Ancien Testament 1. Aix-en-Provence: Kerygma, 1978.

Campbell, Joseph. *The Masks of God*. Vol. 4, *Creative Mythology*. New York: Viking, 1968.

Caputo, John D., editor. *Deconstruction in a Nutshell: A Conversation with Jacques Derrida*. Perspectives in Continental Philosophy 1. New York: Fordham University Press, 1997.

Cassirer, Ernst. *The Philosophy of Symbolic Forms*. Vol. 2, *Mythical Thought*. New Haven: Yale University Press, 1955.

Cassuto, Umberto. *A Commentary on the Book of Genesis: 2. From Noah to Abraham, Genesis 6:9—11:32*. Translated by Israel Abrahams. Jerusalem: Magnes, 1964.

Castellino, G. "The Origins of Civilization according to Biblical and Cuneiform Texts." In *I Studied Inscriptions from before the Flood: Ancient Near Eastern Literary, and Linguistic Approaches to Genesis 1–11*, edited by Richard Hess and David Toshio Tsumura, 75–95. Sources for Biblical and Theological Study 4. Winona Lake, IN: Eisenbrauns, 1994.

———. "Les textes bibliques et les textes cunéiformes." In *Volume du Congrès: Strasbourg, 1956*, 116–37. VTSup 4. Leiden: Brill, 1957.

Charlesworth, James H., editor. *The Old Testament Pseudepigrapha*. Vol. 1, *Apocalyptic Literature and Testaments*. Garden City, NY: Doubleday, 1983.

Childs, Brevard S. *Myth and Reality in the Old Testament*. SBT 1/27. Naperville, IL: Allenson, 1960.

Clifford, Richard. *The Cosmic Mountain in Canaan and the Old Testament*. HSM 4. Cambridge: Harvard University Press, 1972.

Cohen, Ralph, editor. *The Future of Literary Theory*. New York: Routledge, 1989.

Collins John J. *The Bible after Babel: Historical Criticism in a Postmodern Age*. Grand Rapids: Eerdmans, 2005.

Colman, Andrew M. *A Dictionary of Psychology*. Oxford Paperback Reference. Oxford: Oxford University Press, 2003.

Coote, Robert B., and David R. Ord. *The Bible's First History*. Minneapolis: Fortress, 1989.

Couffignal, Robert. "La Tour de Babel: Approches nouvelles de Genèse xi, 1–9." *Revue Thomiste Toulouse* 83/1 (1983) 59–70.

Croatto, J. Severino. "A Reading of the Story of the Tower of Babel from the Perspective of Non-Identity: Genesis 11:1–9 in the Context of Its Production." In *Teaching the Bible: The Discourses and Politics of Biblical Pedagogy*, edited by Fernando F. Segovia and Mary Ann Tolbert, 203–23. Maryknoll, NY: Orbis, 1998.

Crüsemann, Frank. "Die Eigenständigkeit der Urgeschichte: Ein Beitrag zur Diskussion um den 'Jawisten.'" In *Die Botschaft und die Boten: Festschrift für Hans Walter Wolff zum 70. Geburtstag*, edited by Jörg Jeremias and Lothar Perlitt, 11–29. Neukirchen: Neukirchen-Vluyn, 1981.

Derrida, Jacques. *Acts of Religion*. Edited with an introduction by Gil Anidjar. New York: Routledge, 2002.

———. "Coming into One's Own." Translated and edited by James Hulbert. In *Psychoanalysis and the Question of the Text*, edited by Geoffrey H. Hartman, 114–48. Selected Papers from the English Institute, 1976–1977. Baltimore: Johns Hopkins University Press, 1978.

―――. *Deconstruction in a Nutshell: A Conversation with Jacques Derrida.* Edited with commentary by John D. Caputo. Perspectives in Continental Philosophy. New York: Fordham University Press, 1997.

―――. "Des Tours de Babel." In *Acts of Religion*, edited by Gil Anidjar, 102–15. New York: Routledge, 2002.

―――. *Dissemination.* Translated by Barbara Johnson. Chicago: University of Chicago Press, 1981.

―――. *The Ear of the Other: Otobiography, Transference, Translation; Texts and Discussions with Jacques Derrida.* Edited by Christie V. McDonald. Translated by Peggy Kamuf. New York: Schocken, 1985.

―――. *Of Grammatology.* Translated by Gayatri Chakravorty Spivak. Baltimore: Johns Hopkins University Press, 1976.

―――. "Positions." *Diacritics* 2 (1972) 35–43.

―――."Structure, Sign, and Play in the Discourse of Human Sciences." In *Writing and Difference.* Translated with an introduction and notes by Alan Bass, 278–93. Chicago: University of Chicago Press, 1978.

―――. *Writing and Difference.* Translated with an introduction and notes by Alan Bass. Chicago: University of Chicago Press, 1978.

Dijk, Jan van. "'La confusion des langues'. Notes sur le lexique et sur la morphologie d'Enmerkar, 147–155." *Or* 39 (1970) 302–10.

Dostoevsky, Fyodor. *The Brothers Karamazov: A Novel in Four Parts with Epilogue.* Translated and annotated by Richard Pevear and Larissa Volokhonsky. San Francisco: North Point, 1990.

Dozeman, Thomas B., and Konrad Schmid, editors. *A Farewell to the Yahwist? The Composition of the Pentateuch in Recent European Interpretation.* SBLSymS 34. Atlanta: SBL, 2006.

Dunne, Griffin, director. *Fierce People.* Screenplay by Dirk Wittenborn. DVD. Santa Monica, CA: Lions Gate Entertainment, 2005.

Ehrlich, Arnold Bogumil. *Randglossen zur hebräischen Bibel.* Vol. 1, *Genesis und Exodus.* Leipzig: Hinrichs, 1908.

Eliade, Mircea. *Images and Symbols: Studies in Religious Symbolism.* Translated by Philip Mairet. Mythos. Princeton: Princeton University Press, 1991.

―――. *The Myth of the Eternal Return: Cosmos and History.* Translated by Willard R. Trask. London: Kegan Paul, 1955.

―――. *Myths, Dreams, and Mysteries: The Encounter between Contemporary Faiths and Archaic Realities.* Translated by Philip Mairet. The Library of Religion and Culture. Harper Torchbooks. New York: Harper & Row, 1967.

―――. *Patterns in Comparative Religion.* Translated by Rosemary Sheed. Lincoln: University of Nebraska Press, 1996.

―――. *The Sacred and the Profane: The Nature of Religion.* Translated by Willard R. Trask. New York: Harcourt, Brace, 1959.

Emmanuel, Pierre. *Jacob.* Paris: Seuil, 1970.

Ephrem. "Nineteen Hymns on the Nativity of Christ in the Flesh." In *Gregory the Great (II), Ephraim Syrus, Aphrahat*, edited by Philip Schaff and Henry Wace, 221–62. *NPNF*[2] 13. New York: Scribner, 1905.

Exum, J. Cheryl. *Fragmented Women: Feminist (Sub)versions of Biblical Narratives.* Valley Forge, PA: Trinity, 1993.

Fairley, Barker. *A Study of Goethe.* Oxford: Clarendon, 1969.

Faur, José. *Golden Doves with Silver Dots: Semiotics and Textuality in Rabbinic Tradition.* Jewish Literature and Culture. Bloomington: Indiana University Press, 1986.

Fewell, Danna Nolan. "Building Babel." In *Postmodern Interpretations of the Bible: A Reader*, edited by A. K. M. Adam, 1–15. Saint Louis: Chalice, 2001, 1-15.

Finkelstein, J. J., and Moshe Greenberg, editors. *Oriental and Biblical Studies: Collected Writings of E. A. Speiser*. Philadelphia: University of Pennsylvania Press, 1967.

Fishbane, Michael. *Biblical Myth and Rabbinic Mythmaking*. Oxford: Oxford University Press, 2003.

———. *Text and Texture: Close Readings of Selected Biblical Texts*. New York: Schocken, 1979.

Fokkelman, J. P. "Genesis 11.1–9, the Tower of Babel." In *Narrative Art in Genesis: Specimens of Stylistic and Structural Analysis*, 11–45. Studia Semitica Neerlandica 17. Assen: Van Gorcum, 1975.

Forman, H. Buxton, editor. *The Letters of John Keats*. Kessinger Publishing's Rare Reprints. Whitefish, MT: Kessinger, 2007.

Fox, Everett. *The Five Books of Moses: Genesis, Exodus, Leviticus, Numbers, Deuteronomy; A New Translation with Introductions, Commentary, and Notes*. Schocken Bible 1. New York: Schocken, 1995.

Frankfort, Henri A., and Aharon Amir, editors. *Before Philosophy: The Intellectual Adventure of Man; An Essay on Speculative Thought in the Ancient Near East*. Baltimore: Penguin, 1949.

Frankl, Viktor. *The Doctor and the Soul: From Psychotherapy to Logotherapy*. Translated by Richard and Clara Winston. New York: Bantam, 1969.

Freedman, David Noel, et al., editors. *The Anchor Bible Dictionary*. 6 vols. New York: Doubleday, 1992.

Freud, Sigmund. *The Basic Writings of Sigmund Freud*. Translated and edited by A. A. Brill. 1938. Reprint, New York: The Modern Library, 1995.

———. *Beyond the Pleasure Principle*. S.E. 18. Translated by James Strachey. New York: Liverlight, 1950.

———. *Civilization and Its Discontents*. Translated by James Strachey. New York: Norton, 1961.

———. "Creative Writers and Day-Dreaming." In *S.E.* 9:143–53. Translated and edited by James Strachey. London: Hogarth, 1959.

———. "The Dissolution of the Oedipus Complex." In *S.E.* 19:172–79. Translated and edited by James Strachey. London: Hogarth, 1953.

———. "Delusions and Dreams in Jensen's *Gradiva*." In *S.E.* 9:7–95. Translated and edited by James Strachey. London: Hogarth, 1959.

———. "The Ego and the Id." In *S.E.* 19:12–66. Translated by Joan Riviere. London: Hogarth, 1961.

———. *A General Introduction to Psychoanalysis*. Translated by Joan Riviere. Permabooks. Garden City: Doubleday, 1953.

———. *Group Psychology and the Analysis of the Ego*. Translated and newly edited by James Strachey. S.E. 6. The International Psycho-Analytical Library 6. London: Hogarth, 1959.

———. "The Infantile Genital Organization." In *S.E.* 19:140–53. Translated and edited by James Strachey. London: Hogarth, 1953.

———. *Inhibitions, Symptoms and Anxiety*. In *S.E.* 20:87–172. Translated and edited by James Strachey. London: Hogarth, 1986.

————. *The Interpretation of Dreams*. Translated and edited by James Strachey. *S.E.* 4–5. London: Hogarth, 1953.

————. *New Introductory Lectures on Psychoanalysis*. Translated by W. J. H. Sprott. *S.E.* 22. London: Hogarth, 1949.

————. "Notes upon a Case of Obsessional Neurosis" ("The Rat-Man"). In *S.E.* 10:155–320. Translated by James Strachey, Anna Freud, et al. London: Hogarth, 1955.

————. "On the Grounds of Detaching a Particular Syndrome from Neurasthenia under the Description of 'Anxiety Neurosis.'" In *S.E.* 3:315–44. Translated by James Strachey. London: Hogarth, 1961.

————. *An Outline of Psychoanalysis*. Translated by James Strachey. *S.E.* 23. London: Hogarth, 1949.

————. *The Psychopathology of Everyday Life*. Translated with an introduction by A. A. Brill. Mineola, NY: Dover, 2003.

————. "Some Psychical Consequences of the Anatomical Distinction between the Sexes." In *S.E.* 19:243–58. Translated and edited by James Strachey. London: Hogarth, 1953.

————. *Totem and Taboo*. Translated by James Strachey. New York: Norton, 1950.

Friedman, Richard Elliott. *Commentary on the Torah*. San Francisco: HarperSanFrancisco, 2003.

————. *The Hidden Book in the Bible: The Discovery of the First Prose Masterpiece*. San Francisco: HarperSanFrancisco, 1999.

Fromm, Erich. "The Creative Attitude." In *Creativity and Its Cultivation*, edited by Harold H. Anderson, 44–54. New York: Harper, 1959.

Galling, Kurt. *Die Erzählungstraditionen Israels*. BZAW 48. Giessen: Töpelmann, 1928.

Gaster, Theodor H. *Myth, Legend and Custom in the Old Testament*. 2 vols. New York: Harper & Row, 1969.

Gaylord, H. E., Jr., translator. "Third Baruch." In *Old Testament Pseudepigrapha*, edited by James H. Charlesworth, 1:653–79. Garden City, NY: Doubleday, 1983.

Gide, André. *Theseus and Oedipus*. Translated by Andrew Brown. London: Hesperus, 2002.

Ginsberg, H. L. "Babel, Tower of." In *Enc. Jud.* 2007.

Glassner, Jean-Jacques. *Mesopotamian Chronicles*. Edited by Benjamin R. Foster. Writings from the Ancient World 19. Leiden: Brill, 2004.

Goethe, Johann Wolfgang von. *The Tragedy of Faust, Part 1*. Translated by Anna Swanwick. Harvard Classics 19. New York: Collier, 1909.

González Iñárritu, Alejandro, director. *Babel*. Produced by Steve Golin et al. Written by Guillermo Arriaga. Anonymous Content, Central Films, Dune Films, a Zeta Film. Hollywood: Paramount Home Entertainment, 2007.

Gowan, Donald E. *From Eden to Babel: A Commentary on the Book of Genesis 1–11*. ITC. Grand Rapids: Eerdmans, 1988.

————. *When Man Becomes God: Humanism and "Hybris" in the Old Testament*. PittsTMS 6. Pittsburgh: Pickwick, 1975.

Grayson, Albert Kirk. *Assyrian and Babylonian Chronicles*. TCS 5. Locust Valley, NY: Augustin. 1975.

Gressmann, Hugo. *The Tower of Babel*. The Hilde Stich Stroock Lectures at the Jewish Institute of Religion. New York: Jewish Institute of Religion Press, 1928.

Groddeck, Georg. *Das Buch vom Es: Psychoanalytische Briefe an eine Freundin*. Frankfurt: Ullstein, 1978.

———. "The Id in Everyday Life." In *The Unknown Self*. Translated by V. M. E. Collins. London: Vision, 1989.

Grosclaude, P., and Los Deu Larvath. *Un cóp sera*. LP. Béziers, France: Ventadorn, 1976.

Gunkel, Hermann. *Creation and Chaos in the Primeval Era and the Eschaton: Religio-Historical Study of Genesis 1 and Revelation 12*. Translated by K. William Whitney Jr. The Biblical Resource Series. Grand Rapids: Eerdmans, 2006.

———. *Genesis*. HKAT. Göttingen: Vandenhoeck & Ruprecht, 1902.

———. *Genesis*. Translated by Mark E. Biddle. Mercer Library of Biblical Studies. Macon, GA: Mercer University Press, 1997.

———. *Israel and Babylon: The Babylonian Influence on Israelite Religion*. Edited with a new introduction by K. C. Hanson. Eugene, OR: Cascade Books, 2009.

Hallo, William W., and K. Lawson Younger, editors. *Canonical Compositions from the Biblical World*. The Context of Scripture 1. Leiden: Brill, 1997.

Hamilton, Victor P. *The Book of Genesis: Chapters 1–17*. NICOT. Grand Rapids: Eerdmans, 1990.

Heidel, Alexander. *The Gilgamesh Epic and Old Testament Parallels*. Chicago: University of Chicago Press, 1946.

Hempel, Johannes. "Glaube, Mythos und Geschichte im Alten Testament." *ZAW* 65 (1953) 109–67.

Hendel, Ronald S. *The Text of Genesis 1–11: Textual Studies and Critical Edition*. New York: Oxford University Press, 1998.

Henderson, Joseph L. "Ancient Myths and Modern Man." In *Man and His Symbols*, edited by C. G. Jung, 95–156. New York: Dell, 1968.

Herodotus, *The History*. Translated by David Grene. Chicago: University of Chicago Press, 1987.

Hesiod. *Theogony; Works and Days*. Translated by M. L. West. Oxford World's Classics. Oxford: Oxford University Press, 1999.

Hiebert, Theodore. "Babel: Babble or Blueprint? Calvin, Cultural Diversity, and the Interpretation of Genesis 11:1–9." In *Reformed Theology: Identity and Ecumenicity II; Biblical Interpretation in the Reformed Tradition*, edited by Wallace M. Alston Jr. and Michael Welker, 127–45. Grand Rapids: Eerdmans, 2007.

———, editor. *Toppling the Tower: Essays on Babel and Diversity*. Chicago: McCormick Theological Seminary, 2004

———. "The Tower of Babel and the Origin of the World's Cultures." *JBL* 126 (2007) 29–58.

———. *The Yahwist's Landscape: Nature and Religion in Early Israel*. Minneapolis: Fortress, 2008.

Hooke, S. H., editor. *The Labyrinth: Further Studies in the Relation between Myth and Ritual in the Ancient World*. London: SPCK, 1935.

Horton, Robin. "African Traditional Religion and Western Science." *Africa* 37:1–2 (1967) 50–71; 155–87.

Hose, Martin, editor. *Grosse Texte alter Kulturen: Literarische Reise von Gizeh nach Rom*. Darmstadt: Wissenschaftliche Buchgesellschaft, 2004.

Ibn Ezra, Abraham. *Ibn Ezra's Commentary on the Pentateuch*. Vol. 1, *Genesis [Bereshit]*. Translated by H. Norman Stickman and Arthur M. Silver. New York: Menorah, 1988.

Jackson, Jared J., and Martin Kessler, editors. *Rhetorical Criticism: Essays in Honor of James Muilenburg*. PittsTMS 1. Pittsburgh: Pickwick, 1974.

Jacob, Benno. *The First Book of the Bible: Genesis*. Abridged, edited, and translated by
     Ernest I. Jacob and Walter Jacob. Augmented ed. Jersey City, NJ: Ktav, 2007.
Jacobsen, Thorkild. "The Eridu Genesis." *JBL* 100 (1981) 513–29.
———. "Sumerian Mythology: A Review Article." *JNES* 5 (1946) 128–52.
———. "Mesopotamia: The Cosmos of the State, the Function of the State." In *Before
     Philosophy: The Intellectual Adventure of Man; An Essay on Speculative Thought in
     the Ancient Near East*, edited by Henri A. Frankfort and Aharon Amir, 141–44.
     Baltimore: Penguin, 1949.
James, William. *The Varieties of Religious Experience: A Study in Human Nature*. Mentor
     Books. New York: New American Library, 1958.
Jeremias, Jörg, and Lothar Perlitt, editors. *Die Botschaft und die Boten, Festschrift für Hans
     Walter Wolff zum 70. Geburtstag*. Neukirchen: Neukirchen-Vluyn, 1981.
Johnstone, W. "The Mythologising of History in the Old Testament." *Scottish Journal of
     Theology* 24 (1971) 201–17.
Jung, Carl G. "Approaching the Unconscious." In *Man and His Symbols*, edited by Carl G.
     Jung et al., 18–103. Garden City, NY: Doubleday, 1964.
———, et al., editors. *Man and His Symbols*. Garden City, NY: Doubleday, 1964.
———. *The Spirit in Man, Art, and Literature*. Translated by E. C. Hull. Bollingen Series
     20. The Collected Works of Carl Jung 15. Princeton: Princeton University Press,
     1971.
———. *The Symbolic Life: Miscellaneous Writings*. Translated by E. C. Hull. Bollingen
     Series 20. The Collected Works of Carl Jung 18. Princeton: Princeton University
     Press, 1977.
Kafka, Franz. "The Great Wall of China." In *Collected Stories*, edited and introduced by
     Gabriel Josipovici, 374–86. Everyman's Library 145. New York: Knopf, 1993.
Kennedy, George A. *New Testament Interpretation through Rhetorical Criticism*. Studies in
     Religion. Chapel Hill: University of North Carolina Press, 1984.
Kikawada, Isaac M. "The Shape of Genesis 11:1–9." In *Rhetorical Criticism: Essays in
     Honor of James Muilenburg*, edited by Jared J. Jackson and Martin Kessler, 18–32.
     PittsTMS. Pittsburgh: Pickwick, 1974.
Kikawada, Isaac M., and Arthur Quinn. *Before Abraham Was: The Unity of Genesis 1–11*.
     Nashville: Abingdon, 1985.
Kille, D. Andrew. *Psychological Biblical Criticism*. GBS. Minneapolis: Fortress, 2001.
Kirk, G. S. *Myth: Its Meaning and Functions in Ancient and Other Cultures*. Sather Classical
     Lectures 40. Cambridge: Cambridge University Press, 1970.
Kittredge, George Lyman, editor. *Sixteen Plays of Shakespeare with Full Explanatory Notes,
     Textual Notes, and Glossaries*. Boston: Ginn, 1946.
Köhler, Ludwig, and Walter Baumgartner. *Lexicon in Veteris Testamenti libros*. 2nd ed.
     Leiden: Brill, 1958.
Kramer, Samuel Noah. "The 'Babel of Tongues': A Sumerian Version." *JAOS* 88 (1968)
     108–11.
———. *Sumerian Mythology*. Rev. ed. Pennsylvania Paperback 47. Philadelphia: Univer-
     sity of Pennsylvania Press, 1972.
Kugel, James L. *The Bible as It Was*. Cambridge, MA: Belknap, 1997.
Labat, René et al., editors. *Les Religions du Proche-Orient asiatique: Textes et traditions
     sacrés babyloniens, ougaritiques et hittites*. Le trésor spirituel de l'humanité. Paris:
     Fayard-Denoël, 1970.
LaCocque, André. *Esther Regina: A Bakhtinian Reading*. Rethinking Theory. Evanston, IL:
     Northwestern University Press, 2008.

———. "Justice for the Innocent Job!" forthcoming.

———. *Romance, She Wrote: A Hermeneutical Essay on Song of Songs.* Eugene, OR: Wipf & Stock Publishers, 2006.

———. *Onslaught against Innocence: Cain, Abel, and the Yahwist.* Eugene, OR: Cascade Books, 2008

———. *The Trial of Innocence: Adam, Eve, and the Yahwist.* Eugene, OR: Cascade Books, 2006.

LaCocque, André, and Pierre-Emmanuel LaCocque. *Jonah: A Psycho-Religious Approach to the Prophet.* Studies on Personalities of the Old Testament. Columbia, SC: University of South Carolina Press, 1990.

LaCocque, André, and Paul Ricoeur. *Thinking Biblically: Exegetical and Hermeneutical Studies.* Translated by David Pellauer. Chicago: University of Chicago Press, 1998.

La Fontaine, Jean de. *Fables.* Translated by Walter Thornbury. Tunhout, Belgium: Brepols, 1982.

Langdon, Stephen. "Nabopolassar Inscription." In *Die neubabylonischen Königsinschriften*, 60. Translated by Rudolf Zehnpfund. VAT 4. Leipzig: Hinrichs, 1912.

———. *Die neubabylonischen Königsinschriften.* Translated by Rudolf Zehnpfund. VAT 4. Leipzig: Hinrichs, 1912.

Laplanche, Jean. *Essays on Otherness.* Warwick Studies in European Philosophy. London: Routledge, 1999.

———. *Le Primat de l'autre en psychanalyse.* Paris: Flammarion, 1997.

———. *Vie et mort en psychanalyse: Dérivation des entités psychanalytiques.* Nouvelle bibliothèque scientifique. Paris: Flammarion, 1970.

Leach, Edmund. *Genesis as Myth and Other Essays.* Cape Editions 39. London: Cape, 1969.

Leick, Gwendolyn. *Mesopotamia: The Invention of the City.* London: Penguin, 2002.

Levenson, Jon D. *Creation and the Persistence of Evil: The Jewish Drama of Divine Omnipotence.* San Francisco: Harper & Row, 1988.

Levin, Christoph. "Das israelitische Nationalepos: der Yahwist." In *Grosse Texte alter Kulturen: Literarische Reise von Gizeh nach Rom*, edited by Martin Hose, 63–86. Darmstadt: Wissenschaftliche Buchgesellschaft, 2004.

Lévi-Strauss, Claude. *Anthropologie Structurale Deux.* Agora 189. Paris: Pocket, 2003.

———. *Structural Anthropology*, vol. 2. Translated by Monique Layton. Chicago: University of Chicago Press, 1983.

Levy, G. Rachel. *Religious Conceptions of the Stone Age and Their Influence upon European Thought.* Harper Torchbooks. The Cloister Library. New York: Harper & Row, 1963.

L'Heureux, Conrad E. *In and Out of Paradise: The Book of Genesis from Adam and Eve to the Tower of Babel.* New York: Paulist, 1983.

Lord, Albert Bates. *The Singer of Tales.* Harvard Studies in Comparative Literature 24. New York: Atheneum, 1978.

MacIntyre, Alasdair C. *After Virtue: A Study in Moral Theory.* 2nd ed. Notre Dame, IN: University of Notre Dame Press, 1984.

Mahony, Patrick J. *Freud and the Rat Man.* New Haven: Yale University Press, 1986.

Malinowski, Bronislaw. *Magic, Science and Religion, and Other Essays.* Doubleday Anchor Books. Garden City, NY: Doubleday, 1954.

Manguel, Alberto. *The City of Words.* CBC Massey Lecture Series. Toronto: House of Anansi, 2007.

———. *The Library at Night.* New Haven: Yale University Press, 2006.

Margueron, Jean-Claude. "Babylon." In *ABD*, 1:563–65.

Marsh, John. *The Fullness of Time*. London: Nisbet, 1952.

Marx, Karl, and Friedrich Engels. *Kleine ökonomische Schriften*. Bücherei des Marxismus-Leninismus 42 Berlin: Dietz, 1955.

Maslow, Abraham. "Neurosis as a Failure of Personal Growth." *Humanitas* 3 (1967) 153–69.

McKeown, James. *Genesis*. Two Horizons Old Testament Commentary. Grand Rapids: Eerdmans, 2008.

Millard, Alan R. "Assyrian Eponym Chronicle." In *Canonical Compositions from the Biblical World*, edited by William W. Hallo and K. L. Younger, 465–66. The Contexts of Scripture 1. New York: Brill, 1997.

———. "Assyrian King Lists." In *Canonical Compositions from the Biblical World*, edited by William W. Hallo and K. L. Younger, 463–65. The Contexts of Scripture 1. New York: Brill, 1997.

———. "Babylonian Chronicle." In *Canonical Compositions from the Biblical World*, edited by William W. Hallo and K. L. Younger, 467–68. The Contexts of Scripture 1. New York: Brill, 1997.

———. "Babylonian King Lists." In *Canonical Compositions from the Biblical World*, edited by William W. Hallo and K. Lawson Younger, 461–63. The Contexts of Scripture 1. New York: Brill, 1997.

———. "The Weidner Chronicle." In *Canonical Compositions from the Biblical World*, edited by William W. Hallo and K. L. Younger, 468–70. The Contexts of Scripture 1. New York: Brill, 1997.

Miller, Patrick D. *Genesis 1–11: Studies in Structure and Theme*. JSOTSup 8. Sheffield, UK: JSOT Press, 1978.

Milton, John. *Paradise Lost*. 1667. Reprint. Oxford: Oxford University Press, 2005.

Minear, Paul Sevier. *Eyes of Faith: A Study in the Biblical Point of View*. 1965. Reprint, Eugene OR: Wipf & Stock, 2003.

Miscall, Peter D. *The Workings of Old Testament Narrative*. Semeia Studies. Philadelphia: Fortress, 1983.

Montenay, Georgette de. *Emblemes ou devises chrestiennes*. Lyons: Marcorelle, 1571.

Moore, Stephen D. *Poststructuralism and the New Testament: Derrida and Foucault at the Foot of the Cross*. Minneapolis: Fortress, 1994.

Myers, Max A. "Toward What Is Religious Thinking Underway?" In *Deconstruction and Theology*, edited by Thomas J. J. Altizer et al., 109–46. New York: Crossroad, 1982.

Neher, André. *De l'hébreu au français: manuel de l'hébraïsant; la traduction*. Initiation et Méthodes 1. Paris: Klincksieck, 1969.

———. *L'Exil de la parole: Du silence biblique au silence d'Auschwitz*. Paris: Seuil, 1970.

Neusner, Jacob. *Confronting Creation: How Judaism Reads Genesis; An Anthology of Genesis Rabbah*. Columbia: University of South Carolina Press, 1991.

Newsom, Carol. "Bakhtin." In *Handbook of Postmodern Biblical Interpretation*, edited by A. K. M. Adam, 20–27. St. Louis: Chalice, 2000.

Niditch, Susan. *Oral World and Written Word: Ancient Israelite Literature*. Library of Ancient Israel. Louisville: Westminster/John Knox, 1996.

Nietzsche, Friedrich. *The Gay Science: With a Prelude in Rhymes and an Appendix of Songs*. Translated, with commentary, by Walter Kaufmann. New York: Vintage, 1974.

———. *The Philosophy of Nietzsche*. The Modern Library of the World's Best Books. New York: Modern Library, 1927.

Odell-Scott, David W. "Deconstruction" In *Handbook of Postmodern Biblical Interpretation*, edited by A. K. M. Adam, 55–61. St. Louis: Chalice, 2000.

Bibliography

173

Oden, Robert A., Jr. "Myth and Mythology." In *ABD*, 4:946–60.

Oduyoye, Modupẹ. "Balala-balala: The Babel of Tongues." In *The Sons of the Gods and the Daughters of Men: An Afro-Asiatic Interpretation of Genesis 1–11*, 79–82. Maryknoll, NY: Orbis, 1984.

Orwell, George. *Nineteen Eighty-Four: A Novel.* Harmondsworth, UK: Penguin, 1977 [1949].

Panikkar, Raimundo. "The Myth of Pluralism: The Tower of Babel—A Meditation on Non-violence." *Crosscurrents* 29 (1979) 197–230.

Parrot, André. *The Tower of Babel.* Translated by Edwin Hudson. Studies in Biblical Archaeology 2. New York: Philosophical Library, 1955.

———. *Ziggurats et tour de Babel.* Paris: Albin Michel, 1949.

Pascal, Blaise. *Pensées*, vol. 1. Edited by Zacharie Tourneur. Bibliothèque de Cluny 16. Paris: Cluny, 1938.

Pedersen, Joh. *Israel: Its Life and Culture.* Vol. 1. Translated by Joh. Pedersen and Mrs. Aslaug Møller. London: Oxford University Press 1926.

Pettazzoni, Raffaele. "Myths of Beginning and Creation Myths." In *Essays on the History of Religions*, 24–36. Translated by H. J. Rose. SHR 1. Leiden: Brill, 1954.

Phillips, Gary A. "Levinas." In *Handbook of Postmodern Biblical Interpretation*, edited by A. K. M. Adam, 154–59. St. Louis: Chalice, 2000.

Pirandello, Luigi. *Sei Personaggi in Cerca d'Autore: Commedia da Fare.* Florence, Bemporad, 1921.

Poulet, Georges. *Etudes sur le temps humain.* Paris: Plon, 1949.

Preminger Alex, and Edward L. Greenstein, editors. *The Hebrew Bible in Literary Criticism.* A Library of Literary Criticism. New York: Ungar, 1986.

Pritchard, James B. *Ancient Near Eastern Texts Relating to the Old Testament.* 3rd ed. Princeton: Princeton University Press, 1969.

Propp, Vladimir. *Morphology of the Folktale.* Edited by L. A. Wagner. Translated by Laurence Scott. Publications of the American Folklore Society. Bibliographical and Special Series 9. 2nd ed. Austin: University of Texas Press, 1968.

———. *Morphologie du conte; suivi de Les Transformations des Contes merveilleux.* Points. [Essais] 12. Paris: Seuil, 1970.

Pury, Albert de. "Le cycle of Jacob comme légende autonome des origines d'Israël." In *Volume du Congrès: Leuven, 1989*, edited by J. A. Emerton, 78–96. VTSup 43 Leiden: Brill, 1991.

———. "La tour de Babel et la vocation d'Abraham." *ETR* 53 (1978) 80–97.

———. "The Jacob Story and the Beginning of the Formation of the Pentateuch." In *A Farewell to the Yahwist? The Composition of the Pentateuch in Recent European Interpretation*, edited by Thomas B. Dozeman and Konrad Schmid, 51–72. SBLSymS 34. Atlanta: SBL, 2006.

Rad, Gerhard von. *Genesis: A Commentary.* Translated by John H. Marks. Rev. ed. OTL. Philadelphia: Westminster, 1973.

———. *Old Testament Theology.* Vol. 1, *The Theology of Israel's Historical Traditions.* Translated by D. M. G. Stalker. OTL. Louisville: Westminster John Knox, 2001.

———. *The Problem of the Hexateuch and Other Essays.* Translated by E. W. Trueman Dicken. Edinburgh: Oliver and Boyd, 1966.

Rank, Otto. *The Incest Theme in Literature and Legend: Fundamentals of a Psychology of Literary Creation.* Translated by Gregory Richter. Baltimore: Johns Hopkins University Press, 1992.

Raschke Carl A. "The Deconstruction of God." In *Deconstruction and Theology*, edited by T. J. J. Altizer, et al., 1–33. New York: Crossroad, 1982.

Rashkow, Ilona N. *The Phallacy of Genesis: A Feminist-Psychoanalytic Approach*. LCBI. Louisville: Westminster John Knox, 1993.

Ratschow, Carl Heinz. "Anmerkungen zur theologischen Auffassung des Zeitproblems." *ZTK* 51 (1954) 360–87.

Rendsburg, Gary, et al., editors. *The Bible World: Essays in Honor of Cyrus H. Gordon*. New York: Ktav, 1980.

Rendtorff, Rolf. "Hermeneutische Probleme der biblischen Urgeschichte." In *Festschrift für Friedrich Smend zum 70. Geburtstag*, 19–29. Berlin: Merseburger, 1963.

———, editor. *The Problem of the Process of Transmission in the Pentateuch*. Translated by John J. Scullion. The Library of Hebrew Bible / Old Testament Studies. Sheffield, UK: Sheffield Academic, 2009.

———. *Das überlieferungsgeschichtliche Problem des Pentateuch*. BZAW 147. Berlin: de Gruyter, 1977.

Ricoeur, Paul. *De l'interprétation: essai sur Freud*. Paris: Seuil, 1965.

———. *Freud and Philosophy: An Essay on Interpretation*. Translated by Denis Savage. The Terry Lectures. New Haven: Yale University Press, 1970.

———. "Guilt, Ethics and Religion." in *Talk of God*, by the Royal Institute of Philosophy, 100–117. Royal Institute of Philosophy Lectures 2. Glasgow: The Royal Institute of Philosophy, 1969.

———. "The Hermeneutical Function of Distanciation." In *From Text to Action*, translated by Kathleen Blamey and John B. Thompson, 75–88. Essays in Hermeneutics 2. Evanston, IL: Northwestern University Press, 1991.

———. *Histoire et vérité*. Esprit. La condition humaine. Paris: Seuil, 1964.

———. *The Symbolism of Evil*. Translated by Emerson Buchanan. New York: Harper & Row, 1967.

Rilke, Rainer-Maria. *The Letters of Rainer Maria Rilke*. Translated by Jane B. Greene. Gloucester, MA: Smith, 1947.

Robinson, H. Wheeler. *Inspiration and Revelation in the Old Testament*. Westport, CT: Greenwood, 1979.

Rogerson, John W. "Astral Mythology and Anthropological Mythology." In *Myth in Old Testament Interpretation*, 45–51. BZAW 134. Berlin: de Gruyter, 1974.

Róheim, Géza. *The Origin and Function of Culture*. A Doubleday Anchor Book. Garden City, NY: Doubleday, 1971.

Rollins, Wayne G. *Soul and Psyche: The Bible in Psychological Perspective*. Minneapolis: Fortress, 1999.

Rollins, Wayne G., and D. Andrew Kille, editors. *Psychological Insight into the Bible; Texts and Readings*. Grand Rapids: Eerdmans, 2007.

Römer, Thomas. *Israels Väter: Untersuchungen zur Väterthematik im Deuteronomium und in der deuteronomistischen Tradition*. OBO 99. Fribourg: Universitätsverlag, 1990.

Rose, Martin. *Deuteronomist und Jahwist: Untersuchungen zu den Berührungspunkten beider Literarturwerke*. ATANT 67. Zurich: Theologischer Verlag, 1981.

Rousseau, Jean-Jacques. *Essai sur l'origine des langues* [1755]. Introduction and notes by Angèle Kremer-Marietti. La Philosophie Poche. Paris: Aubier Montaigne, 1974.

Rubenstein, Richard L. *After Auschwitz: Radical Theology and Contemporary Judaism*. New York: Bobbs-Merrill, 1966.

———. *The Religious Imagination: A Study in Psychoanalysis and Jewish Theology*. Boston: Beacon, 1968.

Rudnytsky, Peter. *Reading Psychoanalysis: Freud, Rank, Ferenczi, Groddeck*. Cornell Studies in the History of Psychiatry. Ithaca, NY: Cornell University Press, 2002.

Sanford, John A. *The Man Who Wrestled with God: Light from the Old Testament on the Psychology of Individuation*. New York: Paulist, 1981.

Sarna, Nahum. *Understanding Genesis: The World of the Bible in the Light of History*. The Heritage of Biblical Israel 1. New York: Schocken, 1970.

Sartre, Jean-Paul. *Anti-Semite and Jew: An Exploration of the Etiology of Hate*. Translated by George J. Becker. New York: Schocken, 1995.

Sasson, Jack M. "The 'Tower of Babel' as a Clue to the Redactional Structuring of the Primal History [Gen 1–11:9]." In *The Bible World: Essays in Honor of Cyrus H. Gordon*, edited by Gary Rendsburg et al., 211–19. New York: Ktav, 1980.

Scharlemann, Robert. "The Being of God When God Is Not Being God: Deconstructing the History of Theism." In *Deconstruction and Theology*, edited by Thomas J. J. Altizer, et al., 79–108. New York: Crossroad, 1982.

Schmid, Hans Heinrich. *Der sogenannte Jahwist: Beobachtungen und Fragen zur Pentateuchforschung*. Zurich: Theologischer Verlag, 1976.

Schmid, Konrad. "The So-Called Yahwist and the Literary Gap between Genesis and Exodus." In *A Farewell to the Yahwist? The Composition of the Pentateuch in Recent European Interpretation*, edited by Thomas B. Dozeman and Konrad Schmid, 29–50. SBLSymS 34. Atlanta: SBL, 2006.

Seebass, Horst. *Genesis*. Vol. 1, *Urgeschichte (1,1—11,26)*. Neukirchen-Vleuyn: Neukirchener, 1996.

Seely, Paul. "The Date of the Tower of Babel and Some Theological Implications." *WTJ* 63 (2001) 15–38.

Segovia Fernando F., and Mary Ann Tolbert, editors. *Teaching the Bible: The Discourses and Politics of Biblical Pedagogy*. Maryknoll, NY: Orbis, 1998.

Seybold, Klaus. "Der Turmbau zu Babel. Zur Entstehung von Genesis xi, 1–9." *VT* 26 (1976) 453–79.

Sherwood, Yvonne. " Derrida." In *Handbook of Postmodern Biblical Interpretation*, edited by A. K. M. Adam, 69–75. St. Louis: Chalice, 2000.

———. *The Prostitute and the Prophet: Hosea's Marriage in Literary-Theoretical Perspective*. JSOTSup 212. Gender, Culture, Theory, 2. Sheffield: Sheffield Academic, 1996.

Skinner, John. *A Critical and Exegetical Commentary on Genesis*. ICC. Edinburgh: T. & T. Clark, 1910.

Snell, Bruno. *Poetry and Society: The Role of Poetry in Ancient Greece*. Bloomington: Indiana University Press, 1961.

Speiser, Ephraim A., translator. "*Enuma Elish*." In *ANET*, 68–69.

———. *Genesis*. AB 1. Garden City, NY: Doubleday, 1964.

———. "Word Plays on the Creation Epic's Version of the Founding of Babylon." In *Oriental and Biblical Studies: Collected Writings of E. A. Speiser*, edited by J. J. Finkelstein and Moshe Greenberg, 53–61. Philadelphia: University of Pennsylvania Press, 1967.

Spengler, Oswald. *The Decline of the West*. An abridged edition by Helmut Werner; English abridged edition prepared by Charles Francis Atkinson, with a new introduction by H. Stuart Hughes. Oxford Paperbacks. New York: Oxford University Press, 1991.

Steck, Odil Hannes. "Genesis 12,1–3 und die Urgeschichte des Jahwisten." In *Probleme biblischer Theologie: Gerhard von Rad zum 70. Geburtstag*, edited by Hans Walter Wolff, 525–54. Munich: Kaiser, 1971.

Steele, Robert. "Psychoanalysis and Hermeneutics." *International Review of Psychoanalysis* 6 (1979) 389–411.

Steiner, George. *After Babel: Aspects of Language and Translation*. New York: Oxford University Press, 1975.

Stout, Jeffrey. *Ethics after Babel: The Languages of Morals and Their Discontents*. Boston: Beacon, 1988.

Strong, J. T. "Shattering the Image of God: A Response to Theodore Hiebert's Interpretation of the Story of the Tower of Babel." *JBL* 127 (2008) 625–34.

Taylor, Mark C. "Text as Victim" in *Deconstruction and Theology*, edited by Thomas J. J. Altizer et al., 58–78. New York: Crossroad, 1982.

Trilling, Lionel. *The Liberal Imagination: Essays on Literature and Society*. Doubleday Anchor Books A13. Garden City: Doubleday, 1953.

Tylor, Edward Burnett. *Primitive Culture*. 2 vols. London: Murray, 1871.

Uehlinger, Christoph. *Weltreich und "eine Rede": Eine neue Deutung der sogenannten Turmbauerzählung (Genesis 11,1–9)*. OBO 101. Freiburg: Universitätsverlag, 1990.

Van Seters, John. *The Pentateuch: A Social-Science Commentary*. Trajectories 1. Sheffield: Sheffield Academic, 1999.

———. *Prologue to History: The Yahwist as Historian in Genesis*. Louisville: Westminster John Knox, 1992.

Vernant, Jean-Pierre. *Religions, histoires, raisons*. Petite collection Maspero 233. Paris: Maspero, 1979.

Vogels, Walter. *Nos origines: Genèse 1–11*. L'Horizon du croyant. Ottawa: Novalis, 1992.

Wallis, Gerhard. "Die Stadt in den Überlieferungen der Genesis." *ZAW* 78 (1966) 133–48.

Walsh, Jerome T. "Genesis 11:1–9." In *Style and Structure in Biblical Hebrew Narrative* Collegeville, MN: Liturgical, 2001.

Wenham, Gordon J. *Genesis 1–15*. WBC 1. Dallas: Word, 1987.

Wénin, André. *D'Adam à Abraham ou les errances de l'humain: Lecture de Genèse 1,1—12,4*. Lire la Bible 148. Paris: Cerf, 2007.

Westermann, Claus, editor. *Essays on Old Testament Hermeneutics*. Edited by James Luther Mays. Richmond: John Knox, 1963.

———. *Genesis*. Vol. 1, *Genesis 1–11*. BKAT 1. Neukirchen-Vluyn: Neukirchener, 1974.

———. *Genesis 1–11: A Commentary*. Translated by John J. Scullion. Continental Commentary. Minneapolis: Augsburg, 1984.

White, Hayden. "'Figuring the Nature of the Times Deceased': Literary Theory and Historical Writing." In *The Future of Literary Theory*, edited by Ralph Cohen, 19–43. New York: Routledge, 1989.

Wink, Walter. "On Wrestling with God: Using Psychological Insights in Biblical Study." *Religion in Life* 47 (1978) 136–47.

Winnicott, D. W. *Through Paediatrics to Psycho-Analysis: Collected Papers*. The International Psychoanalytical Library 100. London: Hogarth Press & Institute of Psycho-Analysis, 1975

———. "Transitional Objects and Transitional Phenomena." In *Playing and Reality*, 1–30. London: Tavistock, 1971.

Winquist, Charles E. "Body, Text, and Imagination." In *Deconstruction and Theology*, edited by Thomas J. J. Altizer et al., 34–57. New York: Crossroad, 1982.

Witte, Markus. *Die biblische Urgeschichte: Redaktions- und theologiegeschichtliche Beobartungen zu Genesis 1,1—11,26*. BZAW 265. Berlin: de Gruyter, 1998.

Wolde, Ellen van. "The Tower of Babel as Lookout over Genesis 11:1–9." in *Words Become Worlds: Semantic Studies of Genesis 1–11*, 84–109. Biblical Interpretation Series 6. Leiden: Brill, 1994.

Wolff, Hans Walter. "The Kerygma of the Yahwist." *Interpretation* 20 (1966) 131–58.

———, editor. *Probleme biblischer Theologie: Gerhard von Rad zum 70. Geburtstag.* Munich: Kaiser, 1971.

Younghusband, Frances. *Classic Mythology.* New York: Holt, 1883.

Zimmerli, Walter. "Promise and Fulfillment." In *Essays on Old Testament Hermeneutics*, edited by Claus Westermann, 89–122. Edited by James Luther Mays. Richmond: John Kox, 1963.

Zlotowitz, Meir, and Nossom Scherman. *Bereishis = Genesis : A New Translation with a Commentary Anthologized from Talmudic, Midrashic and Rabbinic Sources.* The ArtScroll Tanach Series 1. New York: Mesorah, 1977.

Index of Names

Index of Biblical References

New Testament